After Lisbon: National Parliaments in the European Union

The role of national parliaments in EU matters has become an important subject in the debate over the democratic legitimacy of European Union decision-making. Strengthening parliamentary scrutiny and participation rights at both the domestic and the European level is often seen as an effective measure to address the perceived 'democratic deficit' of the EU – the reason for affording them a prominent place in the newly introduced 'Provisions on Democratic Principles' of the Union (in particular Article 12 TEU). Whether this aim can be met, however, depends crucially on the degree to which, and the manner in which, national parliaments actually make use of their institutional rights.

This volume therefore aims at providing a comprehensive overview of the activities of national parliaments in the post-Lisbon Treaty era. This includes the 'classic' scrutiny of EU legislation, but also parliamentary involvement in EU foreign policy, the use of new parliamentary participation rights of the Lisbon Treaty (Early Warning System), their role regarding the EU's response to the Eurozone crisis, and the, so far under-researched, role of parliamentary administrators in scrutiny processes. This book was originally published as a special issue of *West European Politics*.

Katrin Auel is Associate Professor at the Institute for Advanced Studies, Vienna, Austria. Her research interests include Europeanisation, the democratic legitimacy of multilevel governance and legislative studies with a particular focus on the role of national parliaments in the EU. She has published in journals such as *Journal of Legislative Studies, Journal of Common Market Studies, German Politics, The European Law Journal* and *Comparative European Politics*.

Thomas Christiansen is Professor of European Institutional Politics and Co-Director of the Maastricht Centre for European Governance at Maastricht University, The Netherlands. He is Executive Editor of the *Journal of European Integration* and co-editor of the 'European Administration Governance' book series. Among his recent books are *Constitutionalizing the European Union* (co-authored with Christine Reh, 2009) and *The Maastricht Treaty: Second Thoughts after 20 Years* (co-edited with Simon Duke, 2012).

West European Politics Series

Edited by Klaus H. Goetz, University of Munich, Germany,
Anand Menon, King's College London, UK, and
Wolfgang C. Müller, University of Vienna, Austria

West European Politics has established itself as the foremost journal for the comparative analysis of European political institutions, politics and public policy. Its comprehensive scope, which includes the European Union, makes it essential reading for both academics and political practitioners. The books in this series have originated from special issues published by *West European Politics*.

After Lisbon: National Parliaments in the European Union

Edited by
Katrin Auel and Thomas Christiansen

Routledge
Taylor & Francis Group

LONDON AND NEW YORK

First published 2016
by Routledge
2 Park Square, Milton Park, Abingdon, Oxon, OX14 4RN, UK

and by Routledge
711 Third Avenue, New York, NY 10017, USA

First issued in paperback 2017

Routledge is an imprint of the Taylor & Francis Group, an informa business

British Library Cataloguing in Publication Data
A catalogue record for this book is available from the British Library

ISBN 13: 978-1-138-10663-5 (pbk)
ISBN 13: 978-1-138-93936-3 (hbk)

Typeset in Times New Roman
by RefineCatch Limited, Bungay, Suffolk

Publisher's Note
The publisher accepts responsibility for any inconsistencies that may have
arisen during the conversion of this book from journal articles to book chapters,
namely the possible inclusion of journal terminology.

Disclaimer
Every effort has been made to contact copyright holders for their permission to
reprint material in this book. The publishers would be grateful to hear from any
copyright holder who is not here acknowledged and will undertake to rectify
any errors or omissions in future editions of this book.

Contents

Citation Information

The chapters in this book were originally published in *West European Politics*, volume 38, issue 2 (March 2015). When citing this material, please use the original page numbering for each article, as follows:

Chapter 1
After Lisbon: National Parliaments in the European Union
Katrin Auel and Thomas Christiansen
West European Politics, volume 38, issue 2 (March 2015) pp. 261–281

Chapter 2
To Scrutinise or Not to Scrutinise? Explaining Variation in EU-Related Activities in National Parliaments
Katrin Auel, Olivier Rozenberg and Angela Tacea
West European Politics, volume 38, issue 2 (March 2015) pp. 282–304

Chapter 3
Beyond Institutional Capacity: Political Motivation and Parliamentary Behaviour in the Early Warning System
Katjana Gattermann and Claudia Hefftler
West European Politics, volume 38, issue 2 (March 2015) pp. 305–334

Chapter 4
National Parliaments after Lisbon: Administrations on the Rise?
Anna-Lena Högenauer and Christine Neuhold
West European Politics, volume 38, issue 2 (March 2015) pp. 335–354

Chapter 5
Who Controls National EU Scrutiny? Parliamentary Party Groups, Committees and Administrations
Alexander Strelkov
West European Politics, volume 38, issue 2 (March 2015) pp. 355–374

Chapter 6

National Parliaments and the Eurozone Crisis: Taking Ownership in Difficult Times?
Katrin Auel and Oliver Höing
West European Politics, volume 38, issue 2 (March 2015) pp. 375–395

Chapter 7

Executive Privilege Reaffirmed? Parliamentary Scrutiny of the CFSP and CSDP
Ariella Huff
West European Politics, volume 38, issue 2 (March 2015) pp. 396–415

For any permission-related enquiries please visit:
http://www.tandfonline.com/page/help/permissions

Notes on Contributors

Katrin Auel is Associate Professor at the Institute for Advanced Studies, Vienna, Austria. Her research interests include Europeanisation, the democratic legitimacy of multi-level governance and legislative studies with a particular focus on the role of national parliaments in the EU. She has published in journals such as *Journal of Legislative Studies*, *Journal of Common Market Studies*, *German Politics*, and *The European Law Journal* and *Comparative European Politics*.

Thomas Christiansen is Professor of European Institutional Politics and Co-Director of the Maastricht Centre for European Governance at Maastricht University, Netherlands. He is Executive Editor of the *Journal of European Integration* and co-editor of the 'European Administration Governance' book series. Among his recent books are *Constitutionalizing the European Union* (co-authored with Christine Reh, 2009) and *The Maastricht Treaty: Second Thoughts after 20 Years* (co-edited with Simon Duke, 2012).

Katjana Gattermann is a Post-doctoral Researcher at the Amsterdam Centre for Contemporary European Studies, Netherlands (ACCESS EUROPE). She is academic director of the Erasmus Academic Network on Parliamentary Democracy in Europe (PADEMIA), and co-editor of the LSE 'Europe in Question' Discussion Paper Series (LEQS). Her research interests include comparative politics and political communication with a particular focus on the patterns, drivers and effects of news coverage about EU institutions and politicians as well as legislative behaviour of parliamentarians and the relationship with their represented. Her work has appeared in journals such as the *European Journal of Political Research*, *European Union Politics*, and the *Journal of European Public Policy*.

Claudia Hefftler is a Research Associate and Ph.D. student at the Jean Monnet Chair, University of Cologne, Germany. She has studied political science, history and Portuguese philology. She has published on national parliaments, with a focus on their participation in the Early Warning Mechanism and their control over European Council meetings, and is a co-editor of *The Palgrave Handbook of National Parliaments and the EU*.

Anna-Lena Högenauer is Research Associate at the University of Luxembourg, Luxembourg. She is co-editor of the Pademia Online Papers on Parliamentary Democracy, and book reviews editor for *Regional and Federal Studies*. Her research focuses on multi-level governance, interest representation, multi-level parliamentarism, regional and national parliaments and parliamentary administrations. She has published in journals such as *Comparative European Politics*, *European Political Science Review*, and *Regional and Federal Studies*.

Oliver Höing is Research Associate at the Jean Monnet Chair of the University of Cologne, Germany. His research focuses on the role of national parliaments in the financial and debt crisis as well as the democratic legitimacy of euro crisis management. He has also published on Franco-German relations and the role of the European Council in the EU institutional architecture.

Ariella Huff is a former Post-doctoral Research Associate in the Department of Politics and International Studies, University of Cambridge, UK. Her major research interests include the relationship between member state parliaments and the EU's foreign policy. In particular, she is interested the role of national parliaments in scrutinising the Common Foreign and Security Policy, and non-legislative EU affairs more broadly. In September 2014, she joined the staff of the House of Commons Foreign Affairs Committee as a specialist.

Christine Neuhold is Professor in the Department of Political Science, Faculty of Arts and Social Sciences, Maastricht University, Netherlands. Since May 2013, she has held the Special Chair of EU Democratic Governance. She is co-coordinator of an Initial Training Network on Dynamics of Inter-institutional Cooperation in the EU (INCOOP). Her research focuses on the role of the European Parliament and national parliaments within the EU multi-level system, and the role of unelected officials therein.

Olivier Rozenberg is Associate Professor at Sciences Po, Paris, France, within the Centre d'études européennes. He specialises in legislative studies (legislators' behaviour, comparative studies), European studies (EU institutions, France in Europe) and, between both areas, in the role of parliaments in the governance of the EU. He has published a number of edited volumes, including *Parliamentary Roles in Modern Legislatures* (with Magnus Blomgren, Routledge, 2012) and *The Roles and Function of Parliamentary Questions* (with Shane Martin, Routledge, 2012).

Alexander Strelkov is a junior Lecturer at Maastricht University, Netherlands. After studying Political Science at the Russian State University for the Humanities, Moscow, Russia, at the Freie Universität Berlin, Germany, and at the University of Essex, Colchester, UK, he worked as a research fellow at the Institute of Europe, Russian Academy of Science, Moscow, Russia, on projects relating to European Neighbourhood Policy, conditionality in EU foreign policy and EU–Russia relations. He has contributed to the *Palgrave Handbook on National Parliaments and the European Union*.

Angela Tacea is Temporary Lecturer at Université Paris 2 Panthéon-Assas, Paris, France, and a Ph.D. candidate at the Centre d'études européenne, Sciences Po, Paris, France. Her research and teaching interests are in comparative policies, legislative studies, data protection, and border control. She recently published, with Renaud Dehousse, a book chapter on the French presidential elections, and was involved in the research project 'The Law Factory'.

Acknowledgements

This volume presents research undertaken within OPAL – the Observatory of National Parliaments after Lisbon (http://www.opal-europe.org). OPAL is an international research consortium bringing together research teams based at Sciences Po (Paris), the University of Cologne, Cambridge University and Maastricht University. From 2011 to 2014, it was funded within the Open Research Area in Europe for the Social Sciences. We are very grateful for the generous funding provided by the participating Research Councils of Germany (*Deutsche Forschungsgemeinschaft*), France (*Agence Nationale de la Recherche*), the UK (Economic and Social Research Council) and the Netherlands (*Nederlandse Organisatie voor Wetenschappelijk Onderzoek*). We would also like to thank our many student assistants for their invaluable support with the various data collections undertaken within the project, and in particular Afke Groen and Norma Rose for their administrative support and editorial assistance in bringing this special issue to publication.

Initial ideas and successive drafts of the various papers were presented at workshops and conference panels in Paris (September 2011), Maastricht (February 2012), Berlin (March 2013) and London (March 2014), and we are grateful for the valuable comments we received on these occasions from discussants and participants. Throughout its activity, OPAL has benefited from the advice received from the members of an advisory board – Enrique Barón Crespo, Alain Delcamp, Enikő Győri, Hans Hegeland, Andreas Maurer, Jan Nico van Overbeeke, Lord Roper, Michael Shackleton and Gracia Vara Arribas – who generously devoted their time and expertise to help our research to get on and stay on the right track. Needless to say, any remaining errors and misconceptions would be those of the authors.

Finally, we need to express our gratitude to the editors of *West European Politics* for their continuous support, encouragement and cooperation during the process of peer review, and the anonymous reviewers of each of the submitted papers for their many helpful comments and suggestions.

Katrin Auel and Thomas Christiansen

After Lisbon: National Parliaments in the European Union

KATRIN AUEL and THOMAS CHRISTIANSEN

The role of national parliaments in EU matters has become an important subject in the debate over the democratic legitimacy of European Union decision-making. Strengthening parliamentary scrutiny and participation rights at both the domestic and the European level is often seen as an effective measure to address the perceived 'democratic deficit' of the EU – the reason for affording them a prominent place in the newly introduced 'Provisions on Democratic Principles' of the Union (in particular Article 12 TEU). Whether this aim can be met, however, depends crucially on the degree and the manner in which national parliaments actually make use of their institutional rights. This volume therefore aims at providing a comprehensive overview of the activities of national parliaments in the post-Lisbon era. This includes the 'classic' scrutiny of EU legislation, but also parliamentary involvement in EU foreign policy, the use of new parliamentary participation rights of the Lisbon Treaty (Early Warning System), their role regarding the EU's response to the eurozone crisis and the, so far under-researched, role of parliamentary administrators in scrutiny processes. This introduction provides the guiding theoretical framework for the contributions. Based on neo-institutionalist approaches, it discusses institutional capacities and political motivation as the two key explanatory factors in the analysis of parliamentary involvement in EU affairs.

'Maybe not formally speaking, but at least politically speaking, all national parliaments have become, in a way, European institutions' (Van Rompuy 2012). Whether it is indeed true – or even desirable – that national parliaments have become '*European* institutions' in a narrower sense is open to debate (Cygan 2013: 21). Yet the statement certainly suggests that the former 'losers' of the European integration process have come a long way. For a long time the role of national parliaments was not formally recognised at the European level, and in the domestic arena the integration process provided ample opportunities for the executive actors to bypass legislatures and strengthen their hold on policy-making. Concerns about a growing democratic deficit were addressed through repeated and substantial expansion of the powers of the European Parliament, whereas national parliaments remained on the margins.

However, over time the 'victims' of integration have learned 'to fight back' and obtained new opportunities for participation in domestic European policy-making. It was a slow and uneven process through which they improved their institutional position, but they gained increased rights to scrutinise European affairs and to control the way in which ministers and officials represented national interests in Brussels. Today, the Lisbon Treaty not only mentions the role of national parliaments explicitly (Article 12 TEU), but it also gives them a role within the EU's legislative process, in particular as the new guardians of the subsidiarity principle.

The academic literature on national parliaments in the EU has mirrored these changes quite closely.[1] During the early years of integration, few publications dealt with its impact on national parliaments, but the last two decades have seen them emerge as one of the most salient issues in the debates on the democratic quality of EU governance. Yet the story of national parliaments in the EU is not only one of success: The coming into force of the Lisbon Treaty coincided with one of the greatest challenges national parliaments have yet had to face, the outbreak of the eurozone crisis, which has raised renewed concerns about parliamentary legitimacy in the EU (Fox 2012; Pollak 2014; Puntscher Riekmann, and Wydra 2013). And despite their stronger institutional position in EU affairs, the debate continues as to whether national parliaments can and do actually play an effective role in European policy-making.

This volume seeks to contribute to this debate by presenting the findings of an international research project addressing these questions. It aims at providing a comprehensive overview of the activities of national parliaments in the post-Lisbon era across a range of different policy areas and decision modes, and thus sheds some light on a topic that is widely discussed, but on which only limited comparative empirical knowledge exists.

In the current debate, different and indeed opposing views of the role of national parliaments persist. As Pollak has argued, '[w]ithin the EU's political system the assessment of the role of national parliaments oscillates between hope and frustration' (Pollak 2014: 25). On the one hand, their expanded participation rights give reason to assume that national parliaments have the potential not only to be attentive domestic watchdogs regarding their governments' actions 'in Brussels', but that they also have a capacity to develop into more autonomous players – either individually or jointly – at the EU level. For some, the involvement of national parliaments even seems to go too far already. In early 2012, then Italian prime minister and former EU commissioner Mario Monti (2012) argued that national parliaments, especially those 'to the north of Germany' were something of a spanner thrown into the system: 'If governments let themselves be fully bound by the decisions of their parliaments without protecting their own freedom to act, a breakup of Europe would be a more probable outcome than deeper integration'. While Monti later qualified his statement following severe criticism, it does reveal an attitude that considers a powerful involvement of national parliaments in EU policy-making, and especially in times of economic crisis, as something of a hindrance. On the other hand, authors have consistently, and especially in the context of the eurozone crisis, pointed out the challenges national parliaments face in actually making use of their participation rights, such as the highly technical character and complexity of EU issues, the lack of transparency of EU negotiations, the lack of time and resources required to process information on EU policies adequately or, in particular, the lack of incentives to get involved.

The main reason for such disagreements on the role of national parliaments is arguably the lack of empirical data on parliamentary behaviour in EU affairs. The strengthening of parliamentary scrutiny and participation rights at both the domestic and the European level is often seen as an effective measure to address the perceived democratic deficit in EU decision-making – the reason for affording them a prominent place in the newly introduced 'Provisions on Democratic Principles' of the Union (in particular article 12 TEU). However, whether these aims can be met depends crucially on whether and how national parliaments actually do get involved in EU affairs.

Referring to Lincoln's famous Gettysburg address, Lindseth (2012) has argued that the EU has come a long way in terms of 'government by and for the people', i.e. in terms of input and output legitimacy. However, he argues, 'government *of* the people' requires identification with a polity and a sense of ownership – in other words, a 'political cultural perception that the institutions of government are genuinely the people's own' (Lindseth 2012: 6). National parliaments can only provide this sense of ownership for their citizens in EU affairs if they do fulfil their parliamentary functions in EU politics. This includes not only scrutinising EU policies and controlling the government as an expression of their legislative, or more appropriately, policy-influencing function, but also – and fundamentally – communicating EU politics and holding the government publicly to account (Auel 2007). Unless they actually fulfil these functions, national parliaments will contribute little to the democratic legitimacy of EU policy-making.

The aim of this volume, arising from research conducted by the Observatory of Parliaments after the Lisbon Treaty (OPAL), is therefore to provide comprehensive and comparative empirical data on the way in which national parliaments make use of their powers and intervene in EU affairs.[2] By investigating parliamentary EU activities in practice, it aims at contributing to a better understanding of the conditions under which national parliaments can indeed provide the added value in terms of democratic legitimacy in EU policy-making. In this endeavour it goes beyond the classic focus on the *formal powers* of parliamentary scrutiny by presenting insights into the *actual practice* of parliamentary involvement in EU affairs within the domestic arena. This includes the 'classic' scrutiny of EU legislation, but also parliamentary involvement in non-legislative areas such as EU foreign policy-making, the use of new parliamentary participation rights under the Lisbon Treaty (Early Warning System – EWS) and their role regarding the EU's response to the sovereign debt crisis in the eurozone. In addition, contributors analyse the so far under-researched role of parliamentary administrators in scrutiny processes.

While the contributions investigate different aspects of parliamentary involvement in EU affairs using different types of data, they were guided by a common analytical frame that provided the theoretical lens for the empirical research. In the following, we outline this theoretical framework that draws on the insights of the neo-institutionalist turn in the social sciences. It starts with the recognition that research on national parliaments in the EU needs to be sensitive to both the relevance of formal arrangements and to the way in which actors actually make use of these. Accordingly, the contributors to this volume operate on the assumption that, on the one hand, formal rights, legal rules and existing norms – in other words the *institutional capacities* of parliaments – provide certain opportunities for parliamentary involvement in EU affairs, but, on the other hand, that these do not determine – and thus cannot be equated with – the actual behaviour of parliaments. Therefore, to explain the nature, direction and intensity of parliamentary involvement, the *motivation* of individual members of parliament (MPs) and parliamentary party groups (PPGs) to become involved needs to be studied, and the preferences, incentives and driving forces that guide their actions ought to be examined. Accordingly, we identify institutional capacity and actors' motivation as the two key explanatory factors in the analysis of parliamentary involvement in EU affairs. The following section elaborates in more detail how these factors have been derived and how they have been applied in the context of the empirical research presented in this volume.

Parliamentary Activity in the EU: A Neo-Institutionalist Perspective

Following the well-known argument by March and Olsen, we can distinguish between two logics of human behaviour – a 'logic of consequentiality' and a 'logic of appropriateness' – a basic assumption that can also be applied to the present context of parliamentary activity in the EU. According to the former, actors' behaviour is based on considerations of the consequences of their actions in terms of furthering (their own) preferences and is thus rooted in rationality and efficiency, while the latter is based on considerations of the consistency of their actions with cultural and political norms and rules (March and Olsen 1995: 154).

These two logics of behaviour have given rise to different approaches within a broader neo-institutionalist turn, which recognises that institutions are not neutral containers fulfilling certain functional needs, but interact with, and are subject to, the behaviour of individuals working with and through them. As Fenno has argued (2000: 6), 'representatives are context interpreters. And they will make choices and take actions not in the abstract, but accordingly to what they believe to be rational and/or appropriate in the circumstances or context in which they find themselves'. While neo-institutionalist approaches share the common perspective that behaviour can be explained with both institutional context and actors' preferences or motivations, they differ greatly in their conception of both institutions and the origin or formation of preferences. As a result, they also develop very different hypotheses on the way actors interpret the context they find themselves in and emphasise different explanations for the logic of action, the interpretation of rules, and thus for the motivations and incentives driving behaviour.

The logic of consequentiality is most strongly emphasised by Rational Choice approaches that view actors as rational utility maximisers who have fixed, exogenous preferences. Here, institutions 'merely' act as constraints on or provide opportunities for specific behaviour and strategies to pursue the realisation of these preferences. With this emphasis on individual preferences and incentives rather than group norms and processes of socialisation, actors are conceptualised as fairly independent of their context: 'Rational choice institutionalism consequently sees institutions as providing a context within which individual decisions are set, but places the emphasis on 'individual' rather than 'context' (Aspinwall and Schneider 2000: 11). As will be discussed in more detail below, rational choice institutionalist approaches hypothesise that MPs are mainly motivated by their interest in maximising their chances for re-election, career development and/or policy influence.

From the perspective of a 'logic of appropriateness', emphasised by norma-tive or sociological neo-institutionalist approaches, in contrast, preferences are neither stable, nor precise, nor exogenous (March and Olsen 1989: 163). More-over, institutions 'do not just constrain options; they establish the very criteria by which people discover their preferences' (DiMaggio and Powell 1991: 11). Actors and their context are thus rather closely liked. From this perspective, insti-tutions not only have an impact on preferences but also define what is deemed appropriate behaviour in a given situation. The main hypothesis that can be derived from this perspective is that parliamentary behaviour will be guided by a logic of appropriateness, by formal and informal rules of and norms for parliamentary behaviour and – more generally – by parliamentary culture.

Historical institutionalism emphasises especially the (possibly unintended) consequences of institutional choices and their long-term impact in terms of path dependency. While mainly concerned with long-term institutional or pol-icy development, the approach can also be applied to the study of parliamen-tary behaviour; both from a more rationalist and a more sociological perspective. Institutions are conceptualised as 'sets of regularized practices with a rule-like quality in the sense that the actors expect the practices to be observed; and which, in some but not all, cases are supported by formal sanc-tions' (Hall and Thelen 2009: 3). As a result, actors' strategies and goals become entrenched and thus path-dependent over time as well and relatively resistant to change even under new circumstances.

This distinction between the two logics of action, and the resultant devel-opment of different strands of institutional analysis, is a valuable starting point to approach the study of parliamentary activity in the EU. The contributions to this volume broadly follow the insights of such an approach by investigating both institutional capacities defined by legal and institutional norms and the incentives driving individual and collective actors within parliaments to explain parliamentary behaviour. In the following we develop each of these two broad sets of – complementary rather than competing – explanatory factors further and illustrate the ways in which they can be used towards a more comprehensive empirical analysis of parliamentary activity in the EU.

Institutional Capacity: Institutional Opportunities and Constraints

As discussed in the previous section, what distinguishes historical institutionalist approaches is their emphasis on the long-term – historical – development and resulting resilience and durability of institutions (Pierson 2004). Thus, whether behaviour is assumed to be guided by exogenous rational preferences or by beliefs and norms, cultural traditions and individual role conceptions, the general expectation is that it will be rather resistant to change. Institutional or behavioural repertoires are assumed to act as a barrier to change because actors faced with new situations or challenges will draw on pre-existing institutions or patterns of behaviour rather than considering new ones. As such, the historical institutionalist approach is sensitive not only to new opportunities provided by the institutional framework, but also to the constraints it imposes on actors.

In his analysis of the adaptation of the French, Greek and British parliaments to EU integration, Dimitrakopoulos' (2001: 419–20), for example, shows how change 'has proceeded by means of small, marginal steps based on existing institutional repertoires in a manner that has reproduced the historically defined weaknesses of these Parliaments'. As a result, not only will new institutional provisions reflect given institutional paths, but parliamentary behaviour in EU affairs is also expected to follow the main patterns developed in domestic affairs. As Damgaard and Jensen (2005: 409) show for the Danish Folketing, existing executive–legislative relationships and the modes of decision-making in national politics are indeed replicated in the European context: 'the general patterns of parliamentary decision-making also characterise the field of EU policy. It appears that well-known national policy-making styles are used, with some adjustments, to take care of problems associated with EU policy-making.

With respect to the institutional capacity as an explanatory factor, it is necessary to take these insights about the significance of institutional path dependency on board when studying the context within which parliaments participate in EU affairs. This requires, in addition, a two-fold approach, namely a distinction between the institutional environment present at the EU level as well as at the domestic level. At both levels, a mix between pre-existing and newly changed conditions has had an impact on the opportunities and constraints of national parliaments.

The European Institutional Context

As noted above, in the earlier phase of European integration, the position for national parliaments in the EU in terms of institutional powers had been weak, but over time, and especially with the coming into force of the Lisbon Treaty, institutional provisions were expanded in a number of ways, both directly and indirectly. Regarding the former, the new 'Protocol on the Role of National Parliaments in the European Union' mainly provides national parliaments with better access to information about the European decision-making process. They not only receive a broad range of documents, including non-legislative documents such as the annual reports of the Court of Auditors or the Commission's annual legislative programme, but they also receive these documents directly (rather than via their governments as under the Treaty of Amsterdam).

Second, the 'Protocol on the Application of the Principles of Subsidiarity and Proportionality' provides national parliaments (both chambers in bicameral systems) with a more direct role on the EU legislative process through the so-called Early Warning Mechanism (Kiiver 2012). They have the right to submit – within eight weeks of receiving a legislative proposal – a 'reasoned opinion' to the Commission if they find the proposal to violate the subsidiarity principle (Article 7.1). If one-third of the national parliaments submit a reasoned opinion, the Commission must formally review the proposal and may withdraw or amend it but may also maintain it unaltered (Article 7.2). Thus, in these cases national parliaments can only show the Commission the 'yellow card', but not force it to take their concerns into account. If, however, at least half of the national parliaments submit reasoned opinions on a legislative proposal falling under the ordinary legislative procedure (co-decision), and the Commission maintains the proposal, the legislative proposal will be submitted to both the Council and the European Parliament for review ('orange card'). While national parliaments thus still do not have a right to force the Commission directly to take their opinion into account, this last rule enables parliaments to force the Council and the EP to deal with their concerns.

Third, according to Article 8 of the Protocol the Court of Justice of the European Union (ECJ) will have jurisdiction in actions on grounds of infringement of the principle of subsidiarity by a legislative act, and such action can now also be brought forward by national parliaments through their governments.

Finally, national parliaments also obtained the right to veto the application of the *passerelle* clause (Article 48, para. 7), which covers the transition from unanimity to qualified majority or the transition from special to ordinary legislative procedure. National parliaments have to be informed at least six months before any decision is adopted and can, individually in this case, veto the proposal within this time period.

The Domestic Institutional Context

The introduction – and implementation – of these new participation rights also had an impact on existing institutional provisions within the national context. In particular, national parliaments had to implement their own procedures for the handling of the new instruments of subsidiarity control. Together with the intensified debate over the role of national parliaments in EU politics since the Laeken Declaration and in the context of the Convention on the Future of Europe, this has also led to a general overhaul of institutional scrutiny provisions in a number of parliaments (for an overview of institutional reforms triggered by the Lisbon Treaty provisions in all chambers of the EU see Hefftler *et al.* (2015).

As a result, institutional scrutiny provisions are now more similar, but far from uniform, across the EU member states.[3] All national parliaments have set up one or more European Affairs Committees (EAC), but great differences still remain regarding the involvement of other Standing Committees in EU affairs. Similarly, we can find variation with regard to the scrutiny approach. Although the addressee of the scrutiny procedure is, in the end, the government, systems differ with regard to whether parliament scrutinises EU documents or the government position for the negotiations in the Council or both. While some parliaments issue written statements, others transmit their position on European issues to the government orally during committee sessions, and some use both procedures. Most importantly, the consequences of such statements differ greatly. In some cases, the government is under a legal obligation or strong political pressure to follow the position of their parliaments in the EU negotiations (mandating procedure). In many other cases, however, parliaments can only give their opinion without this having a binding effect on the government. Furthermore, a number of parliaments have established so-called 'scrutiny reserves' aimed at preventing government representatives from agreeing to a proposal in the Council while the parliamentary scrutiny process is on-going (Auel *et al.* 2012). Finally, and often overlooked in the literature, parliaments also differ with regard to administrative support in EU affairs, and their responses to the administrative challenges arising from the Lisbon Treaty have been uneven.

A number of studies have classified and ranked national parliaments according to their institutional strength in EU affairs. Although the rankings differ slightly due to a different emphasis on specific institutional provisions, the overall picture is fairly consistent: As the latest rankings by Karlas (2012), Winzen (2012) as well as Katrin Auel, Olivier Rozenberg and Angela Tacea (2015a) show, we can identify a group of strong, mainly North European, parliaments including those of Denmark, Sweden and Finland, but also Germany, the Netherlands and Austria. In contrast, rather weak parliaments can be found in Southern member states Greece, Malta, Cyprus, Portugal and Spain, but also in Belgium and Luxemburg. France, Italy and the UK fall somewhere in between. Finally, the new constitutions in Central and Eastern Europe tend to accord a greater role for legislatures and, in contrast to their West European counterparts, many of their parliaments can – at least with regard to their formal institutional position – be considered rather strong (see also Karlas 2011; O'Brennan and Raunio 2007; Szalay 2005).

In sum, the institutional capacity of national parliaments has been significantly altered by the provisions of the Lisbon Treaty and the way in which national systems have adapted to these. While in terms of the European level there has been a distinct empowerment of national parliaments, their institutional capacity varies significantly across the member states and depends to a large extent on domestic arrangements and the specific resources and procedures that each individual chamber has available when confronting the challenges of an effective involvement in EU affairs.

Motivation: Incentives and Driving Forces of Parliamentary Actors

Institutional provisions and the overall strength of parliaments play an important role in understanding how legislatures can respond to the challenges arising from an involvement in EU decision-making. At the same time, it is also clear that this is not the whole story, and that we also need to study the way in which parliamentary actors respond to these opportunities and constraints. Drawing on both rational and sociological neo-institutionalist approaches, the following will discuss this motivational dimension in more detail.

MPs as Rational Actors

From a rational choice institutionalist perspective, parliamentarians are rational actors with stable preferences who make decisions based on an analysis of costs and benefits. Given that parliaments are in fact busy institutions with limited resources, the general expectation is that MPs invest these resources – i.e. make use of institutional opportunities – in a way that will advance their preferences. Much of the rational choice literature on legislative behaviour focuses on career goals of legislators to explain behaviour. From this perspective, legislative behaviour can be best understood if legislators are seen as 'single minded reelection seekers' (Mayhew 1974: 5; see also Cox and McCubbins 1993: 100). Other scholars have criticised this purely vote-seeking approach for being too parsimonious and 'not totally persuasive ... It makes little sense to assume that parties value votes for their own sake ... votes can only plausibly be instrumental goals' to achieve policy influence and/or the spoils of office (Strøm and Müller 1999: 9). As Budge and Laver (1986) argue, politicians do pursue policy goals, either intrinsically, because they sincerely care about the policies in question, or instrumentally, as a means for some other goal, for example electoral support. De Swann puts it even more forcefully: 'considerations of policy are foremost in the mind of actors ... the parliamentary game is, in fact, about the determination of major government policy' (De Swann 1973: 88).

On the basis of these considerations, we can assume that the motivation of MPs/PPGs to use institutional opportunities – i.e. to engage in benefits scrutiny of EU affairs – depends (a) on the electoral (and career) benefits that they expect from their activities and (b) the probability MPs assign to their chance of making a difference and actually having a policy impact (Saalfeld 2003).

Regarding the former, it can be assumed that public opinion on EU integration can provide a strong electoral incentive (Raunio 2005; Saalfeld 2005). In member states where EU issues are more salient and public opinion is generally more critical of EU integration, MPs have greater incentives to become active in EU affairs due to the potential electoral impact of EU politics. Where, in contrast, European affairs play no role in voting decisions or where the permissive consensus prevails, there are no electoral benefits to be gained from investing in scrutiny. However, the motivation to engage in scrutiny activities may also vary according to the policy area and specific policy issue (Saalfeld 2003): Given the general preference structure of MPs, they can be expected to engage more actively in the scrutiny of highly salient EU issues, i.e. issues that affect clearly defined (large) groups at the domestic level and that the domestic public is highly aware of.

Second, MPs will get involved in the scrutiny of EU affairs if they expect a payoff in terms of policy influence (Saalfeld 2005; Winzen 2013). Generally, members of the governing PPGs will be more inclined to leave EU politics to their government if they trust the latter to represent their mutual policy preferences in the EU negotiations. This trust can be assumed to be greatest in the case of single-party governments. Although government MPs and ministers may not agree on every single issue, we can expect their interests to be fairly similar – unless the party is deeply internally divided over EU issues. Divergent preferences – and thus less trust – can be expected for coalition governments. Here, coalition partners not only have to negotiate compromises, but they also have a stronger incentive to influence and control the other coalition partners' members of government (Martin and Vanberg 2004). Trust can finally be considered lowest in the case of minority governments, where the government cannot rely on stable support in parliament but has to negotiate majorities for its policies.

While rationalist approaches, and especially agency theory, have been the dominant way to analyse parliamentary involvement in EU affairs, they are also often criticised for their lack of any 'discernible relation to the actual or possible behaviour of flesh-and-blood human beings' (Simon 1976: xxvii). In particular, it has been argued that a rationalist approach is ill-suited to explain parliamentary behaviour as it cannot account for what has to be 'irrational' behaviour in a strategic sense (Rozenberg 2012): In many parliaments, MPs spend several hours per week scrutinising EU documents, presenting parliamentary reports and drafting resolutions despite knowing that their activities will gain little attention from voters and have a limited impact on policy. Thus, it can be argued that MPs need motivations or incentives that go beyond vote- or policy-seeking. According to Searing (1994: 1253), the 'difficulty with economic rational choice models is that their overly cognitive assumptions about self-interest tend to obscure and dismiss the wide variety of desires that shape and reshape our goals – and also our judgments about which courses of action will be most effective [or appropriate] for satisfying these goals'.

The following will therefore discuss alternative approaches to explaining parliamentary behaviour. Given the wide variety of approaches that rely on culture, beliefs, ideas and norms to explain behaviour, the following will not provide an in-depth discussion of the broad literature. Rather, the short overview will highlight some possibilities to conceptualise March and Olsen's 'logic of appropriateness'.

The Role of Norms and Values

From a sociological institutionalism perspective, institutions do not simply provide opportunities or constraints for rational actors. Rather, institutions 'mould their own participants, and supply systems of meaning for their participants in politics' (Peters 1999: 26). Individuals do make conscious choices, but these choices are not purely guided by a personal payoff in terms of exogenous preferences, but rather remain within the parameters established by the dominant institutional values and norms (Peters 1999: 29). One way to conceptualise the 'logic of appropriateness' is parliamentary culture. Political culture has been described as 'a short-hand expression for a "mind set" which has the effect of limiting attention to less than the full range of alternative behaviours, problems, and solutions which are logically possible' (Elkins and Simeon 1979: 128). Therefore, the question of whether and how parliamentarians engage in scrutiny activities touches upon the question of how the process of European integration and its challenges to national parliaments affects these cultural factors, and how, in turn, scrutiny in EU politics is influenced by general parliamentary traditions and political culture. Whether a more cooperative or a more confrontational culture dominates the parliamentary system, for example, has an impact on legislative behaviour and the way parliamentary control and scrutiny of the executive is exercised. As Sprungk (2003) has argued, a cooperative relationship between parliament and the government may hamper intensive parliamentary control: Public confrontation with the government, especially through a more aggressive use of scrutiny rights and/or by exerting pressure on the government to comply with parliamentary policy preferences, may not be considered appropriate. In addition, Sprungk argues that the general attitude of MPs towards European integration may impact their motivation to engage in scrutiny activity. A party favourable to European integration may view parliamentary scrutiny as a factor impeding smooth European policy-making and thus as inappropriate. Such views were readily visible in the plenary debates over the implementation of parliamentary participation rights in the German Bundestag following the German Federal Constitutional Court's decision on the Lisbon Treaty (Auberger and Lamping 2009).

Similarly, MPs' beliefs about the legitimacy of procedures and institutions or their assessment of the relative importance of parliamentary functions can have an impact on the their motivation to become involved in EU affairs. A study by Weßels (2005), for example, reveals the interrelation between parliamentary views about the relative importance of parliamentary functions and their attitudes towards how democratic legitimacy is to be achieved in the EU, on the one hand, and their views on the role national parliaments should play in EU politics, on the other. The findings show, for example, 'that working parliaments – those where the governance function is obviously dominant – regard themselves as powerful enough to play the European policy game in direct contact with the government, informal coordination and bargaining. ... Parliaments that serve more as houses of deliberation, [in contrast] use articulation and voice as the way to react to European policy-making' (Weßels 2005: 463f.). The study's results suggest that different parliamentary norms and beliefs will have an impact not only on the general motivation of MPs to engage in scrutiny, but also, for example, on the extent to which they feel the need to become directly involved in the policy process at the EU level, for example through new instruments such as the Early Warning Mechanism or the Political Dialogue.

Finally, role theory provides a means of incorporating values and beliefs and thus the logic of appropriateness. While our research is not directly concerned with parliamentary roles in EU politics, the notion of 'parliamentary role'[4] is nonetheless helpful, as 'roles are not merely individual beliefs and tastes, but articulate collective norms and values, which might have consequences for MPs' behaviour inside and outside the parliamentary chamber' (Blomgren and Rozenberg 2012b: 211). This emphasis on both shared and individual norms, expectations, ideas or beliefs, enable us to analyse and explain the motivation behind specific patterns of behaviour.

In his influential motivational approach to parliamentary roles, Searing (1991, 1994) famously distinguished between rules and reasons as two drivers for the selection of roles. The former links legislative behaviour to the expectations generated by institutional rules and formal positions of MPs. Thus, the assumption is that general expectations and norms connected to specific parliamentary offices or, more generally, to being a member of the opposition or the governing PPGs will have a – fairly predictable – impact on behavioural patterns. At the same time, parliamentary positions leave – depending on the precise office – more or less leeway to choose between different parliamentary activities MPs may focus on. The latter is driven by preferences that concern both more strategic goals such as career advancement and more emotional goals such as providing good constituency service. Rozenberg (2012), for example, shows that the chairmen of the European Affairs Committees in the House of Commons and the French Assemblée Nationale adopt distinct parliamentary roles, such as 'Chair', 'Clubman', 'Inquisitor and 'the One who rubs shoulders with the Great and Powerful'. These roles, and the underlying motives for adopting them, helps us understand the specific pattern of activity each committee developed, be it special attention to the detailed scrutiny of EU documents, an emphasis on hearings with ministers or a focus on informal participation in decision-making. Such preferences are also not purely endogenous and completely shaped by the institutional environment (Searing 1994). MPs may enter parliament with given preferences yet these preferences may change and adapt to the situation as well as parliamentary institutions and norms (Searing 1994: 483). Preferences and the behaviour in pursuing them are constructed within, but not determined by, the given organisation.

To sum up, we argue that attention to both institutional and actor-centred factors is required to explain how national parliaments operate in the EU, and crucial to understanding the diversity in their involvement in EU policy-making and their responses to the new opportunities arising from the Lisbon Treaty. Answers to questions such as 'How can we explain the variation in the level and type of engagement with EU politics across national parliaments?' or 'Why are some chambers much more active than others in making use of the new powers?' can only be conclusively answered by looking into both capacity and motivation as possible explanatory factors. This has been the approach underlying the empirical research that has been conducted in the context of the OPAL project and which is presented in the contributions to this volume.

The Performance of Parliaments in the European Union

The empirical research presented in the contributions to this volume demonstrates how multi-faceted the role of national parliaments has become. The recent phase of European integration – and in particular the 'double-whammy' of the Lisbon reforms and the eurozone crisis – have created an entirely new set of opportunities and challenges to which parliaments had to respond. The research shows that in many cases parliaments have reacted to these changes but it also shows that these changes are far from uniform and that generalisation across the universe of legislatures in the EU remains highly problematic.

A first observation concerns what one might call the internal impact of Europe: the way in which legislatures have adapted their working mechanisms, procedures, staffing levels, and committee structures to the demands of a more prominent EU. One aspect here is the changing relationship between, on the one hand, elected MPs and, on the other, clerks in committee secretariats and other civil servants working as advisors and technical experts in parliamentary administrations. As Anna-Lena Högenauer and Christine Neuhold (2015) show in their contribution, MPs have, for a variety of reasons, become increasingly dependent on administrative support: the technical expertise required to deal with the growing number of incoming EU dossiers, the dynamic of increasing horizontal cooperation among parliaments in the EU, and the related practice of having parliamentary representatives posted in Brussels. The latter, in particular, have developed an important role in providing informal access to information about developments within the various chambers, thus 'short-circuiting' the coordination of parliamentary action in the context of the EWS. However, the authors also point out that across the EU significant variation remains in the roles that parliamentary officials carry out and that even though the majority of chambers now employ administrators possessing an agenda-shaping role, this remains in the service of, rather than as a replacement for, the primacy of political decision-making.

This ties in with the analysis conducted by Alexander Strelkov (2015) who argues that in the relative balance of 'internal power', parliamentary party groups maintain the upper hand vis-à-vis other parliamentary actors (such as committees and administrators), even if this – privileging party political preferences over technical expertise – leads to a somewhat 'shallow' scrutiny of EU legislation. A further internal dimension of adaption to Europe is the growing 'mainstreaming' of EU affairs (Gattermann *et al.* 2013) – the fact that the scrutiny of EU affairs is increasingly carried out beyond designated European Affairs Committees, as other sectoral committees engage with EU matters that pertain to their portfolio.

These internal developments are remarkable and significant, even if it remains difficult to link their incidence to the standard categories of parliamentary strength or institutional capacity. The contribution by Katrin Auel, Olivier Rozenberg and Angela Tacea (2015b) tackles this question head-on, presenting the data from a large, quantitative analysis testing a number of hypotheses on the link between parliamentary activity and possible explanatory variables based on institutional capacities as well as political motivation. They conclude that in order to understand the driving forces of parliamentary activity it is essential to go beyond the idea of institutional strength and develop more sophisticated models looking at the likely effectiveness of instruments at the disposal of legislatures, and to consider the actual activity – resolutions, reasoned opinions, committee meetings or plenary debates – in more depth. The data shows that strong parliaments are not invariably the most active, and that beyond institutional capacity, motivational factors have significance in explaining parliamentary activity.

Katjana Gattermann and Claudia Hefftler (2015), in their more specific analysis of the driving forces behind the incidence of issuing reasoned opinions in the context of the EWS, come to a similar conclusion: having tested for a range of possible explanatory factors, their paper demonstrates that MPs are more likely to vote for a reasoned opinion under certain conditions (party political contestation, the salience and urgency of EU draft legislation and an adverse macro-economic context). This is further evidence that one must go beyond the formal powers and institutional capacity of chambers in order to understand what drives their engagement with the EU level.

Beyond the narrow confines of the EWS, parliaments have been challenged by the eurozone crisis, be it in terms of voting on proposed bail-out packages or on the conditionality that has come with these packages for the programme countries. The widespread view has been that the technocratic governance and intergovernmental nature of the crisis management carried with it the risk of further 'de-parliamentarisation' – an important question explored by Katrin Auel and Oliver Höing (2015) in their contribution to this volume. Again the finding here is that there is significant variation in the way in which legislatures have responded to the impact from the European level. Unsurprisingly, parliaments in eurozone member states have been more active than those outside, but even within the eurozone certain differences have been identified by the authors: debtor countries have seen much less parliamentary activity than creditor countries, and stronger parliaments have managed to cope better with the increasing demands. There is thus no blanket weakening of legislatures due to the intergovernmental nature of crisis management, but rather the exacerbation of existing strengths and weaknesses. Indeed, some legislatures, such as the German Bundestag, have been able to expand their powers in these circumstances.

Another area of EU policy-making which has seen a greater degree of engagement by national parliaments in recent years has been foreign and security policy, and in her contribution, Ariella Huff (2015) provides an in-depth analysis of the way in which parliaments have performed in this area. Her study adds to the body of evidence demonstrating that formal powers are not the only, and perhaps not even the main, guide to parliamentary activity. Huff shows that the motivations of MPs matter a great deal when it comes to the parliamentary scrutiny of CFSP. Here the normative frame within which MPs perceive their role with regard to foreign policy, as well as the coherence – or lack of it – in party political positions on European integration, have great influence on parliamentary activity: internal divisions among parties or coalitions are seen as a reason why their interest in parliamentary debates, and hence the scrutiny of EU foreign policy, is limited.

Conclusion

Taken together, the contributions to this volume validate the choice in favour of a neo-institutionalist framework that is sensitive to the relevance of both institutional capacity and motivational factors. Much of the past literature on national parliaments has focused on formal powers and defined parliamentary strength in terms of the formal rules and constitutional arrangements. While these are important dimensions, the articles in this volume make clear that the situation is more complex: what matters is not only what powers a legislature has in terms of scrutinising the national executive or the EU decision-making process, but whether MPs are willing and able to make effective use of these. Access to resources – support staff, expertise, time – as well as the political incentives to engage with EU matters, are relevant, and in some cases more so than the formal powers themselves.

The image of national parliaments and their activity in the European Union that emerges from these studies is varied, and does not lend itself to easy generalisation. Parliaments have not emerged from the Lisbon Treaty reforms as being empowered and fully engaged with the European project. There remains much scepticism, ambivalence and even ignorance within national legislatures about developments at the European level. Some of this can be put down to limited capacities, with many MPs either lacking the time to devote the attention required to EU legislation, or else making a calculated decision to focus on higher-profile domestic issues. Inevitably, parliamentary activity on European affairs remains selective, with issue salience and party politics important intervening variables in explaining how (in)active a particular chamber is with regard to Europe.

At the same time, it has to be recognised that there are certain dynamics at play which have fundamentally transformed the situation compared to only a few years ago. The first of these is a discursive change which has seen national parliaments widely regarded as a key part in any future reform of democratic procedures of the European Union – a discourse that includes contributions from both Eurosceptics wanting to 'repatriate' powers from the European level, and advocates of further integration seeking engagement with national parliaments as a way of strengthening the EU's legitimacy. Even though some of these expectations are out of tune with the more modest reality in current practice – as the contributions to this volume also demonstrate – this has not stopped this discourse from developing along these lines in the post-Lisbon era (Groen and Christiansen 2015).

A second dynamic has been that of inter-parliamentary cooperation, building on but moving beyond the traditional and highly formalised mechanisms such as COSAC[5] or the Conference of Speakers. While such long-standing institutions have been upgraded in the context of the Early Warning Mechanism, informal relations between parliaments have become more widespread and more important. This includes collaborations between elected members and between parliamentary officials and clerks, be it to facilitate information exchanges or the coordination of activities in the context of the EWS. To some extent, such exchanges between chambers in different member states is driven by the very divergence that has been alluded to above: those from parliaments in the 'avant-garde', with greater desire and/or resources to make their voice heard at the European level, are looking for support from others in order to achieve a greater impact, or are being approached for access to information or expertise.

A related development concerns the vertical relations between national parliaments and the EP. These have become increasingly formalised, both inside the institutions – the EP now has not one but two Vice-Presidents for Relations with National Parliaments – and through the creation of new bodies bringing together deputies from the national and the European level such as the Article 13 Conference in the area of economic governance or the Inter-parliamentary Conference on CFSP. However, while these enhanced relations between national and European levels is recognition of the importance of cooperation between legislatures – somewhat belatedly in view of decades of administrative 'fusion' on the executive side (Wessels 1997) – it has also made the potential for disagreements between the EP and national parliaments more apparent (Cooper 2014). Far from being natural allies, the EP and national chambers are also competitors in the marketplace for the provision of democratic legitimacy and rivals in the search for voters' attention.

Future reform of the European Union is likely to include an agenda for further structural improvements concerning the legitimacy of decision-making, in particular regarding the area of fiscal stability and economic governance. It is here that institutional solutions to some of the persisting dilemmas facing the Union will have to be found – maintaining decisional efficiency while ensuring democratic legitimacy and transparency. The differentiated nature of economic governance, with more far-reaching decision-making now only affecting the member states of the eurozone, creates increasing tensions for the existing institutional arrangements, raising questions whether EU institutions can continue to serve the eurozone, or whether new bodies – either with mixed national–European membership or sub-committees of the EP – need to be set up for the scrutiny of decision-making in this particular area. It is with a view to this reform agenda that the EP and advocates of greater powers for national parliaments already find themselves on opposite sides of the debate (Deubner 2013).

The involvement of national parliaments in EU affairs has developed significantly since the Lisbon Treaty and the eurozone crisis brought both new opportunities and new challenges. It certainly has come a long way since questions were raised about them being 'victims' (O'Brennan and Raunio 2007), 'losers' or 'latecomers' (Maurer and Wessels 2001). A sizeable number of chambers have chosen to engage with EU affairs as a matter of course, have been adapting their internal procedures and institutional capacity, and are linking up with other parliaments on a regular basis. However, the degree of parliamentary activism remains patchy, and it would be wrong to talk of a generalised empowerment of national parliaments, vis-à-vis either the national executives or the European institutions.

The research presented in this volume sheds some light both on the patterns of variation and on their causes. As such, it advances our knowledge of this complex domain and provides new insights into the possibilities for, and the limitations of, national parliaments to scrutinise and influence EU decision-making in the post-Lisbon era. The findings presented in the articles demonstrate the importance of focusing on both institutional and motivational factors in the research on national parliaments, and to work with both qualitative and quantitative methods in doing so.

At a time when national parliaments have arrived in 'Europe' and are there to stay, the publication of this research will be valuable in gaining a better understanding of the difference that national parliaments can make, under what conditions and at what price. Certain patterns have been identified which help us make sense of the diverse nature of this interaction between national and European actors, between legislatures and executives and between elected politicians and civil servants.

This area remains an aspect of European integration that is bound to develop further, with the search for ways of improving the legitimacy of EU decision-making continuing, not least in the face of the results of the 2014 European elections. High hopes are attached to the role that may be played by national parliaments in this regard, and in this context the contributions to this volume not only advance the scientific discussion, but will also be valuable in the context of future debates about institutional reform.

Disclosure Statement

No potential conflict of interests was reported by the authors.

Notes

1. For excellent overviews see Goetz and Meyer-Sahling (2008), Raunio (2009), Winzen (2010) and Rozenberg and Hefftler (2015).
2. For details about this project, see http://www.opal-europe.org. Contributors draw on both qualitative and quantitative data. In the context of the OPAL project, several large-scale surveys were conducted and unique empirical databases developed. Most important among these are: (a) a qualitative database on institutional provisions in both domestic and European Affairs with contributions from national experts on all 28 parliamentary systems in the EU (including Croatia; for excerpts see http://www.opal-europe.org), and (b) a quantitative data collection of parliamentary activities between 2010 and 2012 in all 40 national chambers across the EU. In addition, members of OPAL have collected quantitative and in-depth qualitative data on a broad range of national parliaments, specific institutional capacities and parliamentary activities.
3. A comprehensive overview of the scrutiny provisions in all national parliaments can be found in Hefftler *et al.* (2015).
4. For an extensive literature overview see Blomgren and Rozenberg (2012a).
5. Conférence des Organes Parlementaires Spécialisés dans les Affaires de l'Union des Parlements de l'Union Européenne.

References

Aspinwall, Mark D., and Gerald Schneider (2000). 'Same Table, Separate Menu. the Institutionalist Turn in Political Science and the Study of European Integration', *European Journal of Political Research*, 38:1, 1–36.

Auberger, Tobias, and Wolfram Lamping (2009). 'Die richtige Aufführung auf der falschen Bühne? Das Bundesverfassungsgericht und die Politisierung der europäischen Integration', *dms – der moderne staat – Zeitschrift für Public Policy, Recht und Management*, 2, 271–91.

Auel, Katrin (2007). 'Democratic Accountability and National Parliaments – Re-Defining the Impact of Parliamentary Scrutiny in EU Affairs', *European Law Journal*, 13:4, 487–504.

Auel, Katrin, and Oliver Höing (2015). 'National Parliaments and the Eurozone Crisis: Taking Ownership in Difficult Times?', *West European Politics*, 38:2, 375–95.

Auel, Katrin, Olivier Rozenberg, and Anja Thomas (2012). 'Lost in Transaction? Parliamentary Reserves in EU Bargains', *OPAL Online Paper Series 10/2012*, available at http://www.opal-eur ope.org/index.php?option=com_content&view=article&id=88.

Auel, Katrin, Olivier Rozenberg, and Angela Tacea (2015a). 'Fighting Back? And If Yes, How? Measuring Parliamentary Strength and Activity in EU Affairs', in Claudia Hefftler et al. (eds.), *Palgrave Handbook of National Parliaments and the European Union*. Houndsmills/Basingstoke: Palgrave Macmillan, 60–93.

Auel, Katrin, Olivier Rozenberg, and Angela Tacea (2015b). 'To Scrutinise or Not to Scrutinise? Explaining Variation in EU-Related Activities in National Parliaments', *West European Politics*, 38:2, 282–304.

Blomgren, Magnus, and Olivier Rozenberg (2012a). 'Legislative Roles and Legislative Studies: The Neo-Institutionalist Turning Point?', in Magnus Blomgren and Olivier Rozenberg (eds.), *Parliamentary Roles in Modern Legislatures*. London: Routledge, 8–36.

Blomgren, Magnus, and Olivier Rozenberg (2012b). 'Bringing Parliamentary Roles Back in', in Magnus Blomgren and Olivier Rozenberg (eds.), *Parliamentary Roles in Modern Legislatures*. London: Routledge, 211–30.

Budge, Ian, and Michael Laver (1986). 'Office Seeking and Policy Pursuit in Coalition Theory', *Legislative Studies Quarterly*, 11:4, 485–506.

Cooper, Ian (2014). 'Parliamentary Oversight of the EU after the Crisis: On the Creation of the 'Article 13' Interparliamentary Conference', *LUISS Working Paper Series* SOG-WP21.

Cox, Gary C., and Matthew D. McCubbins (1993). *Legislative Leviathan: Party Government in the House*. Berkeley: University of California Press.

Cygan, Adam (2013). *Accountability, Parliamentarism and Transparency in the EU: The Role of National Parliaments*. Cheltenham: Edward Elgar.

Damgaard, Erik, and Henrik Jensen (2005). 'Europeanisation of Executive-Legislative Relations: Nordic Perspectives', *Journal of Legislative Studies*, 11:3–4, 394–411.

De Swann, Abram (1973). *Coalition Theories and Cabinet Government. a Study of Formal Theories of Coalition Formation Applied to Nine European Parliaments after 1918*. Amsterdam: Elsevier.

Deubner, Christian (2013). *The Difficult Role of Parliaments in the Reformed Governance of the European Economic and Monetary Union*, Foundation for European Progressive Studies No. 19/2013, Brussels.

DiMaggio, Paul J., and Walter W. Powell (1991). 'Introduction', in Paul DiMaggio and Walter Powell (eds.), *The New Institutionalism in Organizational Analysis*. Chicago/London: University of Cambridge Press, 1–38.

Dimitrakopoulos, Dionyssis (2001). 'Incrementalism and Path Dependence: European Integration and Institutional Change in National Parliaments', *Journal of Common Market Studies*, 39:3, 405–22.

Elkins, David J., and Richard E.B. Simeon (1979). 'A Cause in Search of Its Effect, or What Does Political Culture Explain?', *Comparative Politics*, 11:2, 127–45.

Fenno, Richard F. (2000). *Congress at the Grassroots: Representational Change in the South, 1970–1998*. Chapel Hill: University of North Carolina Press.

Fox, Ruth (2012). 'Europe, Democracy and the Economic Crisis: Is It Time to Reconstitute the 'Assises'?', *Parliamentary Affairs*, 65:2, 463–9.

Gattermann, Katjana, Anna-Lena Högenauer, and Ariella Huff (2013). 'National Parliaments after Lisbon: Towards Mainstreaming of EU Affairs?', *OPAL Online Paper No. 13/2013*, available at http://www.opal-europe.org/tmp/Opal%20Online%20Paper/13.pdf.

Gattermann, Katjana, and Claudia Hefftler (2015). 'Beyond Institutional Capacity: Political Motivation and Parliamentary Behaviour in the Early Warning System', *West European Politics*, 38:2, 305–34.

Goetz, Klaus H., and Jan-Hinrik Meyer-Sahling (2008). 'The Europeanisation of National Political Systems: Parliaments and Executives', *Living Review in European Governance*, 3:2, available at www.livingreviews.org/lreg-2008-2.

Groen, Afke, and Thomas Christiansen (2015). 'National Parliaments in the European Union: Conceptual Choices in the EU's Constitutional Debate', in Claudia Hefftler et al. (eds.), *Palgrave Handbook of National Parliaments and the European Union*. Houndsmills/Basingstoke: Palgrave Macmillan.

Hall, Peter A., and Kathleen Thelen (2009). 'Institutional Change in Varieties of Capitalism', *Socio-Economic Review*, 7:1, 7–34.

Hefftler, Claudia, Christine Neuhold, Olivier Rozenberg, and Julie Smith, eds. (2015). *The Palgrave Handbook of National Parliaments and the European Union*. London: Palgrave Macmillan.

Högenauer, Anna-Lena, and Christine Neuhold (2015). 'National Parliaments after Lisbon: Administrations on the Rise?', *West European Politics*, 38:2, 335–54.

Huff, Ariella (2015). 'Executive Privilege Reaffirmed? Parliamentary Scrutiny of CFSP and CSDP', *West European Politics*, 38:2, 396–415.

Karlas, Jan (2011). 'Parliamentary Control of EU Affairs in Central and Eastern Europe: Explaining the Variation', *Journal of European Public Policy*, 18:2, 258–73.

Karlas, Jan (2012). 'National Parliamentary Control of EU Affairs: Institutional Design after Enlargement', *West European Politics*, 35:5, 1095–113.

Kiiver, Philip (2012). *The Early Warning System for the Principle of Subsidiarity. Constitutional Theory and Empirical Reality*. London: Routledge.

Lindseth, Peter (2012). 'Of the People. Democracy, the Eurozone, and Lincoln's Threshold Criterion', *The Berlin Journal*, 22, 4–7.

March, James G., and Johan P. Olsen (1989). *Rediscovering Institutions: The Organizational Basis of Politics*. New York: Free Press.

March, James G., and Johan P. Olsen (1995). *Democratic Institutions*. New York: Free Press.

Martin, Lanny W., and Georg Vanberg (2004). 'Policing the Bargain: Coalition Government and Parliamentary Scrutiny', *American Journal of Political Science*, 48, 13–27.

Maurer, Andreas, and Wolfgang Wessels eds. (2001). *National Parliaments on Their Ways to Europe: Losers or Latecomers?* Baden-Baden: Nomos.

Mayhew, David (1974). *Congress: The Electoral Connection*. New Haven, CT: Yale University Press.

Monti, Mario (2012). 'Interview' in *Der Spiegel*, available at http://www.spiegel.de/international/eur ope/interview-on-the-euro-crisis-with-italian-prime-minister-mario-monti-a-848511.html (accessed 06 August 2012).

O'Brennan, John, and Tapio Raunio eds. (2007). *National Parliaments within the Enlarged European Union: From 'Victims' of Integration to Competitive Actors?* Abingdon: Routledge.

O'Brennan, John, and Tapio Raunio eds. (2007). *National Parliaments within the Enlarged European Union: From 'Victims' of Integration to Competitive Actors?* London: Routledge.

Peters, B. Guy (1999). *Institutional Theory in Political Science: The 'New Institutionalism'*. London/New York: Continuum.

Pierson, Paul (2004). *Politics in Time: History, Institutions, and Social Analysis*. Princeton, NJ: Princeton University Press.

Pollak, Johannes (2014). 'Compounded Representation in the EU: No Country for Old Parliaments?', in Sandra Kröger and Dario Castiglione (eds.), *Political Representation in the European Union: Still Democratic in times of Crisis?* Abingdon: Routledge, 37–69.

Puntscher Riekmann, Sonia, and Doris Wydra (2013). 'Representation in the European State of Emergency: Parliaments against Governments?' *Journal of European Integration*, 35:5, 565–82.

Raunio, Tapio (2005). 'Holding Governments Accountable in European Affairs: Explaining Cross-National Variation', *Journal of Legislative Studies*, 11:3–4, 319–42.

Raunio, Tapio (2009). 'National Parliaments and European Integration: What We Know and Agenda for Future Research', *Journal of Legislative Studies*, 15:4, 317–34.

Rozenberg, Olivier (2012). 'The Emotional Europeanisation of National Parliaments: Roles Played by EU Committee Chairs at the Commons and at the French National Assembly', *OPAL Online Paper No. 7/2012*, available at http://www.opal-europe.org/index.php?option=com_content&view=article&id=84.

Rozenberg, Olivier, and Claudia Hefftler (2015). 'Introduction', in Claudia Hefftler, Christine Neuhold, Olivier Rozenberg, and Julie Smith (eds.), *Palgrave Handbook of National Parliaments and the European Union*. Houndsmills/Basingstoke: Palgrave Macmillan, 1–39.

Saalfeld, Thomas (2003). 'The Bundestag: Institutional Incrementalism and Behavioural Reticence', in Kenneth Dyson and Klaus Goetz (eds.), *Germany*. Europe and the Politics of Constraint, Oxford: Oxford University Press, 73–96.

Saalfeld, Thomas (2005). 'Delegation or Abdication? Government Backbenchers, Ministers and European Integration', *Journal of Legislative Studies*, 11:3–4, 343–71.

Searing, Donald D. (1991). "Roles', *Rules, and Rationality in the New Institutionalism'*, *American Political Science Review*, 85:4, 1239–60.

Searing, Donald D. (1994). *Westminster's World*. Understanding Political Roles: Cambridge MA, Harvard University Press.

Simon, Herbert A. (1976). *Administrative Behavior: A Study of Decision-Making Processes in Administrative Organization*, 3rd ed. New York: The Free Press.

Sprungk, Carina (2003). 'National Parliamentary Scrutiny in the European Union: The German Bundestag and the French Assemblée Nationale – Key Players or Side-Shows?', Paper presented at the EUSA Conference, Nashville, TN, 27–30 March 2003.

Strelkov, Alexander (2015). 'Who Controls National EU Scrutiny? Party Groups, Committees and Administrations', *West European Politics*, 38:2, 355–74.

Strøm, Kaare, and Wolfgang C. Müller (1999). 'Political Parties and Hard Choices', in Wolfgang C. Müller and Kaare Strøm (eds.), *Policy, Office or Votes? How Political Parties in Western Democracies Make Hard Decisions*. Cambridge: Cambridge University Press, 1–35.

Szalay, Klára (2005). *Scrutiny of EU Affairs in the National Parliaments of the New Member States: Comparative Analysis*. Budapest: Hungarian National Assembly.

Van Rompuy, Herman (2012). 'Speech to the Interparliamentary Committee Meeting on the European Semester for Economic Policy Coordination', Brussels, available at http://europa.eu/rapid/press-release_PRES-12-68_en.htm?locale=en (accessed 27 February 2012).

Wessels, Wolfgang (1997). 'An Ever Closer Fusion? A Dynamic Macropolitical View on Integration Processes', *Journal of Common Market Studies*, 35:2, 267–99.

Weßels, Bernhard (2005). 'Roles and Orientations of Members of Parliament in the EU Context: Congruence or Difference? Europeanisation or Not?', *Journal of Legislative Studies*, 11:3–4, 446–65.

Winzen, Thomas (2010). 'Political Integration and National Parliaments in Europe', *Living Reviews in Democracy 2*, available at http://www.livingreviews.org/lrd-2010-5.

Winzen, Thomas (2012). 'National Parliamentary Control of European Union Affairs: A Cross-National and Longitudinal Comparison', *West European Politics*, 35:3, 657–72.

Winzen, Thomas (2013). 'European Integration and National Parliamentary Oversight Institutions', *European Union Politics*, 14:2, 297–323.

To Scrutinise or Not to Scrutinise? Explaining Variation in EU-Related Activities in National Parliaments

KATRIN AUEL, OLIVIER ROZENBERG and ANGELA TACEA

There is an on-going debate in the literature as to whether national parliaments can and do play an active role in EU policy-making. The main reason for persistent disagreement is the lack of comparative empirical data on parliamentary behaviour in EU affairs. The article aims to contribute to this debate by presenting the first comparative quantitative data on European affairs activities of national parliaments and by explaining the empirical variation. The development of a unique dataset including all 27 national parliaments allows a series of explanatory variables to be tested for the level of parliamentary activity at both the committee and the plenary levels. The analysis shows that institutional strength in EU affairs plays an important role. Overall, however, EU activities can be better explained with a mix of institutional capacities and motivational incentives. The specific combinations vary for different types of activities.

Over recent years, the role of national parliaments has advanced to one of the most salient questions in the general debate over the democratic legitimacy of the EU. Yet, as outlined in more detail in the introduction to this volume (Auel and Christiansen 2015), there is still little agreement in the by now broad literature whether national parliaments can and do actually play an active role in European policy-making. On the one hand, national parliaments have certainly undergone a profound process of formal Europeanisation and are now generally in a much better position to become involved in EU affairs (Winzen 2013). This adaptation has also followed roughly similar institutional patterns. National parliaments have all established specialised committees – the European Affairs Committees (EACs) – and they have obtained extended rights to be informed about and to give their views on European legislative proposals. These similarities can largely be understood as the result of a 'transnational learning process' (Karlas 2011: 258). Differences do remain, however. For example, some parliaments are famous for mandating their ministers in the Council, while others can do little more than express an opinion.

On the other hand, we know little about what parliaments actually do in EU affairs given the lack of detailed comparative empirical data on their involvement in EU politics. The academic debate has so far mainly focused on explaining variation in institutional adaptation and used the institutional provisions, at least implicitly, as a proxy for actual legislative behaviour in EU affairs. Even though this research generated important results, it needs to be completed by explaining why parliaments act rather than why they *are able to* act. National parliaments are complex institutions, made up of individuals faced with a number of different opportunities, constraints and incentives. Institutional capacities are thus not necessarily automatically translated into behaviour.

The paper therefore aims at outlining and explaining the empirical variation regarding parliamentary EU activities. It draws on a unique and rich quantitative dataset of various types of activities in all lower chambers[1] across the EU over three years (2010 to 2012). Our general assumption is that European activities depend on both the institutional capacities of the parliaments and MPs' motivation to act. In addition, we expect that both institutional strength and motivations have a varying impact on different types of activities: activities related to the influencing and scrutiny function, such as mandates or resolutions, are more likely to depend on institutional capacities, while (electoral) incentives can be expected to be more important for activities relating to the communication function such as plenary debates. The paper is organised as follows. The first section presents our data on different types of activities and discusses the literature on the institutional adaptation of national parliaments in EU affairs. This literature puts emphasis on two major factors to explain institutional variation: the institutional strength of parliament independent of EU affairs as well as public and elite Euroscepticism. Drawing on this literature, we then develop explanations for parliamentary activity in EU affairs. After providing an overview of the data for our dependent and independent variables in section five, the following section presents the regression models used to test the hypotheses and the discussion of our findings. The last section concludes.

Dealing with EU Politics from the Backbenches

Fighting back: Parliamentary Activities in EU Affairs

Parliaments are multi-taskers that fulfil a variety of functions. Although both classic (Bagehot [1867] 2009) and modern catalogues (e.g. Norton 1990; Packenham 1970) have identified a large number of parliamentary functions, most agree on four fundamental ones: (s)election of the government, legislation (which includes both policy formulation and giving final assent to collectively binding decisions), oversight (scrutiny and control) and communication. Within

EU affairs, these functions are not all equally important. Parliaments do, of course, select the government, but they rarely do so with regard to EU politics. In addition, national parliaments have delegated part of their legislative function, in terms of both policy formulation and giving final assent, to the European level. To compensate for this loss of legislative competences, they have developed provisions to scrutinise and influence their government's EU policy. In addition, they now also have, albeit limited, opportunities to influence policy-making directly at the EU level through the Early Warning System (EWS) and the Political Dialogue.[2] Scrutiny and influence are therefore generally considered the most important functions in parliament. However, the communication function of parliaments remains just as important in EU affairs as it is in domestic politics. By communicating EU issues to their citizens, national parliaments are in a unique position to ensure that people are more connected with 'Europe' by making the EU more visibly present in national politics and more accessible to and for their national publics.

Accordingly, we focus our analysis on four main types of activities: mandates and/or resolutions (depending on the type of scrutiny system), EAC meetings, plenary debates and the number of opinions submitted to the European Commission within the Political Dialogue. While mandates and resolutions as well as opinions capture the policy-influencing function with regard to both their own government and the European level, time spent in EAC meetings captures the 'working' aspect of national parliaments that relates to scrutiny and developing expertise in EU affairs. Plenary debates, finally, measure the extent to which parliaments fulfil their communication function. We excluded reasoned opinions sent within the Early Warning System from the analysis as they are a fairly new instrument, established only with the Treaty of Lisbon, where parliaments may not yet have established routines to the same extent as for other types of activities.

Before presenting our data in Table 1, two caveats need to be addressed. First, the data does omit other activities, especially activities of the specialised standing committees as well as more informal means of influence and control. This omission is due to unavailable data. While the standing committees are involved in EU affairs in many parliaments, it is impossible to obtain data on the share of committee time spent on scrutinising and debating EU issues compared to domestic issues. The omission of more informal means of influence and control is, unfortunately, part of the trade-off between large and small N studies. Investigating informal strategies not only relies on qualitative data sources, but is also difficult to quantify.

Second, simply measuring the level of activity reveals little about the *impact* of parliamentary involvement, i.e. whether more active parliaments succeed in controlling and influencing their governments effectively. Since the actual impact of parliamentary activity in terms of influence is extremely difficult to measure, we can only capture what parliaments do, but not whether they are actually successful.

TABLE 1
PARLIAMENTARY ACTIVITIES IN EU AFFAIRS (2010–2012)

| | Mandates and resolutions | EAC meetings | | Political Dialogue opinions | EU plenary debates | |
		Number (meetings)	Time (hours)		Number (debates)	Time (hours)
Absolute number	3,153	3,658	5,590	802	1,079	2,104
Mean/year	38.9	44.6	69.2	9.9	13.3	26.1
Min/year	0	8	19.5	0	0	0
Max/year	220	126	154.5	197	51	112.5
Standard deviation	44.4	25.7	31.6	28.3	11.7	25.3

Note: Data for the lower houses of the 27 national parliaments in the EU.
Source: Author's data.

As Table 1 shows, European activities are far from being marginal in parliaments. On average, their EACs met once a working week for more than one hour, and chambers issue about 50 European statements per year: 39 addressed to the government and ten to the European Commission. Yet parliaments differ greatly when it comes to EU activities. The number of resolutions passed by individual parliaments ranges from 0 to 220 per year over the three years. Similarly, the duration of plenary debates spent on EU issues ranges from 0 to over 112 hours, the number of opinions from 0 to 197.[3]

That parliaments not only differ regarding their overall level of activity in EU affairs, but also tend to emphasise different activities, is shown in Table 2 which presents the correlation coefficients between the four types of activity (see also Auel et al. 2015). For example, parliaments that spend long hours scrutinising EU affairs in the EAC are not systematically as active when it comes to debating EU issues in the plenary. The only somewhat stronger correlation can be found between resolutions/mandates and Political Dialogue opinions. Indeed, a number of parliaments tend to forward their resolutions simultaneously to the government and the European Commission. Overall, however, the results suggest that the emphasis on different parliamentary functions varies.

Assessing the Gap between Rules and Behaviour

The last two decades have seen the development of a large and rich body of literature on the cross-national variation regarding the institutional capacities of national parliaments in EU affairs. Despite the diversity of the methods employed and the data used, the studies have generated rather converging results. Most of them agree on the importance of two factors: domestic institutional strength and Euroscepticism. The former has been measured with different variables such as the overall institutional strength of parliaments prior to and independent of integration or the power balance in legislative–executive relations (Bergman 1997, 2000; Dimitrakopoulos 2001; Karlas 2011, 2012; Martin 2000; Maurer and Wessels 2001; Raunio 2005; Saalfeld 2005). The main argument is 'that the overall strength of the legislature "spills over" to

TABLE 2
CORRELATIONS BETWEEN DIFFERENT TYPES OF PARLIAMENTARY ACTIVITIES IN EU AFFAIRS (2010–2012)

	Mandates resolutions	EAC meetings	Plenary debates
EAC meetings	0.260*	1	
Plenary debates	0.133	0.041	1
Political Dialogue	0.340**	−0.028	0.007

Note: Correlations based on Pearson's r, $n = 81$.
*$p < 0.05$; **$p < 0.01$; ***$p < 0.001$. Portugal was excluded from the Political Dialogue opinions given its outlier status ($N = 78$).

European affairs, with stronger control of the government in domestic matters producing also tighter cabinet scrutiny in European affairs' (Raunio 2009: 330, fn. 11). However, the literature has also indicated that domestic institutional strength is more likely to lead to tighter scrutiny procedures in EU affairs where members of parliament (MPs) or parliamentary party groups (PPGs) have additional incentives. The second factor therefore draws on motivation-based explanations and can be summarised under the heading of public and/or elite opinion, including the degree of public support for the EU in the member state and/or the existence of Eurosceptic parties (Bergman 1997, 2000; Raunio 2005; Raunio and Wiberg 2000; Winzen 2013). As Raunio has shown for the EU-15, the power of parliament independent of integration was the only necessary condition (for the Central and Eastern European member states see Karlas 2011), whereas the combination of having a powerful parliament and a Eurosceptic electorate were sufficient conditions for producing tighter procedures for the control of the government in EU matters.

As argued in the introduction, however, much of the literature so far is based on the, mainly implicit, assumption that the resulting parliamentary scrutiny provisions equal legislative scrutiny behaviour. This is rather surprising, given that the literature has clearly established that additional incentives are important to explain the very development of these provisions. In part, using institutional rights as a proxy for actual scrutiny activity is, of course, due to the previous lack of comparative empirical data on parliamentary activities in EU affairs. As a result, studies have mainly focused on comparing institutional provisions, where data is more easily accessible. Yet a number of studies have pointed out that national parliaments do not always make use of their institutional rights (e.g. Auel 2007; Pollack and Slominski 2003; Saalfeld 2003). In fact, parliaments are famous for not systematically doing what they are allowed to: 'what is remarkable about the legislatures is not their power to say no to government but rather their reluctance to employ that power' (Norton 1998: 192).

In a first step, we therefore investigated whether there is a systematic relationship between parliamentary strength in EU affairs (measured by the OPAL score of formal rights, see Auel *et al.* 2015 and below) and our different types of activities. As Figure 1 illustrates, stronger parliaments do tend to be more active, but this is far from being systematic. Institutional strength matters most for mandates/resolutions, but the relationship is weaker for plenary debates or time spent in EAC meetings – and it is non-existent for opinions sent within the Political Dialogue. This not only suggests that institutional strength cannot simply be taken as a proxy for actual parliamentary activity, but also that taking MPs' motivations into account as well may provide overall better explanations for legislative behaviour.

In the following, we develop our theoretical framework based on the discussions and findings above. We first develop general hypotheses on the impact of both institutional and motivational factors on parliamentary activity

FIGURE 1
INSTITUTIONAL STRENGTH AND LEVEL OF ACTIVITY IN EU AFFAIRS, BY TYPE OF
ACTIVITY (MEANS BY YEAR FOR 2010–2012)

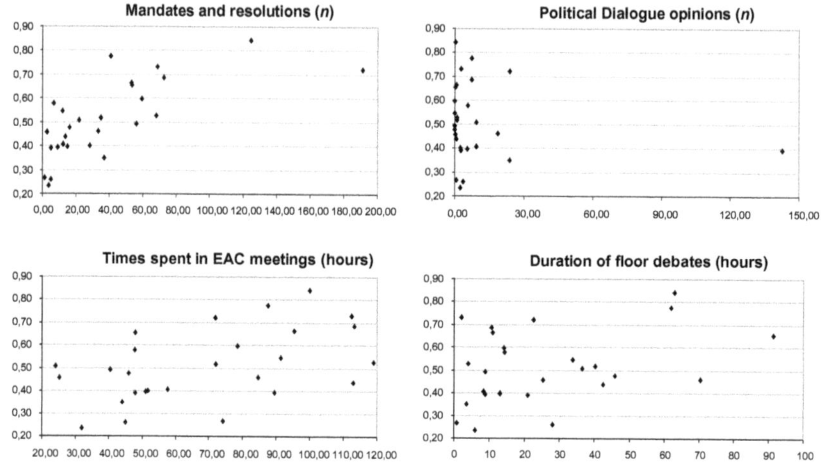

in EU affairs and then discuss our assumptions on the variation in the impact of different types of factors on different types of activities.

Why Are They Fighting Back? Explaining Parliamentary Activities in EU Affairs

To understand why some national parliaments are more active than others in EU affairs, we develop a set of hypotheses based on agency theory and the principal–agent model, which have served as the conceptual framework for several important studies analysing parliamentary control in EU affairs (e.g. Bergman 2000; Saalfeld 2005; Strøm 2003; Winzen 2012). The underlying general assumption is that members of parliament (or parliamentary party groups) as principals delegate EU affairs to their agents, the government, and then can employ various means of control to prevent agency loss. This raises two fundamental questions. First, what are the institutional (legal and formal) means of national parliaments to exercise this control, or, in other words, what are their *capacities* for control and influence? The second question is whether MPs or PPGs have the necessary political will or motivation to exercise control. The paper therefore develops hypotheses on both assumptions about the impact of institutional factors (H1 to H3) and about factors that impact the motivation of actors to become involved in EU affairs (H4 and H5). Finally, it also takes into account the fact that the EU was hit by the eurozone crisis during our period of investigation (H6).

Institutional Capacities

Based on the literature and the findings above, we expect formal institutional rights to have a significant (albeit not necessarily dominant) impact on the level of parliamentary activity in EU affairs. MPs and PPGs can, of course, also find ways to compensate for a lack of formal rights through other, and possibly more informal, strategies (Auel and Benz 2005). Yet it can clearly be expected that institutional provisions enshrined in the Constitution, ordinary legislation or standing orders provide institutional opportunities and thus facilitate the involvement of parliaments in EU affairs.

H1: The stronger the institutional prerogatives of national parliaments in EU affairs, the greater their level of activity in EU affairs.

Since constitutionally strong parliaments developed tighter scrutiny provisions on EU matters, we can expect strong parliaments to be generally more active on EU issues as well. Although there is little agreement within legislative studies on how to define and measure parliamentary strength (Sieberer 2011), there is no doubt that the direct influence over policy-making is essential to it. Given that EU norms greatly affect, directly or indirectly, domestic legislative agendas, it seems plausible to assume that legislatures with greater general policy-influencing power will also be more active regarding EU issues.

H2: The greater the institutional power of national parliaments in domestic affairs, the greater their level of activity in EU affairs.

The third assumption addresses the broader institutional context. Parliaments are embedded in complex political systems where their formal institutional power is only one factor impacting the overall balance of power in executive–legislative relations. Thus, we take into account Lijphart's famous conceptualisation of consensus vs. majoritarian systems, which, in its first 'executives–parties dimension' (Lijphart 2012: 3), embraces the nature of the party system, the type and stability of the government and electoral rules as decisive factors. According to Lijphart (2012: 2), the aim of a consensus system is to 'share, disperse and limit power in a variety of ways'. We assume that within such an institutional setting, MPs and PPGs are better able to control the government in EU affairs. One aspect of consensus democracies in particular supports this view: due to the larger number of parties, governments are more likely to be formed by coalitions. As a result, majority MPs have to 'police the bargain' (Martin and Vanberg 2004, see also Saalfeld 2005) – i.e. to control what ministers from other coalition PPGs are actually doing – while supporting their 'own' ministers vis-à-vis the other coalition partners.

H3: The greater the degree of consensus orientation of the political system, the more active national parliaments are in EU affairs.

Motivational Incentives

The remaining hypotheses deal with MPs' motivations for using their prerogatives in EU affairs. As outlined above, the literature has emphasised that even domestically strong parliaments generally need additional incentives to develop strong institutional scrutiny rights. One of the important characteristics of the chain of delegation in parliamentary systems is that MPs are both principals of the government and agents of their voters or citizens (Strøm 2003). As a result, an investigation of the preferences and incentives of MPs to become involved in EU affairs needs to take both 'roles' of MPs into account. As agents, MPs' most important preference is to secure the continuation of the delegation relationship, i.e. to be re-elected. As principals, the most important preference of MPs is to induce their agent (the government) to act in accordance with their policy interests, i.e. to minimise agency loss. We can thus assume that the motivation of MPs/PPGs to use institutional opportunities – i.e. to engage in parliamentary scrutiny of EU affairs – depends on (a) voters' expectations and (b) incentives that impact their motivation to exert policy influence (see also Saalfeld 2005).

Regarding voter expectations, we test the established hypothesis advanced by previous research, namely that opposition to the EU within public opinion creates an electoral incentive for MPs to control their government.

H4: The stronger the opposition to EU integration/membership in public opinion, the more active parliaments are in EU affairs.

In addition, the literature has suggested that the presence of Eurosceptic parliamentary party groups or party factions within parliament has had a positive impact on the development of tighter scrutiny procedures (e.g. Raunio and Wiberg 2000; Winzen *et al.* 2015). Accordingly, we assume that they also have an incentive to make use of these institutional capacities for both electoral and policy impact reasons: in general, Eurosceptic MPs can be assumed to be more interested in controlling the government on EU matters. Governing parties, however, generally tend to support their governments, at least publicly (Auel 2007), and thus to exert control though more informal means. As a result, we expect parliamentary Euroscepticism to have the greatest impact on formal activities, where we find strong Eurosceptic parties in parliament or a large difference in the position on EU integration between the governing and the opposition parties.

H5: The stronger the opposition to EU integration/membership within parliament, the more active parliaments are in EU affairs.

Finally, we also need to take into account that the time period under investigation (2010 to 2012) was by no means business as usual in the EU due to the eurozone crisis. In fact, as Auel and Höing (2015) have shown, national parliaments have been rather active when it comes to scrutinising crisis management at the EU level. This is not surprising, given the high stakes – especially for countries within the eurozone that had to shoulder large financial guarantees for the European Financial Stability Facility (EFSF) or the European Stability Mechanism (ESM), guarantees that may severely limit their future financial room for manoeuvre. We therefore expect that the level of integration in the Economic and Monetary Union (EMU), and especially the status as donor countries within the eurozone, will have a positive impact on EU activities.[4]

H6: The more integrated their countries are in the EMU, the more active parliaments are in EU affairs.

Different Means of Fighting Back: Parliamentary Communication vs. Policy Influence

The hypotheses developed above address the factors we expect to impact parliamentary activity more generally. However, as outlined, different types of activities relate to different types of parliament functions, and we can assume that institutional capacities as well as motivational incentives vary in how they impact the fulfilment of such functions. Above, we distinguished between activities serving the influencing and scrutiny function (resolutions/mandates, opinions, time spent in the EAC), on the one hand, and the function of communication and public accountability (plenary debates) on the other. With regard to the former, we expect much of the parliamentary scrutiny activity to depend on institutional capacities to scrutinise and influence the government effectively. Parliaments dominated by the executive that lack strong information and oversight rights or an effective infrastructure to deal with EU affairs are less likely to become involved in EU politics. In addition, resolutions or mandates are instruments that require a parliamentary majority. As a result, incentives to 'police the bargain' between governing parties are more likely to have an impact than conflicts between the governing and the opposition parties over EU integration. The same is true for Eurosceptic parties, which are often found at the fringes of the party system and too small to exert influence on their own.

HI: The impact of institutional factors on EU activity will be stronger for activities relating to the influencing function of parliaments.

Plenary debates, in contrast, serve precisely the function of communicating EU issues to the electorate. They are more likely to gain media attention and thus to reach a larger audience. As a result, conflicts between the governing and opposition parties over EU issues can have a greater impact in the plenary than in deliberations behind (often closed) doors of committees. Plenary debates provide opposition parties, and Eurosceptic parties in particular, an opportunity to sharpen their electoral profile by attacking the government parties over their EU policies. Finally, the politicisation of EU affairs through the eurozone crisis (see, for example, Puntscher Riekmann and Wydra 2013) also seems to have had an impact, especially on the debating activity of national parliaments: while crisis-related parliamentary statements accounted for only a little over 10 per cent of all statements on EU matters on average, debates on crisis-related issues made up over 40 per cent of all EU debates (Auel and Höing 2015). We therefore also expect the level of EMU integration to have an impact on plenary debates.

HII: The impact of motivational incentives on EU activity will be stronger for activities relating to the communication function.

Figure 2 provides a synthesised overview over our conceptual framework.

Data

Dependent Variables

Our dependent variables consist of the number of resolutions or mandates, the time spent in EAC meetings, the time spent debating EU issues on the plenary as well as the number of opinions sent within the Political Dialogue – each by parliament (lower houses only) and year. Data on resolutions and mandates, debates and opinions was collected in the context of the OPAL research project, using parliamentary websites, the European Commission's website for the relation with national parliaments (the so-called Political Dialogue)[5] and IPEX[6] as sources.[7] In addition, coders requested and confirmed data directly with parliamentary information offices. Data on the number and duration of EAC meetings, as well as on the average length of EU plenary debates, was collected by sending out a questionnaire to the EACs of all chambers.[8]

FIGURE 2
MPS' ACTIVITIES IN EU AFFAIRS: A CONCEPTUAL FRAMEWORK

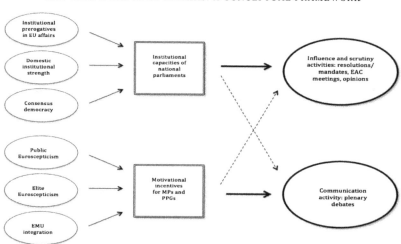

Independent Variables

Institutional strength in EU affairs: With regard to measuring the institutional strength of national parliaments in EU affairs, we draw on the OPAL score of institutional strength (Auel *et al*. 2015). It measures parliamentary strength in EU affairs based on 11 indicators organised along three dimensions: access to information (access to documents, explanatory memorandum, ex ante reports on councils), parliamentary infrastructure (type of EAC, role of standing committees, share of MPs involved) as well as oversight and influence rights (binding character of the opinions, reserve, scope, ex post reports on councils). Figure 3 provides the scores for all 27 parliaments.

Domestic strength of the legislature: We decided to assess the domestic strength using the strength of the committee system. As indicated by a number of converging studies over the last decades (for an overview, see Martin 2014), committees appear to constitute one of the most relevant proxies for capturing the degree of independence of a given legislature vis-à-vis the government. Inspired by Karlas (2012), we draw on two different measures of committee strength: Martin and Depauw (2009) and Yläoutinen and Hallerberg (2009). The two measures were normalised and aggregated into a single score. Data on Cyprus are missing for this variable. Therefore we tested the model for 26 parliaments.

Consensus vs. majority democracy: We used an updated and complete time-variant proxy for Lijphart's (2012) first dimension, 'parties–executives', developed by Armingeon *et al*. (2013), which focuses on the core elements of political systems (government, legislatures, parties and electoral rules).

Public Euroscepticism: To measure public Euroscepticism, we used Eurobarometer data on the percentage of citizens who stated that they tend not to trust the European Union.[9]

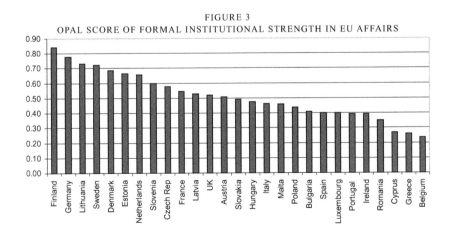

FIGURE 3

OPAL SCORE OF FORMAL INSTITUTIONAL STRENGTH IN EU AFFAIRS

Note: Average score of institutional strength 2010–2012.
Source: Authors' data.

Opposition to EU integration within parliament is captured by two different variables. To measure the strength of *Eurosceptic parties* within parliaments, we calculated their seat share for each parliament based on the Chapel Hill 2010 dataset (Bakker *et al.* 2012).[10] To capture the *opposition to EU integration* more broadly, we calculated the average Chapel Hill scores for the governing and the opposition parties and then subtracted the latter from the former. Thus, the greater the resulting value, the larger the gap between the governing and the opposition parties' position on EU integration.

EMU involvement, finally, is captured by a variable that assigns the value 1 for participation in the Treaty on Stability, Coordination and Governance (TSCG), the Euro Plus Pact (EUPP), the eurozone as well as for EFSF/ESM donor status. This takes into account that participation in different EMU treaties (TSCG, EUPP) varies within non-eurozone countries, while eurozone countries can be distinguished according to donor and debtor status. Values range from 0 to 4 (see also Auel and Höing 2015).

Table 3 provides an overview of the independent variables.

Results

To test the hypotheses developed above, we ran a linear regression analysis using STATA version 13. Standard estimation methods of linear regression analysis do not account for the fact that our observations are nested within parliaments. Consequently, we use a clustered standard error technique (Primo *et al.* 2007), which allows us to adjust for clustering at the parliament level and to avoid overstating the statistical significance of coefficient estimates. Variables were introduced in two sets. We ran a regression with the institutional variables first and then with the whole model. The results of the regressions are reported in Tables 4 and 5.

Discussion

As expected, formal rights in EU affairs (H1) do have an impact on activity related to resolutions, EAC meetings or plenary debates. The effect is also considerable. An increase of 0.1 on the scale of institutional strength (ranging

TABLE 3
OVERVIEW OVER THE INDEPENDENT VARIABLES

Variable	Mean	Std. dev.	Min	Max
OPAL score institutional strength EU	0.510	0.157	0.235	0.842
Committee strength	1.358	0.4103	0.3472	2
Consensus vs. majority system	−0.0411	0.9394	−2.28	1.9
Public Euroscepticism	46.64	12.06	22	80
Strength of Eurosceptic parties	13.66	13.89	0	48.58
Gov.–opp. dissent over EU integration	0.684	1.23	−2.06	2.92
EMU Involvement	2.92	1.34	0	4

TABLE 4

REGRESSION ANALYSIS FOR INSTITUTIONAL VARIABLES

Variables	Number of resolutions	Duration debates	Time spent in EAC meetings	Number of opinions
Institutional strength in EU affairs	176.137***	57.649*	73.313**	−3.650
	(46.29)	(24.34)	(23.95)	(10.48)
Domestic strength of the legislature	−0.154	−20.314	6.747	4.239
	(10.35)	(16.02)	(17.13)	(3.31)
Consensus vs. majority system	10.460*	−0.154	0.554	0.328
	(4.12)	(6.74)	(7.72)	(1.22)
Constant	−50.274	24.736	21.774	1.283
	(27.52)	(22.92)	(23.24)	(6.02)
R^2	0.476	0.195	0.155	0.061

Notes: Entries are coefficients with standard errors adjusted for country clusters in parentheses. $N = 78$. Cyprus was excluded from the entire analysis due to missing data; Portugal was excluded from the analysis of Political Dialogue opinions due to its outlier status (here, $N = 75$).
*$p < 0.05$; **$p < 0.01$; ***$p < 0.001$.

TABLE 5

REGRESSION ANALYSIS FOR INSTITUTIONAL AND MOTIVATION VARIABLES

Variables	Number of resolutions	Duration debates	Time spent in EAC meetings	Number of opinions
Institutional strength in EU affairs	174.134***	53.268**	72.389**	-4.310
	(38.05)	(16.75)	(25.94)	(9.17)
Domestic strength of the legislature	-2.671	-3.651	7.232	5.483
	(11.67)	(11.50)	(23.19)	(3.44)
Consensus vs. majority system	14.614**	-1.864	0.740	1.036
	(4.53)	(4.88)	(8.48)	(1.42)
Public Euroscepticism	1.124*	0.063	0.154	0.130
	(0.44)	(0.22)	(0.44)	(0.10)
Eurosceptic parties	-0.968	1.017**	-0.007	-0.107
	(0.63)	(0.35)	(0.69)	(0.15)
Gov.–Opp. Dissent	6.163	-4.632	1.633	-1.009
	(6.50)	(3.70)	(4.25)	(1.75)
EMU involvement	-9.611	10.438*	-0.038	-1.619
	(8.04)	(4.13)	(5.96)	(1.84)
Constant	-61.098	-39.729	13.361	0.940
	(31.19)	(19.76)	(50.65)	(6.98)
R^2	0.566	0.413	0.161	0.160

Notes: See Table 4.

from 0 to 1), which corresponds, for example, to the difference in strength between the Dutch Tweede Kamer and the, less powerful, French Assemblée Nationale, will increase the number of resolutions by 17.4. The only exceptions are the Political Dialogue opinions, where the predictor has no impact. This result is not too surprising, however, given that all parliaments have the same formal rights regarding participation in the Political Dialogue. The political impact of resolutions or mandates, in contrast, largely depends on formal rules, in particular on rules concerning their legally binding character.

Regarding the domestic rights of the parliament (H2) – using the strength of the standing committees as a proxy for the general influence of the parliament – we find little evidence that domestically strong parliaments are especially active in EU affairs. We confirmed this somewhat unexpected result by using alternative ways of measuring domestic parliamentary strength, such as the Woldendorp *et al.* (2000) index of constitutional balance or the Fish and Kroenig (2009) score of institutional strength. The domestic strength of parliaments may thus play an indirect role[11] as strong parliaments are generally among the most powerful in EU affairs[11], but it is not directly reflected in the level of activities in EU affairs. This may partly result from our quantitative assessment of the activities: domestically strong parliaments may not be especially more active, but they may indeed be much more *influential* in EU affairs. We can expect, for instance, that governments are more willing to anticipate and accommodate parliamentary views when parliaments are constitutionally powerful, which may reduce the need to issue formal resolutions or mandates. Similarly, demanding accountability provisions regarding, for example, the participation of the head of government in European Council meetings (systematic organisation of hearings, personal presence of the PM, no advance notice of the questions, questions and answers rather than long statements), may reduce the need to spend hours in the EAC on that issue (Wessels and Rozenberg 2012). An exception to the above is the degree of consensus orientation of the political system (H3), but it plays a role in the case of resolutions only. This means that where a political system is generally organised to limit the ability of the government (or governing party leaders) to impose decisions, parliaments do indeed tend to be more active policy-influencers in EU affairs.

Regarding MPs' motivations to become involved in EU affairs, we distinguished between electoral and policy incentives. Regarding the former (H4), public opinion on the EU does have a positive impact on resolutions, but it is relatively weak. A 1 per cent increase in public Euroscepticism will only increase the number of resolutions issued by about 1. In turn, opposition to EU integration within parliament – i.e. the share of Eurosceptic parties and conflicts between governing and opposition parties over the EU (H5) – impact on the duration of plenary debates only and again weakly. Here, a 1 per cent increase in the share of Eurosceptic parties will lead to an increase of debates by about one hour. Taken together, these results suggest that Euroscepticism, both in public opinion and among political elites, constitutes a limited incentive for engaging in EU affairs. This is, again, a rather unexpected result given past analyses of the Europeanisation of national parliaments. In part, the weak relation between Euroscepticism and EU activities in parliament may be explained by the often de-politicised way of addressing EU issues in parliaments (Auel and Raunio 2014). When it comes to the scrutiny of specific EU documents and decisions or to the general search for consensus in EACs or standing committees, many Eurosceptic MPs seem to choose the 'exit' rather than the 'voice' option, to echo Hirschman's (1970) famous categories.

This brings us to the final aspect, the impact of the eurozone crisis (H6). Our findings indicate that the parliaments of member states more integrated into the EMU, and thus especially the eurozone members with donor status regarding the EFSF and ESM, tended to spend more time debating EU issues in the plenary. Given the fact that between 2010 and 2012, the eurozone crisis, the future of the common currency and the control over domestic deficits were highly topical issues, these parliaments were thus clearly willing to poke the famous 'sleeping giant' (Van der Eijk and Franklin 2004). On the other activities, in contrast, EMU integration had no effect. This reflects the results of Auel and Höing (2015), who found that the crisis had a great impact on plenary debates, especially in donor countries, while the crisis management was dealt with more as 'business as usual' regarding resolutions or Political Dialogue opinions.

Turning to the comparison of explanatory patterns for different types of activities (HI and HII), our expectation that they follow different logics is only partly confirmed. Institutional factors do impact the adoption of resolutions more strongly than plenary debates. With the exception of Political Dialogue opinions, however, the institutional strength of a parliament in EU affairs has a decisive impact on all types of activities, be they related to the influencing or the communication function. At the same time, the motivational factors affect activities differently: public Euroscepticism increases only the number of resolutions, and MPs' Euroscepticism only the duration of floor debates.

Thus, we have indeed a fairly clear idea of why mandates and resolutions are adopted on EU issues.[12] The limited increase in the R^2 from 0.476 to 0.566 after introducing the predictors related to motivational incentives indicates that motivational incentives do matter, but that resolutions are first and foremost driven by the institutional capabilities. In contrast, we are able to explain less than 20 per cent of the variation regarding the duration of floor debates when we take only institutional variables into account; but the explanatory power more than doubles to over 41 per cent in the complete model. This indicates that how much time was spent on debating EU issues in the plenary also depends both on parliamentary Euroscepticism and on the salience of the eurozone crisis. Yet it is the strength of Eurosceptic parties that matters (albeit weakly), rather than the more general conflict over EU issues between governing and opposition parties. Again, the eurozone crisis could be an important reason: opposition parties may have been under pressure to agree with crisis-related measures both for reasons of time pressure and their 'entrapment in the European rescue discourse' (Puntscher Riekmann and Wydra 2013: 579).

While our final two hypotheses (HI and HII) are partly, and only partly, confirmed in the case of resolutions and floor debates, this is not the case for the two other types of activities that we largely fail to explain. For both the time spent in EAC meetings and the number of Political Dialogue opinions we can explain only about 16 per cent of the variation. Regarding EACs, the institutional strength of the legislatures on EU issues is the only variable that has an impact. This does confirm our assumption about the importance of institutional capacities for the level of activities related to scrutiny and influence. But it still raises the question why other variables have no impact at all and why the overall explanatory value of our model is so limited. Two reasons can be brought forward. First, despite the similarity in name, EACs differ from one parliament to another on many dimensions: size, existence of sub-committees, political profile of the members, responsibilities, openness and relations to the standing committees. This last aspect is especially significant, as some EACs are the main bodies responsible for conducting the parliament's EU business while others are mainly 'clearing houses' in charge of selecting important EU documents for standing committees and acting as the coordinating body. Therefore it may be difficult to identify common explanations for EAC activities simply because the term 'EAC' refers to very different kinds of bodies. Second, as with any other type of parliamentary body, EAC organisation depends on general rules, routines and capacities that are unrelated to the EU dimension, such as general meeting schedules for committees, the length of parliamentary sessions or whether the EAC can meet during parliamentary recesses. We therefore need further analyses that take both such patterns and differences in the type of EACs into account.

Regarding the opinions sent within the Political Dialogue with the European Commission, none of the variables we identified were significant at the 95 per cent level. Overall, it seems that parliamentary engagement in the Political Dialogue with the European Commission follows a rather different logic than other EU activities. What we can infer from the results is that the opinions are neither an instrument used mainly by strong parliaments to extend their influence to the EU level nor mainly by weak parliaments to compensate for their lack of influence at the domestic level. One explanation could be that the system is still relatively new. As illustrated by a comparison of two parliaments that make very active use of the instrument, namely the Portuguese Assembleia and the Swedish Riksdag, the rationale for sending opinions also seems to vary greatly between parliaments: from a purely bureaucratic notification on the result of the subsidiarity check to the submission of a fairly comprehensive assessment of the Commission proposals. Another factor may be how effective and useful MPs believe the Political Dialogue to be in terms of policy influence. As shown by a recent COSAC[13] report, a majority of parliaments feel that it 'could be strengthened or enhanced and advanced a number of ways of improving it. In general, parliaments/chambers would welcome more prompt and substantive responses by the Commission to concerns raised by them' (COSAC 2012: 1). Finally, as those opinions, in contrast to resolutions, are addressed to a body that is external to the domestic political game, they may, in fact, be neglected by MPs and largely delegated to clerks.

Conclusion

This paper has shed light on different European activities within the lower houses of the national parliaments of the EU. It shows that the formal Europeanisation of national legislatures over the last decades has not been vain. While we can still find a few 'scrutiny laggards', many chambers are now rather actively involved in EU affairs, and this is all the more the case where they have obtained stronger formal rights regarding their access to information or their ability to issue resolutions and mandates, and have established an effective infrastructure to deal with EU matters. Formal rights appear to constitute crucial preconditions especially for activities related to the functions of scrutiny and influence, such as issuing resolutions on EU draft legislation or mandating their government's negotiation position. Yet our findings show that European activities result not only from institutional opportunities but also from electoral and policy considerations. In the specific context of the economic crisis, this has been especially the case for EU plenary debates, and thus for a more public activity related to the communication function.

If we compare the explanatory variables for the development of institutional capacities emphasised in the literature on national parliaments in the EU and our results for their actual EU activities, we find both similarities and differences. The findings converge with regard to the fact that it is a mix of institutional and motivational factors that provides an overall better explanation for both dynamics than purely institutional ones. Yet we find differences with regard to the types of institutional and motivational factors that play a role: The *domestic* strength of the parliaments impacts European activities only indirectly, through their formal prerogatives in EU affairs. Domestically strong parliaments are not systematically among the most active, possibly because they do not need to be very active to be influential. Similarly, public Euroscepticism, one of the main factors identified for institutional adaptation, only plays a limited role regarding parliaments' activity. For parliamentary activities related to the communication function, in particular, we found parliamentary Euroscepticism, and especially the salience of the eurozone crisis, to be more important. In addition, our findings suggest that some parliamentary provisions are embedded in general institutional rules and routines and therefore largely independent of on-going, parliamentary or public, controversies about the EU. This seems to be especially the case for EAC meetings that we largely fail to explain.

To conclude, our results on EU activities in parliaments also shed light on their institutional adaptation to the EU. It has been demonstrated that institutional reforms do have consequences regarding different types of parliamentary activities. MPs are rational animals who are all the more willing to become involved in EU affairs if they have the institutional means to do so at their disposal. This suggests, however, that the level of activity will most likely also depend on the *effectiveness* of the respective instruments, for example whether resolutions actually do have an impact on the government's EU position and on EU policies, whether EU debates do reach the citizens and whether the European Commission does take opinions sent by national parliaments into account. This impact could also provide the missing link that accounts – together with endogenous institutional routines – for the variations that we were not able to explain in our model. Assessing the impact of parliamentary activities comprehensively and comparatively thus constitutes an ambitious field of research for the future.

Acknowledgements

The research for this article has been conducted as part of the OPAL (Observatory of Parliaments after Lisbon) research consortium and was funded by the Agence Nationale de la Recherche (10-ORAR-003-01). We also thank our OPAL partners at the Universities of Cambridge, Cologne and Maastricht, the coders who have supported us with the data collection, and the anonymous reviewers as well as Flora Chanvril-Ligneel, Martial Foucault, Peter Grand, Simon Otjes, Jan Rovny and Nicolas Sauger for their helpful advice. All errors remain our own.

Disclosure Statement

No potential conflict of interests was reported by the authors.

Notes

1. Our analysis does not include the newest member state, since Croatia only acceded in 2013.
2. For details on the Early Warning System – the parliamentary subsidiarity check introduced with the Lisbon Treaty – see the introduction (Auel and Christiansen 2015) as well as Gattermann and Hefftler (2015). The Political Dialogue was introduced with the Barroso initiative in 2006 and aims at establishing a dialogue between national parliaments and the European Commission early in the policy-making process and not, as in the EWS, limited to aspects of subsidiarity (see Jančić 2012).
3. However, the numbers for the political opinions have to be viewed with some caution, as they are mainly due to the activity of the Portuguese Assembleia, which adopts opinions within the Political Dialogue on a very large number of documents sent by the European Commission (on average over 140 opinions per year). Given that most of these opinions do not include any comments on the document – other than a statement that the Assembleia has not found a breach of the subsidiarity principle – this inflates the overall and average number of opinions for all parliaments.
4. In comparison to MPs' or citizens' views on the EU, the level of involvement of a member state in the EMU can be considered as an indirect factor for the involvement of MPs in EU activity. Given the salience of the eurozone crisis during the period of investigation, it acted as an external shock that can be expected to have refocused MPs' attention. We therefore consider this variable as a motivational incentive as well.
5. http://ec.europa.eu/dgs/secretariat_general/relations/relations_other/npo/index_en.htm.
6. IPEX (InterParliamentary EU information eXchange, http://www.ipex.eu) is an internet platform that provides detailed information on parliamentary scrutiny by EU document and aims at facilitating information exchanges between national parliaments.

7. The data collection took place between May 2012 and February 2013 on the basis of a detailed codebook. The 25 coders are mostly native speakers and received training in two workshops.

8. The return rate was 100 per cent, although specific data was missing in a few cases, which was added through our own calculations.

9. We used data for the question: 'For each of the following institutions, please tell me if you tend to trust it or tend not to trust it: the European Union?' (answers for 'tend not to trust' only), calculating the mean for the two waves/year covering the period 2010–2012 (Standard Eurobarometer Surveys 73 to 78). Data was retrieved through the interactive Eurobarometer search system, http://ec.europa.eu/public_opinion/cf/index_en.cfm. As there may be a bias linked to the wording of questions that gauge Euroscepticism, we also used an aggregate measure based on including data from three questions related to public opinion on the EU but our results remained the same.

10. The Chapel Hill data is based on expert surveys; respondents were asked to assess 'the general position on European integration that the party leadership took over the course of 2010' on a scale from 1 = strongly opposed to 7 = strongly in favour. A party was considered Eurosceptic if it had a score of 3.5 or below. Missing data (Cyprus, Luxembourg and Malta, new parties in parliaments after 2010) was added on the basis of information country experts supplied.

11. Yet it should be noted that there are no problems of collinearity between both variables in our models.

12. Results are similar when we omit the two most active parliaments, the Finnish Eduskunta and the Swedish Riksdag.

13. Conférence des Organes Parlementaires Spécialisés dans les Affaires de l'Union des Parlements de l'Union Européenne.

References

Armingeon, Klaus, Romana Careja, David Weistanner, Sarah Engler, Panajotis Potolidis, and Marlène Gerber (2013). *Comparative Political Data Set III 1990–2011*. Berne: University of Berne, Institute of Political Science.

Auel, Katrin (2007). 'Democratic Accountability and National Parliaments – Re-Defining the Impact of Parliamentary Scrutiny in EU Affairs', *European Law Journal*, 13:4, 87–504.

Auel, Katrin, and Arthur Benz (2005). 'The Politics of Adaptation: Europeanisation of National Parliamentary Systems', *The Journal of Legislative Studies*, 11:3–4, 372–93.

Auel, Katrin, and Thomas Christiansen (2015). 'After Lisbon: National Parliaments in the European Union', *West European Politics*, 38:2, 261–81.

Auel, Katrin, and Oliver Höing (2015). 'National Parliaments and the Eurozone Crisis: Taking Ownership in Difficult Times?' *West European Politics* 38:2, 375–95.

Auel, Katrin, and Tapio Raunio (2014). 'Introduction: Connecting with the Electorate? Parliamentary Communication in EU Affairs', *The Journal of Legislative Studies*, 20:1, 1–12.

Auel, Katrin, Olivier Rozenberg, and Angela Tacea (2015). 'Fighting Back? And if Yes, How? Measuring Parliamentary Strength and Activity in EU Affairs', in Claudia Hefftler, Christine Neuhold, Olivier Rozenberg and Julie Smith (eds.), *The Palgrave Handbook of National Parliaments and the European Union*. London: Palgrave Macmillan.

Bagehot, Walter (2009 [1867]). *The English Constitution*. Oxford: Oxford University Press.

Bakker, Ryan, Catherine de Vries, Erica Edwards, Liesbet Hooghe, Seth Jolly, Gary Marks, Jon Polk, Jan Rovny, Marco Steenbergen, and Milada Vachudova (2012). 'Measuring Party Positions in Europe: The Chapel Hill Expert Survey Trend File, 1999–2010'. *Party Politics* (published before print).

Bergman, Torbjörn (1997). 'National Parliaments and EU Affairs Committees: Notes in Empirical Variation and Competing Explanations', *Journal of European Public Policy*, 4:3, 373–87.

Bergman, Torbjörn (2000). 'The European Union as the Next Step of Delegation and Accountability', *European Journal of Political Research*, 37:3, 415–29.

COSAC (2012). 17th Bi-annual Report on EU Practices and Procedures, available at http://www.cosac.eu/documents/bi-annual-reports-of-cosac/

Dimitrakopoulos, Dionyssis (2001). 'Incrementalism and Path Dependence: European Integration and Institutional Change in National Parliaments', *Journal of Common Market Studies*, 39:3, 405–22.

Fish, M. Steven, and Matthew Kroenig (2009). *The Handbook of National Legislatures: A Global Survey*. New York, NY: Cambridge University Press.

Gattermann, Katjana, and Claudia Hefftler (2015). 'Beyond Institutional Capacity: Political Motivation and Parliamentary Behaviour in the Early Warning System', *West European Politics*, 38:2, 305–34.

Hirschman, Albert (1970). *Exit, Voice, and Loyalty: Responses to Decline in Firms, Organizations, and States*. Cambridge, MA: Harvard University Press.

Jančić, Davor (2012). 'The Barroso Initiative: Window Dressing or Democratic Boost?', *Utrecht Law Review*, 8:1, 78–91.

Karlas, Jan (2011). 'Parliamentary Control of EU Affairs in Central and Eastern Europe: Explaining the Variation', *Journal of European Public Policy*, 18:2, 258–73.

Karlas, Jan (2012). 'National Parliamentary Control of EU Affairs: Institutional Design after Enlargement', *West European Politics*, 35:5, 1095–113.

Lijphart, Arend (2012 [1999]). *Patterns of Democracy: Government Forms and Performance in Thirty-Six Countries*, 2nd ed. New Haven, CT: Yale University Press.

Martin, Lisa L. (2000). *Democratic Commitments: Legislatures and International Cooperation*. Princeton: Princeton University Press.

Martin, Shane (2014). 'Committees', in Shane Martin, Thomas Saalfeld and Kaare Strøm (eds.), *The Oxford Handbook of Legislative Studies*. Oxford: Oxford University Press, 352–68.

Martin, Shane, and Sam Depauw (2009). 'Coalition Government and the Internal Organization of Legislatures', paper presented at the Annual APSA Meeting, Toronto, Canada, available at http://webpages.dcu.ie/*martins/committees1.pdf.

Martin, Lanny W., and Georg Vanberg (2004). 'Policing the Bargain: Coalition Government and Parliamentary Scrutiny', *American Journal of Political Science*, 48:1, 13–27.

Maurer, Andreas, and Wolfgang Wessels, eds. (2001). *National Parliaments on their Ways to Europe: Losers or Latecomers?* Baden-Baden: Nomos.

Norton, Philip (1990). *Legislatures.* Oxford: Oxford University Press.

Norton, Philip (1998). 'Conclusion: Do Parliaments make a Difference?', in Philip Norton (ed.), *Parliaments and Governments in Western Europe.* London: Frank Cass, 190–208.

Packenham, Robert A. (1970). 'Legislatures and Political Development', in Allan Kornberg and Lloyd D. Musolf (eds.), *Legislatures in Developmental Perspective.* Durham, NC: Duke University Press, 521–82.

Pollak, Johannes, and Peter Slominski (2003). 'Influencing EU Politics? The Case of the Austrian Parliament', *JCMS: Journal of Common Market Studies*, 41:4, 707–29.

Primo, David M., Matthew L. Jacobssmeier and Jeffrey Milyo (2007). 'Estimating the Impact of State Policies and Institutions with Mixed-Level Data.' *State Politics & Policy Quarterly* 7: 4, 446–59.

Puntscher Riekmann, Sonja and Doris Wydra (2013). 'Representation in the European State of Emergency: Parliaments against Governments?', *Journal of European Integration*, 35:5, 565–82.

Raunio, Tapio (2005). 'Holding Governments Accountable in European Affairs: Explaining Cross-national Variation', *The Journal of Legislative Studies*, 11:3–4, 319–42.

Raunio, Tapio (2009). 'National Parliaments and European Integration: What We Know and Agenda for Future Research', *Journal of Legislative Studies*, 15:4, 317–34.

Raunio Tapio and Matti Wiberg (2000). "Does Support Lead to Ignorance?', National Parliaments and the Legitimacy of EU Governance', *Acta Politica*, 35:2, 146–68.

Saalfeld, Thomas (2003). 'The Bundestag: Institutional Incrementalism and Behavioural Reticence', in Kenneth Dyson and Klaus Goetz (eds.), *Germany. Europe and the Politics of Constraint*, Oxford: Oxford University Press, 73–96.

Saalfeld, Thomas (2005). 'Delegation or Abdication? Government Backbenchers, Ministers and European Integration', *The Journal of Legislative Studies*, 11:3-4, 343–71.

Sieberer, Ulrich (2011). 'The Institutional Power of Western European Parliaments: A Multidimensional Analysis', *West European Politics*, 34:4, 731–54.

Strøm, Kaare (2003). 'Parliamentary Democracy and Delegation', in Kaare Strøm, Torbjörn Bergman and Wolfgang C. Müller (eds.), *Delegation and Accountability in Parliamentary Democracies.* Oxford: Oxford University Press, 55–106.

Van der Eijk, Cees, and Mark N. Franklin (2004). 'Potential for Contestation on European Matters at National Elections in Europe', in Marco R. Steenbergen and Gary Marks (eds.), *European Integration and Political Conflict.* Cambridge: Cambridge University Press, 32–50.

Wessels, Wolfgang, and Olivier Rozenberg (2012) 'Democratic Control in the Member States of the European Council and the Eurozone Summits', report requested by the European Parliament's Committee on Constitutional Affairs, European Parliament, Brussels, http://www.europarl. europa.eu/studies.

Winzen, Thomas (2012). 'National Parliamentary Control of European Union Affairs: A Cross-national and Longitudinal Comparison', *West European Politics*, 35:3, 657–72.

Winzen, Thomas (2013). 'European integration and National Parliamentary oversight institutions', *European Union Politics*, 14:2, 297–323.

Winzen, Thomas, Christilla Roederer-Rynning, and Frank Schimmelfennig (2015). 'Parliamentary Co-Evolution: National Parliamentary Reactions to the Empowerment of the European Parliament', *Journal of European Public Policy*, 22:1, 75–93.

Woldendorp, Jaap, Hans Keman, and Ian Budge (2000). *Party Government in 48 Democracies (1945–1998).* Dordrecht: Kluwer.

Yläoutinen, Sami, and Mark Hallerberg (2009). 'The Role of Parliamentary Committees in the Budgetary Process in the Central and Eastern European Countries', in Steffen Ganghof, Christoph Hönnige and Christian Stecker (eds.), *Parlamente, Agendasetzung und Vetospieler.* Wiesbaden: VS Verlag für Sozialwissenschaften, 147–73.

Beyond Institutional Capacity: Political Motivation and Parliamentary Behaviour in the Early Warning System

KATJANA GATTERMANN and CLAUDIA HEFFTLER

The Early Warning System gives national parliaments the right to intervene in European Union policy-making. This article investigates their incentives to submit reasoned opinions. It analyses the reactions of 40 parliamentary chambers to 411 draft legislative acts between 1 January 2010 and 31 December 2013 by ReLogit models. The article argues that, beyond institutional capacity, political motivation explains cross-chamber and inter-temporal variation. Higher levels of party political contestation over EU integration have a positive effect, but greater party dispersion on the left–right dimension negatively affects submissions. Furthermore, salient and urgent draft legislative acts incentivise parliaments to become active in the Early Warning System. Finally, some findings suggest that minority governments and economic recession represent positive conditions for unicameral parliaments and lower chambers to submit reasoned opinions. The findings are discussed with reference to the role of national parliaments in EU democracy.

With the rising impact of European Union decision-making on European citizens' daily lives, the question of an adequate democratic order at Union level becomes ever more pressing. The most recent treaty changes introduced the 'Early Warning System' (EWS), providing national parliaments with the right to intervene in EU policy-making by submitting reasoned opinions on draft legislative acts as part of the subsidiarity procedure (Protocol on the role of national parliaments in the European Union, Treaty on European Union [TEU]).[1] In the literature the merits of the EWS are hotly debated. Some scholars see the chance of national parliaments forming a 'virtual third chamber' at Union level (Cooper 2012), or potentially acting as 'Conseil d'état' of the EU (Kiiver 2011). Others argue that the EWS would reduce the role of national parliaments to gatekeepers of EU integration that are unable to actively shape policy outcomes at the EU level (see Raunio 2011; Sprungk 2013).

First empirical assessments of the EWS have indeed shown a very limited use of the new instrument (see de Wilde 2012: 12; Hefftler 2013; Neuhold 2011; Raunio 2010). Thus far, the threshold for a 'yellow card', i.e. by one-third of national parliaments' votes, has been met only twice: in case of the Monti II regulation,[2] which was then withdrawn, and the proposal to establish the European Public Prosecutor's Office,[3] which the European Commission maintained. While these developments underline the rather limited impact on EU legislation, national parliaments nonetheless continue to submit reasoned opinions in the EWS: Between 1 January 2010 and 31 December 2013, they have raised their concerns through 286 reasoned opinions in response to an overall number of 411 draft legislative acts. This number is indeed very low, but the focus of this article lies not on assessing impact. Rather, we are interested in the conditions under which national parliaments submit reasoned opinions and ask: what explains the variation in the extent to which national parliaments become active in the EWS? To answer this question, we designed a large-N dataset which comprises the reactions of 40 parliamentary chambers to 411 draft legislative acts ($N = 16,440$) and estimate our results by logistic regression for rare events data (see King and Zeng 2001a, 2001b).

Thus far, existing research has argued that it is mainly the institutional capacity – or lack thereof – that determines whether parliamentary chambers submit reasoned opinions within the EWS. The main challenges for national parliaments comprise the short time period of eight weeks (e.g. Knutelská 2011: 335), lack of resources (e.g. Fraga 2005: 499; Paskalev 2009: 6), the central role of the European Affairs Committee (EAC) vis-à-vis sectoral committees (e.g. Hegeland and Neuhold 2002; Winzen 2012: 660) and the indispensable coordination between parliaments in order to meet the threshold of a yellow card (e.g. Cooper 2012; Neuhold 2011). However, with the exception of studies which show that the common majority–opposition divide represents a problem in the EWS (Cooper 2012: 449; Raunio 2009, 2010), we know little about the extent to which political incentives influence national parliaments to become active in the EWS.

Taking a rational choice perspective, we assume that members of national parliaments (MPs) are mainly motivated to submit reasoned opinions in order to enhance their chances for policy influence and ultimately re-election (see also Auel and Christiansen 2015). Some maintain that European affairs hardly represent electoral incentives (Raunio 2009: 328), while others show that electoral institutions matter for MPs to engage in European affairs via formal channels of inter-parliamentary cooperation (Gattermann 2013). We argue that – beyond institutional capacity – the political motivation of national parliaments plays a key role in explaining variation in the extent to which national parliaments become active in the EWS. Controlling for institutional capacity, the article finds that higher levels of political contestation over EU integration inside parliamentary chambers increase the probability of them submitting reasoned opinions. Greater party dispersion on the left–right dimension, however, has a negative effect once the Swedish Riksdag, an outlier, is omitted from the models. Furthermore, salient and urgent draft legislative acts incentivise parliaments to become active in the EWS. Lastly, there is some evidence in our findings for the circumstance that minority governments and economic recession represent a positive condition for unicameral and lower chambers to submit reasoned opinions.

In the following section we discuss our hypotheses with respect to the political motivation of national parliaments. Afterwards, we present the data and method as well as the operationalisation of our variables before we proceed with the analysis of the results. In the conclusions we discuss the implications of our findings with regard to the role of national parliaments in the EU political system.

National Parliaments' Political Motivation to Submit Reasoned Opinions

All national parliaments in the EU have the right to participate in the EWS by submitting reasoned opinions to the European Commission on matters that they believe infringe the subsidiarity principle (Protocol on the role of national parliaments in the European Union, Art. 3, TEU). They receive the same amount of information directly from the European Commission (Art. 8c, TEU) and are able to rely on support from the European Parliament (EP). Although one main criticism of the EWS concerns the short time period of eight weeks (e.g. Knutelská 2011: 335), it poses similar challenges for all parliaments. Indeed, the institutional capacity of national parliaments is considered a key determiner of whether a chamber is able to submit a reasoned opinion or not. Many scholars have argued that parliamentary resources (e.g. Fraga 2005: 499; Paskalev 2009: 6), intra-parliamentary divisions of labour (e.g. Neuhold 2011) as well as the coordination between chambers (e.g. Cooper 2012, 2013) matter for the extent to which parliaments become involved in the EWS.

However, we contend that – beyond institutional capacity – the political motivation of national parliaments is a crucial determiner of their involvement in the EWS. From a rational choice perspective, this motivation is driven by policy influence and re-election prospects. This is why the literature expects national parliaments that support a majority government to be less incentivised to submit reasoned opinions (Cooper 2012: 449; Raunio 2009, 2010). The parliamentary majority is unlikely to turn against the government it supports. MPs might be concerned about their re-selection and election prospects if their support for a reasoned opinion entails public disagreement with their party leadership. They are more likely to submit a reasoned opinion if the government is also concerned about a potential subsidiarity breach. The parliamentary opposition is expected to openly challenge the government's stances, but they lack the numbers to vote in favour of submitting a reasoned opinion. However, parliaments which tolerate minority governments are more independent from the executive. Since in this case the opposition parties have the voting power to turn against the government, they are more likely to submit a reasoned opinion than parliaments under a majority government.

> H1: National parliaments are more likely to submit a reasoned opinion under a minority government than under a majority government.

Intra-parliamentary conflict not only evolves along the divide between the majority and opposition, but is also apparent in the dispersion of party political stances. Existing research has demonstrated that divergent party positions towards European integration affect party competition in the domestic electoral arena. In their seminal work on the politicisation of EU integration, Hooghe and Marks (2009) show that mainstream political parties rather avoid the issue of EU integration in domestic debates as it runs counter to the left–right logic and endangers intra-party cohesion. Conversely, small extremist parties on either side of the political spectrum with a coherent position have an incentive to place EU issues on the agenda (see also, de Vries 2007; Green-Pedersen 2012).

Previous research on variation in formal parliamentary control rights in EU affairs suggests that the presence of Eurosceptic parties has a positive, albeit very small, effect (Karlas 2012: 270; Raunio 2005: 335). Eurosceptic MPs are more incentivised to become active on EU issues in order to be rewarded by their voters at the next election for their EU scrutiny. The degree to which the EU is contested inside parliaments might therefore become relevant to explain the actual use of their formal rights to scrutinise EU legislation. Schuck *et al.* (2011) found that higher levels of party political contestation over EU integration had a positive effect on the volume of EU news coverage during the 2009 EP election campaigns. Gattermann (2013) applies their argument to the parliamentary context and shows that higher levels of intra-parliamentary political contestation have a positive effect on the incentives of MPs to participate in committee meetings in Brussels. Similarly, Finke and Dannwolf (2013) investigate the scrutiny activities on EU legislation in the Czech and German parliaments and argue that party competition in respective policy areas has a positive effect on parliamentary scrutiny of EU laws.

We thus also expect that contestation over EU integration matters for parliamentary activity in the EWS. Within the EWS MPs assess the proper allocation of competencies either to the EU or the member state level (Cooper 2012: 450; Knutelská 2011: 331). This not only entails a mere judicial question, but also a political evaluation of EU integration (cf. Fraga 2005). Conflicting ideas about European integration are likely to spur parliamentary debates on the question of subsidiarity and are therefore likely to lead to higher levels of scrutiny.

> H2a: Higher levels of party political contestation over EU integration are likely to increase the probability of a parliament submitting a reasoned opinion.

Parliamentary politics are also structured along the traditional left–right cleavage. De Wilde (2011) argues that both the pro-/anti-EU and the left–right dimensions of conflict are visible in plenary debates about the EU multiannual budget in the Danish Folketing and the Dutch Tweede Kamer. However, subsidiarity control might escape the left–right conflict line since assessing compliance with the subsidiarity principle differs considerably from the usual legislative work whereby parliamentarians evaluate the political desirability of a policy proposal (see Kiiver 2011). Yet subsidiarity complaints can be used strategically as an instrument of criticism on the content of a policy (see COSAC 2012). In his assessment of the first successful yellow card, Cooper (2013: 5) argues that '[w]hile the opponents to Monti II within the [national parliaments] came from across the political spectrum, and many were motivated more by protecting national autonomy than workers' rights per se, there is on balance a leftward tilt to the campaign against it'. This suggests that MPs do not neglect their policy preferences when assessing draft legislative acts. Thus, while policy influence as an incentive for EU scrutiny is limited, it is not irrelevant. Left–right contestation may constrain agreement over the question of whether or not to delegate competences to the EU. We therefore expect that political parties are less likely to agree to submit a reasoned opinion if there is greater disagreement over the substance of draft legislative acts.

> H2b: Higher levels of party political contestation inside a national parliament over the left–right scale are likely to decrease the probability to submit a reasoned opinion.

The EWS has been criticised for not providing positive means of direct policy influence at the EU level as national parliaments only have a take-it-or-leave it option and are formally limited to subsidiarity review (see Raunio 2011; Sprungk 2013). However, despite these limitations, their incentives may still be driven by their political motivation to respond to salient and urgent policies. Finke and Dannwolf (2013) find that issue salience has a positive effect on the parliamentary scrutiny of EU laws. We thus expect the salience of draft legislative acts to raise the incentives for national parliaments' activity in the EWS. Here, draft legislative acts which introduce new legislation are likely to be more frequently scrutinised than legislation that amends or repeals existing legislation. New legislation is likely to cause more significant changes than the revision of existing legislative acts (see de Ruiter 2013: 4; Finke and Dannwolf 2013: 17). We therefore expect MPs to be more motivated to scrutinise these acts, which may return higher benefits in terms of policy impact.

> H3: National parliaments are more likely to submit a reasoned opinion if the draft legislative act proposes new legislation rather than amends or repeals existing legislation.

Additionally, and assuming that MPs have complete information, the engagement of the EU institutions with respect to individual draft legislative acts might impact on the incentives of parliamentary chambers to submit reasoned opinions. Finke and Dannwolf (2013) argued that an early vote in the EP indicates that the legislative proposal is highly politicised at the EU level, which they found to matter for the likelihood of the German and Czech parliaments to scrutinise EU law. However, Warntjen (2012: 172) contends that procedural aspects of EU legislative proposals cannot necessarily be equated with salience but should rather be defined as a 'consequence of salience'. The behaviour of the Council or the EP before the end of the eight-week deadline might nevertheless indicate the urgency of a draft legislative act. Time pressure might apply when a draft legislative act is discussed in the Council debates before the deadline, or when the EP schedules a vote on the matter during the scrutiny period. MPs are likely to be more motivated to scrutinise urgent legislative proposals as they imply high relevance and policy impact. Furthermore, a government might urge its parliament to submit a reasoned opinion in order to support its negotiation strategy.

> H4a: National parliaments are more likely to submit a reasoned opinion if the draft legislative act is debated in the Council before the end of the scrutiny period.

> H4b: National parliaments are more likely to submit a reasoned opinion if the European Parliament votes on the draft legislative act before the end of the scrutiny period.

Related to salience and urgency is the circumstance that the financial and economic crisis hit Europe at about the same time the Lisbon Treaty came into force. We expect that in countries that undergo economic recession, parliamentarians will focus on resolving the economic downturn and the social and political consequences thereof. One could argue that EU issues have gained more salience through the crisis (e.g. see Saurugger 2014). However, assuming that the primary goal of MPs is re-election (see Strøm 1997), they are likely to concentrate on ways to overcome the crisis in their home country and care less about subsidiarity issues. In short, resources will less likely be used for a subsidiarity review of Commission proposals under these circumstances.

> H5: National parliaments are less likely to submit a reasoned opinion when a country experiences economic recession.

Data and Method

Dependent Variable and Model

According to the complementary information provided by the Legislative Dialogue Unit of the European Parliament and by IPEX,[4] 425 draft legislative acts were transmitted by the European Commission to national parliaments in the EWS with a deadline between 1 January 2010 and 31 December 2013. One legislative act was withdrawn before the closing date; and the *lettre de saisine*, i.e. the official referral by the Commission, was missing for 13 proposals. Hence, we excluded these and consider a total of 411 draft legislative acts in our analysis; namely 82 from 2010, 151 from 2011, 78 from 2012 and 100 from 2013.

To test our argument, we designed a dataset which comprises the responses of individual parliamentary chambers to each draft legislative act.[5] In the EWS reasoned opinions by unicameral parliaments count twice compared to submissions from individual upper or lower chambers in bicameral systems. Since we are interested in their motivation to submit a reasoned opinion and not the likelihood of reaching the threshold, we treat all reasoned opinions equally and count each as one submission per chamber. Our dependent variable is a binary variable which is 1 when a chamber has provided a reasoned opinion and 0 if it has not done so. We consider all 40 chambers in 27 EU countries (excluding Croatia). Hence our overall N for the dependent variable is 16,440. With a total of only 286 reasoned opinions submitted during the time period of investigation, which represents only 1.47 per cent of all cases, our dependent variable is extremely biased towards zero ($M = 0.02$; $SD = 0.13$). Figure 1 shows

FIGURE 1
PERCENTAGE OF INSTANCES PER YEAR IN WHICH REASONED OPINIONS WERE SUBMITTED

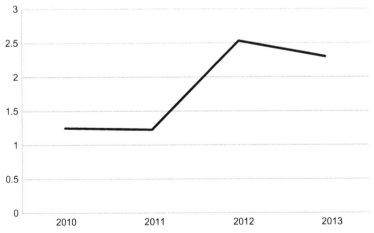

Note: The year is taken from the official document reference.

that while there was a slight increase in the number of reasoned opinions relative to the number of legislative proposals between 2010 and 2012, the ratio only lies between 1.25 and 2.53 per cent.

This inter-temporal variation in the dependent variable is comparable to what King and Zeng (2001a: 138) define as the occurrence of rare events: 'binary dependent variables with dozens to thousands of times fewer ones (events, …) than zeros ("nonevents")'. They argue that ordinary logistic regression procedures would underestimate the probability of these events and propose logistic regression for rare events (ReLogit), which estimates bias-corrected coefficients instead of logit coefficients (King and Zeng 2001b: 702). We follow King and Zeng's (2001a, 2001b) suggestion and apply ReLogit models. For this, we conducted our analysis in Stata 12 with the ReLogit software designed by Tomz *et al.* (1999).

Secondly, we find considerable cross-sectional variation in the dependent variable. Figure 2 depicts the total number of reasoned opinions each chamber has submitted during the period of investigation. It shows that the Swedish Riksdag is by far the most active chamber in the EWS with 47 submissions in total; followed by the French Senate (18 reasoned opinions) and the Dutch Tweede Kamer (17). The remaining chambers have voiced their concerns over a draft legislative act at least once, with the exception of the Slovenian upper house.

Furthermore, we also need to account for the variation within chambers because we investigate their reactions to 411 legislative proposals over time. Consequently, we cluster the standard errors by chamber. We acknowledge that we do not take variation at the country level into account. However, the majority of countries (14 out of 27) have unicameral chambers and for these a distinction between the country and the chamber level becomes redundant. This is also why the inclusion of country dummies would entail multicollinearity problems. Several control variables consider that observations are not independent within and across countries, which we present further below. In addition, we estimate all models once without the Swedish Riksdag to test whether our results are robust without this outlier. As a second robustness check, we provide jack-knife tests of the main model (Model 6, see below) in the appendix: each model omits one of the years under investigation.

Main Independent Variables

Our main independent variables of interest correspond to our hypotheses and measure the motivation of national parliaments and their members to submit reasoned opinions. We generally consider three types of variation in the data, namely at the chamber level, at the level of legislative proposals and at the country level. Our first hypotheses are measured at the chamber level. The dummy variable *Majority government* serves to test H1. We do not include it in all of our models, because in most countries the government is electorally dependent only on the lower house or unicameral chamber. We also disregard caretaker governments.

FIGURE 2
NUMBER OF REASONED OPINIONS PER CHAMBER DURING THE TIME PERIOD OF
INVESTIGATION. http://epp.eurostat.ec.europa.eu/statistics_explained/index.php/Glossary:
Country_codes

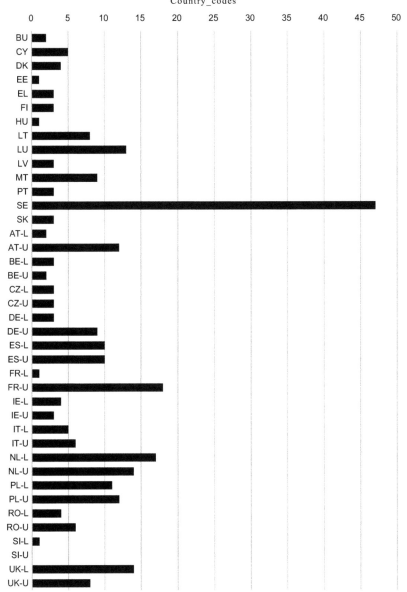

Notes: The time period of investigation lies between 1 January 2010 and 31 December 2013; the maximum number of reasoned opinions which could have possibly been submitted by a chamber is 411 in our data. 'L' stands for lower house and 'U' for upper house.

We operationalise party political contestation over the EU (H2a) by the weighted parliamentary party system dispersion (WPPSD). For this we rely on Schuck *et al.* (2011: 45), but contrary to them we consider the seat share of a respective parliamentary party as opposed to the vote share (see also Gattermann 2013).

$$WPPSD = \sqrt{\sum_{j=1} SS_{jk}(P_{jk} - \overline{P}_k)^2} \tag{1}$$

where SS_{jk} is the seat share and P_{jk} is the position of party j in country k towards EU integration, and $\overline{P}_k$ is the weighted mean of all party positions in country k. We obtained information on the general orientation of the party leadership towards EU integration from the Chapel Hill expert surveys of 2006 and 2010 (Bakker *et al.* 2012; Hooghe *et al.* 2010). We employ a similar measure to calculate party political contestation on the left–right dimension inside parliamentary chambers (H2b). For this, we took the party position on the left–right scale from the respective Chapel Hill expert surveys. Both variables (*EU dispersion* and *Left–right dispersion*) were re-calculated after each legislative election. Unfortunately, the Chapel Hill expert surveys do not include Cyprus, Luxembourg or Malta and do not yet consider newer political parties that stood at some of the latest elections (e.g. Greece in June 2012). Hence, both variables have a few missing values (see Appendix).

At the proposal level, we operationalise the salience of a draft legislative act by the dummy variable *New legislation* which corresponds to H3. It is 1 in 27 per cent of all cases. Two additional dummy variables measure the urgency of draft legislative acts: *Debate in Council* indicates whether a Commission proposal was debated in the Council before the end of the deadline (H4a); to operationalise H4b we include the dummy *EP vote*, which considers votes in the plenary. We obtained information on these variables from the Legislative Observatory of the EP. The only problem with these variables, however, is that we assume that national parliamentarians have complete information.

We operationalise H5 on the impact of the crisis as a dummy variable (*Recession year*) at the country level. We not only account for debtor states within the eurozone but for all countries that have undergone economic recession. To calculate this variable we obtained information on GDP growth compared to the previous year for each country from Eurostat (2014) and coded negative values as 1. It includes four observations per country which vary over time.

Control Variables

Our control variables are also measured at the chamber, proposal and country level, respectively. We begin with the former. As we briefly discussed above, previous research has argued that the institutional capacity of parliamentary chambers represents one indicator of the extent to which national parliaments become active in the EWS. Institutional capacity mainly concerns resources, coordination and time. Paskalev (2009: 6) argues that national parliaments 'need significant administrative and expert capacity for a meaningful engagement' in the EWS (see also Fraga 2005: 499; Högenauer and Neuhold 2015). Thus, we include the number of staff relative to the statutory chamber size in our models, which allows for cross-chamber comparison. It ranges from 0.51 (Malta) to 8.06 (Austrian Bundesrat). We obtained this information from the Interparliamentary Union (2013), but the variable has a few missing values (see Appendix). Hence, we do not include it in all of our models.

A second indicator of institutional capacity is the division of labour between parliamentary committees. In many parliaments, the EAC is often the first point of reference for the scrutiny of EU affairs, especially regarding matters of the subsidiarity principle. However, scholars argue that when sectoral committees become involved, the effectiveness of EU affairs scrutiny increases (see Hegeland and Neuhold 2002; Neuhold 2011; Raunio 2005; Winzen 2012: 660). Here, more MPs add resources and expertise to the scrutiny process. One would thus expect that the chances for submitting a reasoned opinion become greater if a sectoral committee is in charge of the review process. We therefore include the dummy *Sectoral committee drafts RO* in our models (Legislative Dialogue Unit of the European Parliament 2013). The reference category comprises European Affairs committees, the administration (e.g. Belgian Chamber of Deputies), the joint responsibilities of both committees and a joint committee between two houses (Spanish Parliament).

The capacity of a parliament to mandate its government position before Council meetings might also play a role for parliamentary behaviour in the EWS (see Auel 2007; Raunio 2005: 322). Those parliaments that are able to exert strong control over their governments in EU affairs are supposedly less inclined to use their resources to directly influence policy outcomes at the EU level. We test this by the dummy variable *Mandating*, which is 1 when a chamber either has the right to provide a binding mandate or can request its government to provide ex post justifications following the classifications of Karlas (2012: 1102).

The dummy variable *Election* indicates whether legislative elections for a given chamber were held during the eight weeks before a respective deadline, which is likely to have a negative effect on the ability of national parliaments to submit a reasoned opinion. Finally, two dummies, *Lower house* and *Upper house* (reference category: unicameral parliament) serve to control for variation across different types of chambers.

At the proposal level, the scrutiny period of eight weeks is officially extended by the number of days in the period which fall into the month of August, which we took into account in our dataset. The Christmas break, however, is not considered for an extension, which is said to constrain the ability of national parliaments to review certain draft legislative acts (Knutelská

2011: 335). Hence, we include the dummy variable *Christmas*, which is 1 when any day between 24 December and 1 January falls into the scrutiny period.

Institutional capacity not only concerns intra-parliamentary resources. Research suggests that inter-parliamentary cooperation plays an important role in the EWS, because one-third of parliaments are required to submit reasoned opinions in order to reach the threshold for a 'yellow card' (e.g. see Cooper 2012; Neuhold 2011). Cooper (2013) argues that COSAC meetings provide an opportunity for exchanging views on draft legislative acts in the EWS, as in the case with the Monti II regulation. To assess the impact of formal coordination activities between national parliaments we include the variable *COSAC* in the models. It is 0 in the case where no such meeting took place during the scrutiny period, and 1 when either the chairpersons or the ordinary members of EACs have met. Furthermore, for each legislative proposal we include the number of *Other reasoned opinions* that have been submitted in addition to the one (or none) by the respective chamber. Given the design of the EWS, one would expect that individual chambers are more likely to submit a reasoned opinion when they see that others have done so already. It ranges from 0 to 14 and includes the two aforementioned yellow cards. We are aware that this variable is a crude measure, since we are unable to consider sequences of submissions. It nevertheless provides an indicator of coordination and accounts for interdependencies across parliamentary chambers (as well as within countries with bicameral parliaments). Lastly, we also include the *Year* from the document reference of draft legislative acts to capture potential linear time trends.

At the country level, *EU member* is a continuous variable measuring the duration of EU membership for a given country in a respective year. The dummy variable *Presidency* indicates whether a country was responsible for the rotating EU presidency at a given time. A chamber might be less likely to submit a reasoned opinion under these circumstances either because it has less time to scrutinise a draft proposal or because it finds other channels of influence during the presidency.

Results

The ReLogit models provided in Table 1 serve to explain the conditions under which parliamentary chambers submit reasoned opinions. Models 1 to 4 comprise all applicable chambers; Models 5 to 8 are similar to the previous ones but omit the Swedish Riksdag. Since our dispersion variables have missing values we exclude them from Model 1 and 5. For similar reasons the variable *Majority government* is only included in Models 4 and 8; and the controls *Mandating* and *Relative number of staff* are only added to Models 3 and 4, and 7 and 8, respectively. Table 2 provides the predicted probabilities of the main effects reported in Models 2, 4 and 6. The complete table can be found in Appendix Table A2.

To begin with our first hypothesis, our results suggest that national parliaments which tolerate a minority government are more inclined to submit

TABLE 1
RELOGIT MODELS

	Model 1	Model 2	Model 3	Model 4	Model 5	Model 6	Model 7	Model 8
Majority gov.				-1.12**				-0.34
				(0.50)				(0.27)
EU dispersion		0.06*	0.08**	0.11***		0.05**	0.04	0.05
		(0.04)	(0.04)	(0.05)		(0.03)	(0.02)*	(0.03)
Left–right dispersion		-0.01	-0.02	-0.08		-0.09***	-0.12***	-0.16***
		(0.05)	(0.04)	(0.05)		(0.03)	(0.03)	(0.03)
New legislation	0.15	0.22*	0.20*	0.24	0.16	0.26*	0.25	0.30
	(0.12)	(0.12)	(0.12)	(0.16)	(0.14	(0.15)	(0.15)	(0.23)
Council debate	0.16	0.12	0.14	0.04	0.16	0.12	0.13	0.00
	(0.12)*	(0.13)	(0.14)	(0.16)	(0.14	(0.16)	(0.18)	(0.25)
EP vote	0.62*	0.75*	0.88*	0.36	0.62	0.74	0.89*	0.24
	(0.36)	(0.38)	(0.37)	(0.46)	(0.44)	(0.48)	(0.46)	(0.79)
Recession year	-0.25	-0.14	-0.29	0.18	-0.1	0.21	0.35	0.53*
	(0.26)	(0.29)	(0.36)	(0.34)	(0.23)	(0.23)	(0.30)	(0.25)
Controls								
Rel. no. of staff			-0.21	-0.45			0.12*	0.17
			(0.19)	(0.31)			(0.06)	(0.13)
SC drafts RO	0.81	0.98	1.13	1.59***	-0.23	-0.77	-2.10***	-1.61**
	(0.74)	(0.80)	(0.79)	(0.52)	(0.4	(0.49)	(0.39)	(0.51)
Mandating			-0.12				0.40	
			(0.54)				(0.37)	
Election	-0.68	-0.52	-0.51	-0.41	-0.73	-0.54	-0.43	-0.31
	(0.51)	(0.62)	(0.63)	(0.86)	(0.62)	(0.82)	(0.80)	(1.06)
Lower House	-0.27	-0.02	-0.06	0.74*	0.13	0.84***	1.08***	1.43*
	(0.43)	(0.50)	(0.46)	(0.43)	(0.36)	(0.32)	(0.28)	(0.28)
Upper house	-0.05	0.27	0.53		0.46	1.42***	1.66***	
	(0.40)	(0.56)	(0.62)		(0.34)	(0.31)	(0.41)	
Christmas	-0.23	-0.27	-0.21	-0.21	-0.32*	-0.43*	-0.42	-0.35
	(0.16)	(0.20)	(0.20)	(0.20)	(0.18)	(0.23)	(0.26)	(0.31)

(Continued)

TABLE 1
(Continued)

	Model 1	Model 2	Model 3	Model 4	Model 5	Model 6	Model 7	Model 8
COSAC	-0.20	-0.27	-0.23	-0.33	-0.11	-0.19	-0.13	-0.12
	(0.16)	(0.17)	(0.18)	(0.25)	(0.16)	(0.19)	(0.19)	(0.29)
Other ROs	0.36***	0.37***	0.36***	0.41***	0.36***	0.37***	0.37***	0.41**
	(0.02)	(0.03)	(0.03)	(0.04)	(0.02)	(0.03)	(0.03)	(0.04)
Year	0.03	0.00	-0.01	-0.01	-0.01	-0.07	-0.13	-0.15
	(0.08)	(0.10)	(0.11)	(0.12)	(0.09)	(0.12)	(0.13)	(0.17)
EU member	0.00	0.00	0.00	0.01	0.01*	0.02*	0.02***	0.01
	(0.01)	(0.01)	(0.01)	(0.01)	(0.01)	(0.01)	(0.01)	(0.01)
Presidency	-0.56	-1.55**	-1.98*	-1.13	-0.47	-1.50**	-1.84*	-1.35
	(0.62)	(0.72)	(1.04)	(0.96)	(0.6)	(0.71)	(1.04)	(1.04)
Constant	-58.47	-4.36	18.80	24.03	11.10	143.72	258.89	290.87
	(160.88)	(200.30)	(222.43)	(236.97)	(184.29)	(237.38)	(260.10)	(332.79)
df	14	16	18	17	14	16	18	17
N chambers	40	33	30	23	39	32	29	22
N	16,440	12,887	11,757	8660	16,029	12,476	11,346	8249

Notes: *p < 0.1; **p < 0.05; ***p < 0.01.
Clustered standard errors in parentheses; dependent variable: binary variable indicating whether a chamber has submitted a reasoned opinion or not for each draft legislative act; Models 4 and 8 exclude all upper houses.

TABLE 2
PREDICTED PROBABILITIES

	Model 2		Model 4		Model 6	
	Prob.	**90% CI**	**Prob.**	**90% CI**	**Prob.**	**90% CI**
Majority gov.						
No	–		0.009	0.004; 0.022	–	
Yes	–		0.003	0.001; 0.007	–	
EU dispersion						
Minimum	0.005	0.002; 0.011	0.001	0.000; 0.004	0.003	0.001; 0.006
Mean	0.009	0.005; 0.015	0.003	0.001; 0.007	0.004	0.002; 0.007
Maximum	0.014	0.007; 0.026	0.006	0.003; 0.013	0.006	0.004; 0.009
Left–right dispersion						
Minimum	0.010	0.005; 0.019	0.007	0.002; 0.021	0.009	0.005; 0.019
Mean	0.009	0.005; 0.015	0.003	0.001; 0.007	0.004	0.002; 0.007
Maximum	0.008	0.003; 0.022	0.002	0.001; 0.005	0.002	0.001; 0.004
New legislation						
No	0.009	0.005; 0.015	0.003	0.001; 0.007	0.004	0.002; 0.007
Yes	0.011	0.007; 0.019	0.004	0.002; 0.009	0.005	0.003; 0.009
Council debate						
No	0.009	0.005; 0.015	0.003	0.001; 0.007	0.004	0.002; 0.007
Yes	0.010	0.006; 0.019	0.003	0.001; 0.008	0.005	0.003; 0.008
EP vote						
No	0.009	0.005; 0.015	0.003	0.001; 0.007	0.004	0.002; 0.007
Yes	0.019	0.008; 0.042	0.004	0.002; 0.011	0.008	0.003; 0.022
Recession year						
No	0.009	0.005; 0.015	0.003	0.001; 0.007	0.004	0.002; 0.007
Yes	0.008	0.004; 0.014	0.003	0.001; 0.009	0.005	0.003; 0.008
Other ROs						
0	0.007	0.004; 0.012	0.002	0.001; 0.005	0.003	0.002; 0.005
5	0.042	0.025; 0.071	0.017	0.008; 0.035	0.020	0.013; 0.030
10	0.215	0.129; 0.353	0.120	0.065; 0.220	0.118	0.077; 0.177
Max	0.540	0.365; 0.710	0.407	0.242; 0.622	0.377	0.263; 0.511

Notes: Predicted probabilities of submitting a reasoned opinion (versus not doing so); all other variables are kept at their mean or median; the lower and upper values of confidence intervals are reported at a 90 per cent level as some effects are not statistically significant at higher levels; see Appendix Table A2 for the full data.

a reasoned opinion, holding everything else constant and considering lower houses and unicameral chambers only (Model 4). The difference between minority and majority government is only 0.6 per cent in the probability to submit a reasoned opinion, but considering the rare occasion of submissions, this effect is not as small as it suggests. While this finding supports the assumption that the control of the government over its parliamentary majority constrains an active use of the EWS (e.g. see Raunio 2009, 2010), it does not hold when the Swedish outlier is excluded (Model 8).

We do, however, find wide-ranging support for our argument that party political contestation inside parliamentary chambers plays a role for their activity in the EWS. With respect to H2a, our results suggest that higher levels of dispersion over EU integration have a positive effect on submitting reasoned opinions, holding everything else constant. The change in the predicted probabilities is rather small – the difference between minimum and maximum levels of contestation is about 1 per cent in Model 2 (Table 2). Yet, considering that national parliaments have submitted reasoned opinions in only 1.47 per cent of all cases, this effect is rather strong. Furthermore, the findings are robust amid numerous control variables and the effect remains significant when we remove the Swedish Riksdag from the models (Model 6, the effects in Models 7 and 8 are significant at the 85 per cent level), and conduct the jack-knife tests (Table A2). This finding underlines our expectations that the more the EU is contested inside parliamentary chambers, the greater the incentives of their members to raise their voices against legislative proposals of the European Commission. Moreover, it suggests that despite the predominant legal consideration of subsidiarity compliance, the EWS is politicised with respect to the pro-/anti-EU cleavage.

Also in line with our expectations (H2b) is the finding that party political contestation over the traditional left–right cleavage has a negative effect on our dependent variable. The effects do not comply with conventional levels of statistical significance in the first set of models, but the results from Models 6 to 8, which disregard Sweden, suggest that rising levels of political contestation decrease the probability of submitting reasoned opinions, controlling for everything else. The predicted probabilities reported in Table 2 (Model 6) show that maximum levels of dispersion over the left–right dimension are responsible for a 0.7 per cent decrease in the probability to submit a reasoned opinion compared to low levels of contestation. Figure 3 shows that these effects are even stronger than for the political contestation over EU integration, once the Swedish outlier is omitted. These results are also robust to the jack-knife tests

FIGURE 3
PROBABILITY OF SUBMITTING A REASONED OPINION FOR DIFFERENT DEGREES OF DISPERSION

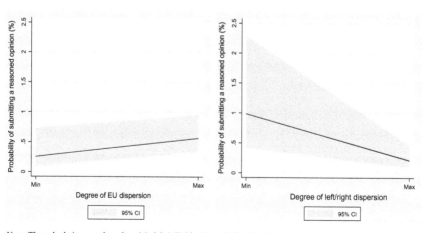

Note: The calculations are based on Model 6 (Table 1), excluding Sweden.

(Table A2). Following our argumentation above, this suggests that disagreement over the substance of draft legislative acts constrains the subsidiarity review.

We also find support for the relevance of the salience of draft legislative acts. The probability of submitting a reasoned opinion is 0.2 per cent higher if a draft legislative act specifies new legislation as opposed to proposals that amend or repeal existing legislation (Model 2, Table 2). The effect holds when omitting the Swedish outlier (Model 6), with a predicted probability of 0.1 per cent. This finding lends support to our expectations (H3) and is plausible if we assume that new legislation entails more dramatic changes to the status quo and represents an opportunity for MPs to influence EU policy-making (see de Ruiter 2013: 4; Finke and Dannwolf 2013: 17). As regards urgency, the results show that if the EP plenary votes on a given draft legisla-tive act the probability of a reasoned opinion being submitted is about 1 per cent higher compared to legislative acts which have not been subject to a vote during the eight-week period (Model 2, Table 2). The effect holds without Sweden (Model 7, Table 1) and lends support to H4b. However, it does not make a difference whether or not a proposal was debated in the Council before the end of the deadline as none of the effects are statistically signifi-cant. H4a thus has to be rejected.

Lastly, we expected that national parliaments are less likely to submit reasoned opinions at times a country experiences economic recession (H5). The effect hardly complies with conventional levels of statistical significance except in Model 8, which excludes Sweden and upper houses. Here, the probability of submitting a reasoned opinion increases by about 0.7 per cent under economic recession compared to periods in which a country's econ-omy is doing fairly well (Table A2). We expected that in times of crisis MPs would have more important problems to solve than the question of competences in EU decision-making. The lack of support for our hypothesis may indicate that the EWS is not a mere technical procedure of judicial control over subsidiarity, but is considered a potential channel to voice concerns.

Regarding the control variables, we generally find little support for the explanatory power of institutional capacity. At the chamber level, the relative number of support staff has the expected effect, albeit only in Model 7 which excludes the Swedish parliament. Here, the difference in the predicted proba-bilities between the minimum and the maximum number of staff is about 0.4 per cent (Table A2). The effects of the sectoral committee having the right to draft a reasoned opinion are mixed. In the sample including Sweden, it has a positive effect (Model 4), but its involvement is negative in Models 7 and 8. Furthermore, whether a chamber has the right to provide a binding mandate or to demand ex-post justification does not affect its activity in the EWS. Nor do legislative elections taking place during the scrutiny process have any effect.

Considering variation at the level of the draft legislative act, our results show that if the scrutiny period coincides with the Christmas holidays, the probability to submit a reasoned opinion decreases by about 0.1 to 0.2 per cent compared to all other periods during the year when disregarding the Swedish parliament (Models 5 and 6, Table A2). COSAC meetings that take place during the scrutiny period do not have any effect, but our results indicate that parliamentary chambers are influenced by the activities of other parliaments in the EWS. The probabilities to submit a reasoned opinion are about 21 per cent higher if ten other chambers have submitted one as well compared to instances in which no reasoned opinion was submitted at all (Model 2, Table 2). The effect holds throughout the models (even with the jack-knife tests in Table A2), keeping everything else constant, and is greater than the remaining effects, which is not surprising since coordination in the EWS is indispensable to meet the threshold for a yellow card. It also suggests that informal coordination between national parliaments, such as through IPEX or via national parliaments' Permanent Representatives might have a positive impact on their incentives to submit a reasoned opinion (see Cooper 2013; Neuhold 2011).

Lastly, the two control variables at the country level produce significant effects. The length of EU membership positively affects the probability to submit reasoned opinions when Sweden is excluded from the model, albeit only marginally: the difference between five and 25 years of membership is only 0.2 per cent in the predicted probabilities (Model 5, Table A2). Yet it suggests that parliaments in the older member states have been slightly more active than those which joined the EU more recently – with the exception of Sweden. In addition, the probability of submitting a reasoned opinion is between 0.2 to 0.8 per cent lower for chambers under the rotating presidency compared to others, regardless of whether the Swedish parliament is included in the models or not. Here, national parliaments may be constrained in terms of resources due to the organisational tasks of the presidency or are able to find other means for influence.

Conclusions

The article set out to study the conditions under which national parliamentary chambers submit reasoned opinions in the EWS. Thereby it – for the first time – investigated a large set of draft legislative acts and considered all parliamentary chambers in the EU-27 between 1 January 2010 and 31 December 2013. It argued that – beyond institutional capacity – the political motivation of national parliaments plays a crucial role in explaining variation in the extent to which national parliaments become active in the EWS. Our point of departure rested on the assumption that their political motivation is determined by policy influence and re-election prospects. Thus far, the literature has only identified one explanatory factor related to political motivation by arguing that national parliaments that support a majority government are less likely to submit reasoned opinions (Cooper 2012: 449; Raunio 2009, 2010), which our findings partially confirmed. Our argument also considers additional determiners of parliamentary activity in the EWS in terms of the dispersion of party political stances inside parliamentary chambers, the salience and urgency of draft legislative acts as well as unfavourable economic conditions during the eurozone crisis.

Our argument is substantiated by the positive effect of party political contestation over EU integration on the likelihood of submitting reasoned opinions. The degree of political contestation over the left–right dimension has a negative impact once we remove the Swedish outlier. Our results imply that reasoned opinions are motivated by the politicisation of European integration inside parliamentary chambers, but constrained by disagreements over the substance of draft legislative acts. Our tentative finding that economic recession seems to represent a positive condition for unicameral and lower chambers to submit reasoned opinions supports this interpretation if we assume that national parliaments have become more sensitive to EU policy-making (see Saurugger 2014). Furthermore, salient and urgent draft legislative acts incentivise national parliaments to submit reasoned opinions: the article found that the probability of submitting a reasoned opinion is higher for new legislation and when it is voted upon by the EP plenary before the end of the scrutiny period. Taken together, it is MPs' incentives and awareness which encourage proactive scrutiny in the EWS. We showed that institutional capacity in terms of resources, inter-parliamentary exchange via COSAC and formal scrutiny rights has limited explanatory power for the likelihood of the submission of reasoned opinions. Future research should therefore take into account the relevance of party political contestation and the salience and urgency of draft legislative acts for parliamentary involvement in EU affairs.

The advantages of our study, which lie in the systematic, large-N study of the incentives of 40 parliamentary chambers across Europe, represent pitfalls at the same time. We are, for instance, unable to account for the path dependence of an individual chamber. Some national parliaments might become disheartened over time when seeing that their reasoned opinions hardly have any impact (see Raunio 2010). The Commission withdrew the Monti II proposal, but maintained its proposal for a European Public Prosecutor's Office despite a yellow card. Conversely, some national parliaments might develop new, cost-efficient internal procedures over time to participate in the EWS. Moreover, our analysis rests on the assumption – in line with rational choice theory – that national parliaments and their members have complete information about the developments at the EU level suggesting that they are able to assess the urgency of a legislative proposal. Our results imply they are well informed, but our findings could also be triggered by additional explanatory factors. Future research might also find a way to statistically disentangle within- and between-country effects in order to investigate potential interaction effects between political motivation and institutional capacity. The EWS has only been in force for a few years since the Lisbon Treaty was enacted in December 2009. Furthermore, our time period of investigation coincides with the eurozone crisis. Our findings must therefore be interpreted with some caution regarding their representativeness for explaining variation in the participation in the EWS in the long run. Future research should investigate whether the relevance of political motivation holds over time.

The EWS gave national parliaments a new opportunity to actively scrutinise the allocation of competences between member states and the EU. From a normative perspective, the EWS is considered a tool to more actively engage national parliaments in order to strengthen the legitimacy of EU legislation. Despite the low frequency of reasoned opinions by national parliaments, we show that it is mainly their political motivation, rather than sheer capacity, which matters for the degree to which they become involved. Føllesdal and Hix (2006) call for more contestation at the EU level in order to combat the democratic deficit. At the national level, we find that parliamentary activity in the EWS is particularly triggered by party political contestation over EU integration and is dependent on the salience and urgency of draft legislative acts themselves. Thereby national parliamentary chambers may be able to provide a political linkage between EU policy-making and their represented in the domestic context.

Acknowledgements

We wish to thank Katrin Auel, Thomas Christiansen, Benjamin Egerod, Andreas Hofmann, Mads Dagnis Jensen, Alison Johnston, Haris Kountouros, Jonas Lefevere, Eric Miklin, Christine Neuhold, the participants of the 2013 OPAL Conference in Berlin and the 2013 ECPR General Conference in Bordeaux, Linda Dieke and Na-Hyeon Shin for their research assistance as well as the anonymous reviewers for their helpful comments. Any errors or omissions remain our own.

Disclosure Statement

No potential conflict of interests was reported by the authors.

Funding

This work was funded by the DFG [grant number WE 954/13-1] as part of an Open Research Area Fund (ARN-DFG-ESRC-NWO) and the 'Nachwuchs-Professorinnenprogramm' at the University of Cologne.

Notes

1. For detailed information about the EWS, see Auel and Christiansen (2015).
2. 'Proposal for a Council regulation on the exercise of the right to take collective action within the context of the freedom of establishment and the freedom to provide services', COM (2012) 130 final (21.3.2012).
3. 'Proposal for a Council regulation on the establishment of the European Public Prosecutor's Office', COM (2013) 534 final (17.7.2013).
4. 'Inter-parliamentary EU information exchange', http://www.ipex.eu.
5. The data are available from the authors upon request.

References

Auel, Katrin (2007). 'Democratic Accountability and National Parliaments: Redefining the Impact of Parliamentary Scrutiny in EU Affairs', *European Law Journal*, 13:4, 487–504.

Auel, Katrin and Thomas Christiansen (2015). 'After Lisbon: National Parliaments in the European Union', *West European Politics*, 38:2, 261–81.

Bakker, Ryan, Catherine de Vries, Erica Edwards, Liesbet Hooghe, Seth Jolly, Gary Marks, Jonathan Polk, Jan Rovny, Marco Steenbergen, and Milada Anna Vachudova (2012). 'Measuring Party Positions in Europe: The Chapel Hill Expert Survey Trend File, 1999–2010', *Party Politics*, 1–16. doi:10.1177/1354068812462931.

Cooper, Ian (2012). 'A 'Virtual Third Chamber' for the European Union? National Parliaments after the Treaty of Lisbon', *West European Politics*, 35:3, 441–65.

Cooper, Ian (2013). *A Yellow Card for the Striker: How National Parliaments Defeated EU Strikes Regulation.* Baltimore, MD: European Union Studies Association Meeting.

COSAC (2012). 'Eighteenth Bi-Annual Report: Developments in European Union Procedures and Practices Relevant to Parliamentary Scrutiny', available at http://www.cosac.eu/documents/bi-annual-reports-of-cosac/ (accessed 22 May 2014).

De Ruiter, Rik (2013). 'Under the Radar? National Parliaments and the Ordinary Legislative Procedure in the European Union', *Journal of European Public Policy*, 20:8, 1196–212.

de Vries, Catherine E. (2007). 'Sleeping Giant: Fact or Fairytale?: How European Integration Affects National Elections', *European Union Politics*, 8:3, 363–85.

de Wilde, Pieter (2011). 'Ex Ante Vs. Ex Post: The Trade-off between Partisan Conflict and Visibility in Debating EU Policy-Formulation in National Parliaments', *Journal of European Public Policy*, 18:5, 672–89.

De Wilde, Pieter (2012). 'Why the Early Warning Mechanism Does Not Alleviate the Democratic Deficit', OPAL Online Paper Series, 2012/6, available at http://www.pademia.eu/wp-content/uploads/2014/02/6.pdf.

Eurostat. GDP and main components – volumes (2014). available at http://appsso.eurostat.ec.europa.eu/nui/show.do?dataset=nama_gdp_k (accessed 21 May 2014; last updated on 20 May 2014).

Finke, Daniel, and Tanja Dannwolf (2013). 'Domestic Scrutiny of European Union Politics: Between Whistle Blowing and Opposition Control', *European Journal of Political Research*, 52:6, 715–46.

Føllesdal, Andreas, and Simon Hix (2006). 'Why There is a Democratic Deficit in the EU: A Response to Majone and Moravcsik', *JCMS: Journal of Common Market Studies*, 44:3, 533–62.

Fraga, Ana (2005). 'After the Convention: The Future Role of National Parliaments in the European Union (and the Day after … Nothing Will Happen)', *The Journal of Legislative Studies*, 11:3-4, 490–507.

Gattermann, Katjana (2013). *Brussels Calling!? Understanding National Parliamentarians' Participation in Inter-Parliamentary Committee Meetings*. Baltimore, MD: European Union Studies Association Meeting.

Green-Pedersen, Christoffer (2012). 'A Giant Fast Asleep? Party Incentives and the Politicisation of European Integration', *Political Studies*, 60:1, 115–30.

Hefftler, Claudia (2013). 'Nationale Parlamente', in Werner Weidenfeld and Wolfgang Wessels (eds.), *Jahrbuch Der Europäischen Integration 2012*. Baden-Baden: Nomos, 355–60.

Hegeland, Hans, and Christine Neuhold (2002). 'Parliamentary Participation in EU Affairs in Austria, Finland and Sweden: Newcomers with Different Approaches', European Integration Online Papers, 6, 10, available at http://eiop.or.at/eiop/pdf/2002-010.pdf.

Högenauer, Anna-Lena, and Christine Neuhold (2015). 'National Parliaments after Lisbon: Administrations on the Rise?', *West European Politics*, 38:2, 335–54.

Hooghe, Liesbet, and Gary Marks (2009). 'A Postfunctionalist Theory of European Integration: From Permissive Consensus to Constraining Dissensus', *British Journal of Political Science*, 39:1, 1–23.

Hooghe, Liesbet, Ryan Bakker, Anna Brigevich, Catherine de Vries, Erica Edwards, Gary Marks, Jan Rovny, and Marco Steenbergen (2010). 'Reliability and Validity of Measuring Party Positions: The Chapel Hill Expert Surveys of 2002 and 2006', *European Journal of Political Research*, 42:4, 684–703.

Interparliamentary Union (2013). 'Global Parliamentary Report'. available at http://www.ipu.org/gpr-e/data/index.htm (accessed 16 July 2013).

Karlas, Jan (2012). 'National Parliamentary Control of EU Affairs: Institutional Design after Enlargement', *West European Politics*, 35:5, 1095–113.

Kiiver, Philipp (2011). 'The Early-Warning System for the Principle of Subsidiarity: The National Parliament as a Conseil D'Etat for Europe', *European Law Review*, 36:1, 98.

King, Gary, and Langche Zeng (2001a). 'Logistic Regression in Rare Events Data', *Political Analysis*, 9:2, 137–63.

King, Gary, and Langche Zeng (2001b). 'Explaining Rare Events in International Relations', *International Organization*, 55:3, 693–715.

Knutelská, Viera (2011). 'National Parliaments as New Actors in the Decision-Making Process at the European Level', *Journal of Contemporary European Research*, 7:3, 327–44.

Legislative Dialogue Unit of the European Parliament/ Directorate for Relations with National Parliaments (2013). 'National Parliaments' Internal Procedures for Subsidiarity Checks'. available at http://www.europarl.europa.eu/webnp/webdav/site/myjahiasite/shared/Publications/subsidiarity%20procedures/Table%20internal%20procedures%20for%20subsidiarity%20check%2008.04.13.pdf (accessed 28 August 2013).

Neuhold, Christine (2011). 'Late Wake-up Call or Early Warning? Parliamentary Participation and Cooperation in Light of the Lisbon Treaty'. UACES Conference, London.

Paskalev, Vesselin (2009). 'Lisbon Treaty and the Possibility of a European Network Demoi-Cracy', European University Institute Working Paper, LAW 2009/20.

Raunio, Tapio (2005). 'Holding Governments Accountable in European Affairs: Explaining Cross-National Variation', *The Journal of Legislative Studies*, 11:3-4, 319–42.

Raunio, Tapio (2009). 'National Parliaments and European Integration: What We Know and Agenda for Future Research', *The Journal of Legislative Studies*, 15:4, 317–34.

Raunio, Tapio (2010). 'Destined for Irrelevance? Subsidiarity Control by National Parliaments', *Real Instituto Elcano Working Paper*, 36:2010, 1–9.

Raunio, Tapio (2011). 'The Gatekeepers of European Integration? The Functions of National Parliaments in the EU Political System', *Journal of European Integration*, 33:3, 303–21.

Saurugger, Sabine (2014). 'Europeanisation in times of Crisis', *Political Studies Review*, 12:2, 181–92.

Schuck, Andreas R.T., Georgios Xezonakis, Matthijs Elenbaas, Susan A. Banducci, and Claes H. de Vreese (2011). 'Party Contestation and Europe on the News Agenda: The 2009 European Parliamentary Elections', *Electoral Studies*, 30:1, 41–52.

Sprungk, Carina (2013). "A New Type of Representative Democracy? Reconsidering the Role of National Parliaments in the European Union', *Journal of European Integration*, 35:5, 547–63.

Strøm, Kaare (1997). 'Rules, Reasons and Routines: Legislative Roles in Parliamentary Democracies', *The Journal of Legislative Studies*, 3:1, 155–74.

Tomz, Michael, Gary King, and Langche Zeng (1999). *RELOGIT: Rare Events Logistic Regression, Version 1.1.* Cambridge, MA: Harvard University, available at http://gking.harvard.edu/ (accessed 1 October 2013).

Warntjen, Andreas (2012). 'Measuring Salience in EU Legislative Politics', *European Union Politics*, 13:1, 168–82.

Winzen, Thomas (2012). 'National Parliamentary Control of European Union Affairs: A Cross-National and Longitudinal Comparison', *West European Politics*, 35:3, 657–72.

APPENDIX

TABLE A1
DESCRIPTIVE STATISTICS

	Valid N	Missing	M	SD	Min	Max	Notes
Reasoned opinion	16,440	n/a	0.02	0.13	0	1	
EU dispersion	12,887	3553	11.13	4.58	1.42	17.78	Missing: LU,
Left–right dispersion	12,887	3553	18.76	4.06	8.40	26.27	CY, MT, DE-U, SI-U; and EL June 2012, IT 2013, RO 2012, SK 2012, SI-L2011
Majority gov.	10,864	5576	0.86	0.35	0	1	Disregards caretaker governments (IT 2011– 2013, EL 2012) and upper houses
New legislation	16,440	0	0.27	0.44	0	1	
Council debate	16,440	0	0.23	0.42	0	1	
Vote in EP plenary	16,440	0	0.02	0.14	0	1	
Recession year	16,440	0	0.34	0.47	0	1	
Lower house	16,440	0	0.33	0.47	0	1	
Upper house	16,440	0	0.33	0.47	0	1	
Election	16,440	0	0.05	0.21	0	1	
SC drafts RO	16,440	0	0.18	0.38	0	1	
Rel. no of staff	14,796	1644	2.83	1.57	0.51	8.06	Missing: NL-U, IT-U, IE
Mandating	16,440	0	0.325	0.47	0	1	
Christmas	16,440	0	0.23	0.42	0	1	
COSAC	16,440	0	0.64	0.48	0	1	
No. of other ROs	16,440	0	0.68	1.67	0	14	
Year	16,440	0	2011.47	1.07	2010	2013	
Length EU member	16,440	0	28.25	21.90	3	61	
Presidency	16,440	0	0.05	0.21	0	1	

Note: Cell entries are rounded to two decimals where applicable.

TABLE A2
PREDICTED PROBABILITIES

	Model 1		Model 2		Model 3		Model 4	
	Prob.	90% CI	Prob.	90% CI	Prob.	90% CI	Prob.	90% CI
Majority gov.								
No	–		–		–		0.009	0.004; 0.022
Yes	–		–		–		0.003	0.001; 0.007
EU dispersion								
Minimum	–		0.005	0.002; 0.011	0.005	0.002; 0.013	0.001	0.000; 0.004
Mean	–		0.009	0.005; 0.015	0.009	0.004; 0.020	0.003	0.001; 0.007
Maximum	–		0.014	0.007; 0.026	0.016	0.007; 0.037	0.006	0.003; 0.013
Left–right disp.								
Minimum	–		0.010	0.005; 0.019	0.011	0.004; 0.030	0.007	0.002; 0.021
Mean	–		0.009	0.005; 0.015	0.009	0.004; 0.021	0.003	0.001; 0.007
Maximum	–		0.008	0.003; 0.022	0.008	0.003; 0.022	0.002	0.001; 0.005
New legislation								
No	0.011	0.008; 0.017	0.009	0.005; 0.015	0.010	0.004; 0.019	0.003	0.001; 0.007
Yes	0.013	0.008; 0.019	0.011	0.007; 0.019	0.011	0.006; 0.024	0.004	0.002; 0.009
Council debate								
No	0.011	0.007; 0.017	0.009	0.005; 0.015	0.009	0.004; 0.020	0.003	0.001; 0.007
Yes	0.013	0.009; 0.020	0.010	0.006; 0.019	0.011	0.005; 0.024	0.003	0.001; 0.008
Vote in EP								
No	0.011	0.008; 0.017	0.009	0.005; 0.015	0.009	0.004; 0.020	0.003	0.001; 0.007
Yes	0.020	0.010; 0.041	0.019	0.008; 0.042	0.023	0.010; 0.048	0.004	0.002; 0.011
Recession year								
No	0.011	0.008; 0.017	0.009	0.005; 0.015	0.009	0.004; 0.020	0.003	0.001; 0.007
Yes	0.009	0.006; 0.014	0.008	0.004; 0.014	0.007	0.003; 0.015	0.003	0.001; 0.009
Rel. no. of staff								
Min	–		–		0.014	0.006; 0.031	0.005	0.003; 0.012
Max	–		–		0.003	0.001; 0.019	0.001	0.000; 0.006
SC drafts RO								
No	0.011	0.007; 0.017	0.009	0.005; 0.015	0.009	0.004; 0.020	0.003	0.001; 0.007
Yes	0.026	0.007; 0.094	0.024	0.005; 0.103	0.028	0.005; 0.140	0.014	0.006; 0.032

(*Continued*)

TABLE A2
(*Continued*)

	Model 1		Model 2		Model 3		Model 4	
	Prob.	90% CI	Prob.	90% CI	Prob.	90% CI	Prob.	90% CI
Mandating								
No	–		–		0.009	0.004; 0.020	–	
Yes	–		–		0.008	0.005; 0.015	–	
Election								
No	0.011	0.007; 0.017	0.009	0.005; 0.015	0.009	0.004; 0.020	0.003	0.001; 0.007
Yes	0.006	0.002; 0.016	0.006	0.002; 0.019	0.006	0.001; 0.022	0.002	0.000; 0.009
Lower house								
No	0.011	0.008; 0.016	0.009	0.005; 0.016	0.009	0.004; 0.020	0.003	0.001; 0.007
Yes	0.009	0.005; 0.015	0.009	0.005; 0.016	0.009	0.004; 0.020	0.006	0.003; 0.011
Upper house								
No	0.011	0.007; 0.017	0.009	0.005; 0.015	0.010	0.004; 0.020	–	
Yes	0.011	0.006; 0.018	0.012	0.006; 0.023	0.016	0.009; 0.030	–	
Christmas								
No	0.011	0.008; 0.017	0.009	0.005; 0.015	0.009	0.004; 0.019	0.003	0.001; 0.007
Yes	0.009	0.005; 0.015	0.007	0.003; 0.014	0.008	0.003; 0.018	0.002	0.001; 0.005
COSAC								
No	0.014	0.009; 0.022	0.012	0.006; 0.022	0.012	0.005; 0.029	0.004	0.002; 0.011
Yes	0.011	0.007; 0.017	0.009	0.005; 0.015	0.009	0.005; 0.020	0.003	0.001; 0.007
Other ROs								
0	0.009	0.006; 0.014	0.007	0.004; 0.012	0.007	0.003; 0.016	0.002	0.001; 0.005
5	0.050	0.034; 0.074	0.042	0.025; 0.071	0.043	0.021; 0.084	0.017	0.008; 0.035
10	0.244	0.166; 0.366	0.215	0.129; 0.353	0.218	0.114; 0.377	0.120	0.065; 0.220
Max	0.574	0.429; 0.694	0.540	0.365; 0.710	0.541	0.327; 0.735	0.407	0.242; 0.622
Year								
2010	0.011	0.007; 0.016	0.009	0.005; 0.015	0.009	0.005; 0.019	0.003	0.001; 0.007
2011	0.011	0.007; 0.016	0.009	0.005; 0.015	0.010	0.005; 0.020	0.003	0.001; 0.007
2012	0.012	0.008; 0.018	0.009	0.005; 0.016	0.009	0.004; 0.022	0.003	0.001; 0.008
2013	0.012	0.007; 0.020	0.009	0.004; 0.018	0.009	0.004; 0.024	0.003	0.001; 0.008

(*Continued*)

TABLE A2
(*Continued*)

	Model 1		Model 2		Model 3		Model 4	
	Prob.	90% CI	Prob.	90% CI	Prob.	90% CI	Prob.	90% CI
EU member								
5 years	0.011	0.006; 0.019	0.009	0.004; 0.019	0.009	0.003; 0.024	0.002	0.001; 0.007
15 years	0.011	0.007; 0.017	0.009	0.005; 0.018	0.009	0.004; 0.023	0.003	0.001; 0.007
25 years	0.011	0.007; 0.017	0.009	0.005; 0.016	0.009	0.005; 0.020	0.003	0.001; 0.007
Presidency								
No	0.011	0.007; 0.017	0.009	0.005; 0.016	0.009	0.004; 0.020	0.003	0.001; 0.007
Yes	0.007	0.002; 0.018	0.002	0.001; 0.007	0.001	0.000; 0.007	0.001	0.000; 0.004

	Model 5		Model 6		Model 7		Model 8	
	Prob.	90% CI	Prob.	90% CI	Prob.	90% CI	Prob.	90% CI
Majority gov.								
No	–		–		–		0.015	0.008; 0.028
Yes	–		–		–		0.011	0.007; 0.017
EU dispersion								
Minimum	–		0.003	0.001; 0.006	0.002	0.001; 0.006	0.006	0.003; 0.015
Mean	–		0.004	0.002; 0.007	0.003	0.001; 0.006	0.011	0.007; 0.016
Maximum	–		0.006	0.004; 0.009	0.004	0.002; 0.007	0.015	0.011; 0.021
Left–right disp.								
Minimum	–		0.009	0.005; 0.019	0.010	0.005; 0.021	0.048	0.029; 0.077
Mean	–		0.004	0.002; 0.007	0.003	0.001; 0.007	0.011	0.007; 0.017
Maximum	–		0.002	0.001; 0.004	0.001	0.000; 0.003	0.003	0.002; 0.006
New legislation								
No	0.008	0.005; 0.014	0.004	0.002; 0.007	0.003	0.002; 0.007	0.011	0.007; 0.017
Yes	0.010	0.006; 0.015	0.005	0.003; 0.009	0.004	0.002; 0.008	0.015	0.009; 0.022
Council debate								
No	0.008	0.005; 0.014	0.004	0.002; 0.007	0.003	0.001; 0.007	0.011	0.007; 0.017
Yes	0.010	0.006; 0.017	0.005	0.003; 0.008	0.003	0.002; 0.007	0.011	0.007; 0.018
Vote in EP								
No	0.009	0.005; 0.014	0.004	0.002; 0.007	0.003	0.001; 0.006	0.011	0.007; 0.017
Yes	0.016	0.007; 0.034	0.008	0.003; 0.022	0.007	0.003; 0.018	0.013	0.003; 0.056

(*Continued*)

TABLE A2
(*Continued*)

	Model 1		Model 2		Model 3		Model 4	
	Prob.	**90% CI**	**Prob.**	**90% CI**	**Prob.**	**90% CI**	**Prob.**	**90% CI**
Recession year								
No	0.008	0.005; 0.014	0.004	0.002; 0.007	0.003	0.001; 0.006	0.011	0.007; 0.017
Yes	0.008	0.005; 0.012	0.005	0.003; 0.008	0.004	0.002; 0.007	0.018	0.011; 0.029
Rel. no of staff								
Min	–		–		0.002	0.001; 0.005	0.008	0.005; 0.015
Max	–		–		0.006	0.002; 0.012	0.018	0.009; 0.038
SC drafts RO								
No	0.008	0.005; 0.013	0.004	0.002; 0.007	0.003	0.001; 0.007	0.011	0.007; 0.017
Yes	0.007	0.003; 0.015	0.002	0.001; 0.005	0.000	0.000; 0.001	0.002	0.001; 0.005
Mandating								
No	–		–		0.003	0.001; 0.007	–	
Yes	–		–		0.004	0.003; 0.007	–	
Election								
No	0.008	0.005; 0.013	0.004	0.002; 0.007	0.003	0.001; 0.007	0.011	0.007; 0.017
Yes	0.004	0.001; 0.011	0.003	0.001; 0.008	0.002	0.001; 0.007	0.008	0.001; 0.044
Lower house								
No	0.008	0.005; 0.014	0.004	0.002; 0.007	0.003	0.001; 0.006	0.003	0.007; 0.005
Yes	0.010	0.006; 0.016	0.009	0.006; 0.015	0.009	0.005; 0.017	0.011	0.007; 0.017
Upper house								
No	0.008	0.005; 0.014	0.004	0.002; 0.007	0.003	0.002; 0.007	–	
Yes	0.013	0.009; 0.019	0.017	0.012; 0.024	0.016	0.011; 0.022	–	
Christmas								
No	0.008	0.005; 0.014	0.004	0.002; 0.007	0.003	0.002; 0.006	0.011	0.007; 0.017
Yes	0.006	0.004; 0.010	0.003	0.002; 0.005	0.002	0.001; 0.004	0.008	0.004; 0.016
COSAC								
No	0.009	0.006; 0.015	0.005	0.003; 0.009	0.003	0.002; 0.007	0.012	0.007; 0.019
Yes	0.008	0.005; 0.014	0.004	0.002; 0.007	0.003	0.001; 0.006	0.011	0.007; 0.017
Other ROs								
0	0.007	0.004; 0.011	0.003	0.002; 0.005	0.002	0.001; 0.005	0.008	0.005; 0.013
5	0.040	0.025; 0.062	0.020	0.013; 0.030	0.015	0.008; 0.029	0.062	0.040; 0.088

(*Continued*)

TABLE A2
(*Continued*)

	Model 1		Model 2		Model 3		Model 4	
	Prob.	90% CI	Prob.	90% CI	Prob.	90% CI	Prob.	90% CI
10	0.203	0.135; 0.300	0.118	0.077; 0.177	0.089	0.048; 0.161	0.349	0.227; 0.481
Max	0.515	0.375; 0.648	0.377	0.263; 0.511	0.293	0.169; 0.465	0.733	0.551; 0.858
Year								
2010	0.009	0.005; 0.013	0.005	0.003; 0.007	0.004	0.002; 0.007	0.013	0.008; 0.022
2011	0.008	0.005; 0.013	0.004	0.002; 0.007	0.003	0.002; 0.006	0.011	0.008; 0.017
2012	0.008	0.005; 0.014	0.004	0.002; 0.007	0.003	0.001; 0.007	0.010	0.006; 0.016
2013	0.008	0.005; 0.015	0.004	0.002; 0.007	0.003	0.001; 0.007	0.009	0.005; 0.016
EU member								
5 years	0.006	0.004; 0.011	0.003	0.001; 0.005	0.002	0.001; 0.005	0.009	0.005; 0.015
15 years	0.007	0.004; 0.012	0.003	0.002; 0.006	0.002	0.001; 0.006	0.010	0.006; 0.015
25 years	0.008	0.005; 0.013	0.004	0.002; 0.007	0.003	0.001; 0.007	0.011	0.007; 0.016
Presidency								
No	0.008	0.005; 0.014	0.004	0.002; 0.007	0.003	0.002; 0.006	0.011	0.007; 0.016
Yes	0.005	0.002; 0.015	0.001	0.000; 0.003	0.001	0.000; 0.003	0.003	0.001; 0.018

Notes: predicted probabilities of submitting a reasoned opinion (versus not doing so); all other variables are kept at their mean or median; the lower and upper values of confidence intervals are reported at a 90% level as some effects are not statistically significant at higher levels.

TABLE A3
RELOGIT MODELS – JACK-KNIFE TESTS

	Model 6a	Model 6b	Model 6c	Model 6d
EU dispersion	0.03	0.07**	0.03	0.08***
	(0.03)	(0.03)	(0.03)	(0.03)
Left–right dispersion	−0.09**	−0.07**	−0.09***	−0.10***
	(0.04)	(0.03)	(0.03)	(0.03)
New legislation	0.31	0.32*	0.19	0.15
	(0.19)	(0.19)	(0.18)	(0.22)
Council debate	0.00	0.07	0.20	0.31*
	(0.20)	(0.21)	(0.20)	(0.17)
Vote in EP plenary	0.93*	0.87*	0.56	0.55
	(0.53)	(0.52)	(0.50)	(0.60)
Recession year	0.40	0.34	0.04	0.03
	(0.29)	(0.24)	(0.23)	(0.28)
Controls				
Lower house	0.79***	0.81*	0.84**	0.88**
	(0.29)	(0.44)	(0.39)	(0.40)
Upper house	1.29***	1.36***	1.52***	1.49***
	(0.31)	(0.44)	(0.36)	(0.34)
Election	−0.58	−0.08	−1.45	−0.11
	(1.07)	(0.79)	(1.05)	(0.81)
SC drafts RO	−0.78	−0.78	−0.72	−0.72
	(0.54)	(0.53)	(0.45)	(0.48)
Christmas	−0.53***	−0.06	−0.66*	−0.30
	(0.21)	(0.38)	(0.34)	(0.25)
COSAC	−0.16	−0.27	−0.11	−0.16
	(0.24)	(0.25)	(0.22)	(0.18)
No. of other ROs	0.36***	0.35***	0.37***	0.43***
	(0.03)	(0.03)	(0.03)	(0.04)
Year	−0.09	−0.05	−0.08	−0.10
	(0.13)	(0.14)	(0.12)	(0.15)
Length EU member	0.02**	0.01	0.01**	0.02**
	(0.01)	(0.01)	(0.01)	(0.01)
Presidency	−1.18*	−0.76	−1.79*	−1.93*
	(0.61)	(0.55)	(1.05)	(1.16)
Constant	178.58	97.72	158.32	188.47
	(254.43)	(277.83)	(247.18)	(298.22)
Excluding year	2010	2011	2012	2013
df	16	16	16	16
N chambers	32	32	32	32
N legislative drafts	329	260	333	311
N	9852	7744	10,131	9701

Notes: *$p < 0.1$;**$p < 0.05$;***$p < 0.01$. Clustered standard errors in parentheses; dependent variable: binary variable indicating whether a chamber has submitted a reasoned opinion or not for each draft legislative act; all models exclude the Swedish Riksdag.

National Parliaments after Lisbon: Administrations on the Rise?

ANNA-LENA HÖGENAUER and CHRISTINE NEUHOLD

In the wake of the Lisbon Treaty, much of the academic debate on national parliaments in the EU has focused on the new powers of national parliaments and the potential for the politicisation and parliamentarisation of the EU. In the process, the role of administrators in the parliamentary control of EU affairs has been neglected. This article addresses that gap by comparing parliamentary administrations to a set of ideal types on the basis of in-depth interviews and a comparative survey of parliamentary staff. This leads to the observation that the roles of parliamentary administrators have been further expanded after Lisbon to a range of tasks that go beyond technical support and include elements of agenda-setting.

The role of administrators in the functioning of national parliaments is routinely overlooked in the European integration literature. This is to some extent natural. Parliaments are seen as political arenas, and commentators thus focus on the political actors and their activities – control of the executive, debates and party politics – often with an emphasis on electoral incentives (cf. Auel and Christiansen 2015). This article argues that such a focus obscures the roles of administrators in the functioning of parliaments. This is problematic for two reasons: On the one hand, administrators contribute to the functioning of parliaments through the provision of supporting tasks and are thus part of their capacity for action. Thus, while the European Treaties and national constitutions define the formal powers of parliaments and their margin for manoeuvre, the availability of administrative support affects to what extent committees and plenaries are able to make use of those powers (Auel and Christiansen 2015). On the other hand, if the activity of administrators goes beyond the merely technical or secretarial, it may lead to the 'bureaucratisation' of legislative institutions and diminish the extent to which parliamentary control is in fact *political* in nature (see Christiansen *et al.* 2014).

The Lisbon Treaty has provided national parliaments with a set of opportunities. The protocol on the role of national parliaments guarantees parliaments wide-ranging information rights with regard to Commission consultation documents, instruments of legislative planning and draft legislative acts as well as the agendas and minutes of Council meetings (Articles 1 and 2). In addition, the control and participation rights of national parliaments are improved, especially with the introduction of the Political Dialogue with the Commission in 2006 and under the new 'Early Warning System' (EWS) (see Auel and Christiansen 2015). The introduction of the EWS triggered a vibrant debate about the level of influence that parliaments can have in practice, the coordination problems between national parliaments and the new procedures put in place by parliament in response to the Lisbon provisions (e.g. Christiansen *et al.* 2014; Cooper 2012; Kiiver 2012; Raunio 2010). However, a question that was largely eclipsed within the academic debate is the question of the role of parliamentary administrators in the use of these procedures.

This article thus raises the question of the extent to which parliamentary administrations play an active part in the scrutiny of EU politics with a particular emphasis on to what extent their tasks are purely 'technical' or have the potential to shape the actual outcome of parliamentary scrutiny. While the debate and research on the role of the administrations of national parliaments in European affairs scrutiny is very recent and does not allow for a detailed comparison over time, due to a lack of data or literature on the pre-Lisbon state of affairs, the article will as far as possible try to address the question whether the attempts to politicise and 'democratise' European policy-making by way of the Lisbon Treaty were in fact accompanied by a tendency to bureaucratisation, as argued by Christiansen *et al.* (2014). In order to address these questions, we attempt to classify and capture the tasks and roles of the various administrations in order to be able to see the extent to which they are in fact merely technocratic (or not).

For this purpose, the first section will review the existing literature on delegation to bureaucratic actors and the literature on administrative roles. The second section develops a set of ideal-typical roles that allows for an assessment of the degree of administrative involvement by distinguishing between a range of technical and non-technical tasks. Although the definition of administrative roles in the current literature cannot be applied precisely to parliaments – as opposed to governments – it can be instructive when reflecting on the roles that administrators (could) play in national legislatures. The third section then discusses the findings of the first comparative study of parliamentary administrations in European policy-making in the context of the ideal-typical roles. It argues that parliamentary administrations play an active role in parliamentary scrutiny that goes beyond technical tasks and that can include even agenda-shaping. In conclusion the extent of bureaucratisation of parliamentary scrutiny of EU affairs is discussed and an agenda for further research is presented.

In this quest the study focuses on parliamentary staff rather than the experts employed by party groups or individual MPs. Whereas party group staff or personal assistants are meant to interpret policy issues according to a political stance, parliamentary administrators face the challenge of having to remain unbiased. The research was conducted in two stages: it comprises 39 semi-structured interviews with committee clerks and MPs from 11 member states between September 2010 and June 2013 in the framework of a larger project (Observatory of Parliaments after Lisbon – OPAL): the UK (House of Commons), France, Belgium, Germany (Bundesrat), the Netherlands, Sweden, Austria, Poland, Italy, Slovakia and Romania, as well as parliamentary representatives in Brussels from Slovenia, Finland and Ireland. These cases cover a wide range of parliaments characterised by marked differences as regards geographical location, the size of the respective parliament and the activity of the legislature in EU affairs in general. The complete list of interviews can be found in the appendix. In addition, the authors have received written replies to a questionnaire from 21 chambers that allow for a broader overview. By way of this data collection 28 chambers in 21 member states are covered.[1]

The Problem of Delegation to Administrators and their Roles

The literature on delegation to bureaucrats postulates that the complexity of the modern state and the issues at stake in policy-making require politicians to delegate some tasks and decisions due to a lack of time and expertise. However, the empowerment of bureaucratic actors results in a tension between the desire for political control and the value of bureaucratic expertise (Huber and McCarty 2004). Prime examples are delegation to executive agencies or delegation inside executives, where policies are in practice often drawn up and managed by the bureaucratic layers rather than by politicians.

A similar dilemma faces politicians in legislatures, who also need to delegate certain decisions due to time constraints (Arnold 1987: 279). Delegation to staff within parliaments is also necessitated by the fact that these relatively small institutions have a disadvantage when it comes to expertise compared to the much larger ministries that they are supposed to control.

For political actors, the main risk is that 'the very skills and expertise that bureaucrats enjoy create the possibility that bureaucrats will usurp the rightful role of politicians in policy-making processes' (Huber and McCarty 2004). An 'excessive' amount of bureaucratic influence can ultimately challenge democratic principles, which is why the literature has devoted much attention to questions of political control and oversight. A distinction has been made between measures that can *prevent* transgressions on the part of bureaucrats, such as tight laws authorising administrative action and rules on administrative behaviour and measures that *correct* transgressions after they have occurred, such as hearings and appeals to courts (Arnold 1987; Huber 2000; McCubbins and Schwartz 1984).

However, such measures, which have been developed in the literature on oversight over *executives*, cannot easily be applied to *legislative staff*. Most of them are simply too formal and cumbersome to work in the context of delegation within an institution. The main form of control and oversight available to politicians in parliaments is trust. Accordingly it is in the power of political actors not to accept advice provided by officials if it becomes apparent that the latter are politically 'biased'. Administrators, in turn, will anticipate that their influence depends on the extent to which they are trusted and will try to avoid any blatant bias (De Gregorio 1994: 2; Winzen 2011). Trust is strongest where administrators adhere to a written or unwritten professional code that includes transparency and neutrality as its core principles. However, lack of trust is more likely to have negative consequences on the influence of administrators if bigger – and especially governing – parties mistrust them. Manley's (1968) study of politically biased committee staff in Congress illustrates that the opposition can do little to check staff as long as the staff are supported by the majority.

The fact that political oversight in parliaments thus relies predominantly on informal mechanisms highlights two other aspects about delegation. Firstly, in order for a positive relationship between politicians and staff to develop, it is important that staff act to at least some extent on a *logic of appropriateness* and accept and internalise principles of neutrality and transparency (Olsen 2006). Secondly, when studying these processes it is particularly important to know whether extensive delegation to administrators – beyond merely 'technical' tasks – actually takes place. This is where this article comes in, by seeking to establish what types of tasks are delegated to administrators and to what extent the role of administrators goes beyond technical support.

The literature on delegation suggests that delegation is particularly likely to occur on complex issues and on issues of low salience (Manley 1968) – which would imply a high level of delegation to administrators as EU affairs are perceived by parliaments as complex and of low (electoral) salience. In addition, a further incentive lies in the opportunity to become less dependent on information from the government, which can lead even governing parties to be in favour of independent information gathering (Dutch Lower House, VVD MP, 28 March 2012). Finally, the Lisbon changes and especially the EWS require parliaments to digest an increased amount of information, identify priorities and problems and react within a very narrow time span of only eight weeks. As the EWS is limited to objections on grounds of subsidiarity, the reasoned opinions need to include legal justifications. Thus, if parliaments want to use the new opportunities effectively as means to maximise their influence within EU affairs, delegation to administrators may be necessary (see Christiansen *et al.* 2014).

However, the literature on national parliaments in Europe provides few insights into the *roles* that administrators might play. Parliamentary administrations in Western Europe have thus far been the subject of mainly descriptive analysis (Campbell and Laporte 1981; Harfst and Schnapp 2003; Perez 2007; Ryle 1981). Baron (2013) highlights the emphasis on political neutrality in the French system and mentions both an advisory role and an increasing involvement in the drafting of laws, amendments and reports. Independence and autonomy from governments are essential characteristics not only of the French but also of the British parliamentary administrative system (Campbell and

Laporte 1981; Perez 2007; Ryle 1981). By contrast, in Germany the civil service is covered by the same legal framework as the federal bureaucracy, which is to provide for mobility between the legislative and executive bureaucracy (Blischke 1981). For the administration of the US Congress, Patterson (1970: 26) describes the tasks as information-gathering, the planning of hearings and drafting.

Alternative resources in the literature are the typologies that have been developed with regard to bureaucrats in executives and the nascent literature on the European Parliament (EP). Page and Jenkins, for example, develop a typology of policy roles in the context of mid-level bureaucrats in the UK. They distinguish between three roles: a production role, which encompasses the drafting of policy-related documents; a maintenance role, which relates to the management of policies (i.e. that policies run according to agreed principles); and a service role, which implies that administrators provide advice to politicians (Page and Jenkins 2005: 60–75). However, while the production and service roles are likely also to be relevant in a parliamentary context, the maintenance role seems to be a typical executive role.

The literature on the European Parliament may also be instructive. Even if it is a trans-national body, it is a legislative body. Officials in both the EP and national parliaments have to grapple with the technicalities and complexities of EU legislation and the decision-making process. According to Provan (2001; cited in Neunreither 2006: 55) assistance to EP committees and MEPs can be broken down into technical-administrative assistance, which consists of organisational support, technical-substantive assistance, which involves procedural advice and assistance with drafting, research assistance and, lastly, political assistance, which is defined as political coordination within or across political groups and policy definition. Provan (2001) recommended that political assistance be left to the staff of political groups and the assistants of MEPs. This breakdown is detailed, but the description of all tasks that might fall to the parliamentary administration as 'technical' could downplay the role of administrators and hide the extent to which decisions are delegated. Winzen (2011) questions more openly the extent to which the work of the EP staff is merely technical or also of relevance to public policy, and in the process defines two roles: managing the process and informing the process. This distinction between 'technical' and 'non-technical' is however rather blunt, at least at first glance. Egeberg et al. (2013) also examine the activities of EP staff by way of an online survey ($N = 118$). When zooming in on what officials actually do – i.e. what tasks they (say they) perform – it becomes apparent that providing background information for MEPs ranks at the top, followed by drafting documents (Egeberg et al. 2013).

Finally, Dobbels and Neuhold (2013) have attempted to apply the roles developed by Page and Jenkins (2005) to the EP: for the EP the *production role* would imply mainly the drawing up of documents for meetings, whereas a *service role* would also involve supplying personal knowledge to MEPs on the substance of the draft reports and procedural guidance. Finally, the authors posit that EP officials could perform a *steering role*. This would imply that EP civil servants are substantially influencing the item at stake beyond the instructions of MEPs (or because of the lack thereof).

The concept of the 'steering role', which would suggest that administrators can exercise influence on policy-making, might also be of relevance for national parliaments. However, it would be interesting to take the potential tasks of civil servants in the domain of information processing more explicitly into account, as this is likely to play an important role for national parliaments, which now receive thousands of EU documents every year.

Overall it seems that most of the existing typologies only partially fit the purpose of describing parliamentary staff. Either they are too descriptive or they miss distinctions that could be relevant for the role of parliamentary staff in European affairs scrutiny. As a result, we decided to follow a largely inductive approach to develop a refined typology of roles on the basis of our empirical insights on what administrators actually *do* in the practical political process.

How to Study the Roles of Parliamentary Administrations

If we want to capture the differences between parliamentary administrations in a meaningful way, we need to step back from overly broad and catch-all categories, such as 'technical' and 'non-technical'. Firstly, all cases might fall into the same category. Secondly, we would not be able to capture nuances in the extent to which tasks of parliamentary administrations really are non-technical. Instead, we need a fine-tuned distinction between different administrative roles, especially for the 'non-technical' functions, which might potentially be problematic from a delegation perspective.

As much of the Early Warning System and Political Dialogue, but also mandating, increasingly revolves around the provision of large amounts of information by the European institutions directly to national parliaments, information-processing is likely to form a central part of the tasks of parliamentary administrations. However, this could take different forms that have different implications for administrative input. We essentially distinguish between five ideal types of roles related to information-processing (see Table 1). This distinction is based on an analysis of the Lisbon provisions and possible implications for administrations and our interview data.

Firstly, under an administrative analyst model, the administration would either simply forward the information from the European level or government to the relevant committees and to MPs without further comment, or provide politicians with very short summaries regarding the content of the respective measure. In both cases, the opportunities for steering the discussion in a certain direction would be absent or limited.

Secondly, an analyst-type administration would offer legal and procedural advice on the options available to parliament. In addition, they could be involved in drafting documents on the basis of debates and in the provision of

TABLE I

ROLES AND TASKS OF PARLIAMENTARY ADMINISTRATORS IN EU AFFAIRS

Roles	Administrative assistant	Analyst	Advisor	Agenda-shaper	Coordinator
Tasks	Gathers and forwards information	Provides choice of balanced arguments*	Content-related advice	Pre-selection of documents	Coordination with executive other parliaments EU institutions
	Summarises information	Prepares drafts after debates*	Prepares drafts before debates*		
	Organises committee meetings	Procedural and legal advice			Internal coordination
Extent of involvement in scrutiny	Low	Low–medium	Medium	Medium–high	

Note: *These tasks and distinctions were derived from the in-depth interview data.

limited advice, for example in the form of balanced arguments. This would allow the administration some room to influence parliamentary scrutiny, for example by highlighting certain possible courses of action. However, the political actors would still be in charge of actively selecting priorities and formulating the actual position through deliberation amongst themselves.

Thirdly, the administration could play an advisory role in which its tasks might include the provision of specific content-related advice (for example on whether something constitutes a breach of subsidiarity), which would allow the administration to promote a certain scrutiny outcome. Drafts of opinions and resolutions *prior* to debates would of course also fall into that category of content-related interpretation.

Fourthly, an administration could play the role of agenda-shaper if it were tasked with the pre-selection of documents that are particularly relevant for parliament or specific committees. By recommending certain documents for further consideration, the staff would effectively influence what kind of issues are likely to make it onto the parliamentary agenda.

Finally, a fifth – and slightly distinct – role would be that of coordinator. As the Early Warning System and Political Dialogue are most likely to result in influence if several parliaments push in the same direction, inter-parliamentary coordination becomes increasingly important. Hence, one can expect parliamentary administrations to play a role in the exchange of information between parliaments on who is planning what type of action. The level of influence depends on the precise tasks: coordination can mean information gathering, but it could also imply a representational function vis-à-vis other actors in Brussels or at 'home' and can in the best of cases imply that issues are 'pre-cooked' across national boundaries (French Senate, senior EU clerk, 25 May 2012; Swedish NPR, 17 November 2010; Irish NPR, 13 January 2010).

It is also important to note that the first four roles are likely to be incremental. In other words, staff playing an advisory role may well also perform the tasks in the categories of analyst and assistant.

Parliamentary Administrations in EU Affairs: Mere Paper-Pushers?

As flagged up in the introduction, our empirical data is based on semi-structured interviews that explored the tasks of parliamentary administrations in depth for a number of parliaments. In addition, a written questionnaire tested to what extent a basic set of tasks applied to a wider range of chambers. The main results of the questionnaire are presented in Table 2. They will be discussed in greater depth in connection with the interview data in the following sub-sections.

The background data reflects that the vast majority of administrations have a very extensive set of tasks and play an important supporting role in the scrutiny process. Moreover, we can also discern a general trend of officials providing both procedural guidance and advice as regards content. It is noteworthy that this trend of a certain degree of empowerment of officials not only

TABLE 2
THE TASKS OF STAFF IN EU AFFAIRS

		Tasks of EU staff			
		Selection documents	Procedural advice	Drafting of the final position	Content advice
Austria	Both chambers	Pre-check for subsidiarity	Yes	No	Yes
Belgium	Upper House	Yes	Yes	No	No
	Lower House	Yes	Yes	Yes	Yes
Bulgaria		Yes	Yes	Yes	Yes
Cyprus		Yes	Yes	No	Yes
Czech Republic	Upper House	Yes	n.i.	n.i.	Yes
	Lower House	Yes	Yes	Yes	Yes
Denmark		Yes	Yes	No	Yes
Estonia		Yes	Yes	Yes	Yes
Finland		No	Yes	Yes	Yes
France	Upper House	Yes	Yes	Yes	Yes
	Lower House	Yes	Yes	n.i.	Yes
Germany	Upper House	Yes	Yes	No	Yes
	Lower House	Yes	Yes	Yes	No
Hungary		Yes	Yes	Yes	Yes
Italy	Lower House	Yes	Yes	Yes	Yes
Lithuania		n.i.	Yes	n.i.	Yes
Luxembourg		Yes	Yes	No	No
Netherlands	Upper House	No	Yes	Yes	On request
	Lower House	Yes	Yes	Yes	Yes, but balanced
Poland	Upper House	Yes	Yes	Yes	Yes
	Lower House	Yes	Yes	Yes	Yes
Portugal		No	Yes	Sometimes	Yes
Romania	Lower House	Yes	Yes	Yes	Yes
Slovakia		Yes	Yes	Yes	Yes
Sweden		Yes	Yes	Yes, but only on request	No
UK	Lower House	No	Yes	Yes	Yes

n.i. = no information.

prevails in member states that are seen as 'proactive and engaged' within EU decision-making, such as Denmark (O'Brennan and Raunio 2007: 21), but also in member states that have joined the European Union in the more recent rounds of enlargement. This is in line with the more general verdict that parliaments of the (relative) newcomers to the EU face shortcomings but these are expected to diminish over time (Szalay 2005; Vehar 2007). There thus seems to be a trend of convergence, leaving officials to play rather substantial roles in parliaments across the Union, at least when it comes to parliamentary scrutiny of EU affairs in the post-Lisbon EU.

Procedural Advice and Pre-Selection

As Table 2 shows, the provision of procedural advice is one of the key responsibilities of the administrations of all chambers for which information is available. Thus, due to the complex and legalistic nature of parliamentary involvement, especially under the EWS, all of the administrations play important roles as *analysts* who have to inform MPs of the options that are available to them.

In addition, the new rules on information provision led to national parliaments being swamped with information. Thus, national parliaments receive about 1,000 policy documents (e.g. legislative proposals) per year accompanied by about 24,000 supporting documents (e.g. EP opinions) per year (Höing 2015; Belgian House of Representatives, EAC clerk, 25 May 2012). As a result, all parliaments channel this information flow via their administrations.

The European Affairs staff do not just act as a 'mailbox', but – in at least 21 cases – pre-select documents based on their relevance for the member state and political salience, based on the Commission Work Programme, the weekly list of proposals or both (see Table 2). In quantitative terms, the Belgian European Affairs clerk estimates that about 100–200 out of 1,000 documents are short-listed by the parliamentary staff (Belgian House of Representatives, EAC clerk, 25 May 2012). The Dutch parliament selects about 80 'priority dossiers' on an annual basis (Dutch parliament, NPR, 9 December 2010). These lists of priorities are of course of an advisory nature and usually subject to the approval of the European Affairs Committee, Specialised Committees or the Chair of the European Affairs Committee. Thus, in most cases, parliamentary administrations pre-select the documents in accordance with the relevant committees, and administrators agree that their lists are generally accepted by their political masters (House of Commons, EAC clerk, 23 May 2012; French Senate, advisor, 4 May 2012; Dutch parliament, NPR, 9 December 2010; Italian House of Representatives, European Affairs Service, 9 November 2012; Danish parliament, EU advisor, 19 November 2012; Austrian parliament, NPR, 22 November 2010). The Sejm has for example never issued a reasoned opinion without an earlier suggestion from the Research Bureau (Polish Sejm, Research Bureau, 19 April 2013). In practice, this filtering role thus provides parliamentary staff with an opportunity to act as *agenda-shapers*. In order to ensure that important dossiers get noticed, some parliamentary staff in addition provide specific procedural advice on how to follow the issue up (Dutch Lower House, EU Affairs clerk, 9 December 2011; Romanian parliament, former EU staff, 17 November 2011).

It should be noted that the role of the administration in pre-selection issues is specific to the Early Warning System and document-based scrutiny. In the case of mandating, which is based on the agenda of the Council of Ministers and the draft position of the government on these issues, the tasks of the administration are based around preparatory information provision and analysis rather than selection (Dutch Lower House, EU Affairs clerk, 9 December 2011; Swedish parliament, EAC clerk, 13 March 2012). Nevertheless, the role of administrators is also strengthened in mandating systems insofar as there is now a clear list of priorities that the parliament will focus on and that administrators can prepare for.

Drafting and Advice

As in the case of the filtering of documents, the practices on information provision vary across chambers. Overall, at least 17 chambers allow their administrations to draft the final documents and 21 to provide content-related advice (see Table 2).

The interviews revealed finer variations. The administration of the Dutch Lower House, the Swedish parliament and the French parliament generally provide committees with balanced arguments on an issue. The administration of the Romanian House of Representatives provides an analysis only upon request (Dutch Lower House, EU Affairs clerk, 9 December 2011; Swedish parliament, Social Insurance Committee clerks, 6 March 2012; French Senate, senior EU clerk, 25 May 2012). The advantage of such a system is that administrators support the activities of MPs, but by providing MPs with a range of arguments and alternatives they remain relatively neutral (see Meller 1952: 116). In the case of the Dutch Lower House, this provision of balanced arguments is part of an attempt to get politicians more actively involved in the scrutiny of EU affairs. Before the reform in 2006, the administrators often drafted the actual document before the debate, which could result in the committee simply approving a pre-prepared draft. As the committees are now confronted with potentially contradictory arguments, they have at the very least to choose from amongst the list of arguments (Dutch Lower House, EU Affairs clerk, 9 December 2011).

Those administrations that only provide summaries of documents or a list of different arguments usually also only draft parliamentary documents *after* the debates in the committees. The EAC staff of the German Bundesrat, for example, draft reasoned opinions based on the debates in the Bundesrat (German Bundesrat, EAC clerk, 4 May 2012).

In rare cases parliamentary administrations provide drafts *prior* to debates in the committee, for example the European Affairs clerks of the Belgian House of Representatives, the Romanian Senate and the Polish Sejm (Belgian House of Representatives, EAC clerk, 25 May 2012; Romanian Senate, EAC clerk, 5 May 2012; Polish Sejm, EAC clerk, 23 April 2013), as well as the French parliamentary administration for reasoned opinions (French Senate, senior EU clerk, 25 May 2012) or the Slovak parliament upon request of the chair (Slovak parliament, EAC clerk, 29 May 2013).

The duties of parliamentary staff with regard to mandating are similar to those under parliamentary scrutiny in this regard. Administrators gather information on the Council meeting and government position and advise the relevant committee (Swedish parliament, EAC clerk, 13 March 2012). In the case of the Dutch parliament – and sometimes also the Polish Senate – the administration sometimes even drafts possible questions to the minister (Dutch Lower House, EU Affairs clerk, 9 December 2011; Polish Senate, EAC advisor, 10 April 2013).

A Coordination Function

In addition to the tasks outlined above and in Table 2, parliamentary administrations play an important coordinating function across national parliaments. The key players with regard to inter-parliamentary coordination and exchange between EU institutions and national parliaments are not so much the EU staff in the national parliaments, but rather the permanent representatives of the respective national legislatures in the EP (hereafter: NPRs) in Brussels. Each parliament has a representative at the EP, and some bicameral parliaments have one for each chamber.

The Danish parliament is a forerunner in this respect as it has sent a permanent representative to Brussels to cover EU affairs since 1990. The reason behind this was that the Danish parliament was the first to deal with EU issues quite intensively by way of their system of mandating the respective minister in the Council, so this came rather naturally (Danish NPR, 9 November 2010). The Finnish parliament followed in 1996 (Hegeland 2007). A majority of the representatives have worked in their respective parliaments before, so they have a first comprehensive insight into their legislative system (Swedish NPR, 17 November 2010).

Building on the provisions of the Lisbon Treaty as a legal basis, national parliamentary representatives to the EP have derived the common task of coordinators for themselves, which is the exchange of information on the stance of their respective parliaments towards a possible breach of the principle of subsidiarity from the perspective of one or more member states. The informal network of NPRs is beginning to function by way of the regular 'Monday morning meetings'. It is in this setting that national parliamentary representatives exchange information and 'alert' other parliaments to proposals that could be problematic from the perspective of the subsidiarity principle or from a more political stance. They can thus perform an informal agenda-setting and advisory role. Moreover, the fact that all representatives work in the same building builds a basis for informal information exchange, where this 'bridge-building function' across national parliaments is flagged up as one of the main functions of NPRs (Dutch NPR, 9 December 2010; Slovenian NPR, 16 November 2010).

Apart from contributing to a fruitful information exchange between national parliamentary representatives, the respective parliamentary officials have the main tasks of creating a network of contacts with the European institutions and participating in their respective meetings as well as in meetings of their respective national parliaments. The direct contact with the EU executive is inter alia facilitated by the fact that representatives of the services of the Commission regularly attend the meetings of NPRs (Commission 2010: 7; COSAC clerk, 9 November 2010). Moreover representatives are to supply data for the scrutiny activities of their respective parliaments and in some cases to ensure cooperation with their respective Permanent Representation to the European Union (French NPR, 14 September 2010).

The EU experts in the national parliaments, by contrast, do not have many direct contacts to other national parliaments and only some contacts to EU institutions. They are in regular contact with officials in the national ministries, but rely mostly on the NPRs for contacts with other parliaments and EU institutions (e.g. French Senate, EAC clerk, 12 May 2012; Dutch Senate, 2 EAC clerks, 11 January 2011; Dutch Lower House, EU Affairs clerk, 9 December 2011; House of Commons, EAC clerk, 23 May 2012). This means that de facto most inter-parliamentary cooperation and requests for information run via the NPR network. As the Early Warning System encourages inter-parliamentary cooperation, parliamentary staff have started to see the advantage of an enhanced network of administrators. As a result, due to a Dutch initiative, a meeting of EAC clerks took place after the COSAC meeting of April 2012 (COSAC, 24 May 2012). It was the first meeting in many years and was motivated by the increased need for coordination (Folketing, EU advisor, 19 November 2012).

In the Netherlands, cooperation between the two chambers is also ensured mainly via administrative cooperation. Thus, the EU staff of the Senate take part regularly in the Tuesday morning meetings of the EU staff of the Lower House. Even when the two chambers issue joint reasoned opinions, the coordination takes place mostly via the administration. However, this close cooperation is specific to the Netherlands. Neither the French nor the Belgian chambers work so closely together and thus nor do their administrations (Dutch Senate, 2 EAC clerks, 11 January 2011; Dutch Lower House, EU Affairs clerk, 9 December 2011; Belgian Senate, EAC clerk, 16 April 2012; French Senate, EAC clerk (1), 25 May 2012).

However, parliamentary clerks also play a role in *intra-parliamentary* cooperation: the Dutch EU advisors of all standing committees coordinate horizontally which committees should best discuss a certain issue. If several committees are involved, they facilitate the communication between those fora. In Denmark, where sectoral committees are consulted before the EAC mandates the government, the EU and committee staff are also responsible for compiling the different views and ensuring that the various parliamentary actors are aware of their activities (Danish parliament, Environment clerk, 20 November 2012; Danish parliament, Food, Agriculture and Fisheries clerk, 27 November 2012). Of course the multiple memberships in committees mean that there is usually at least one MP on the EAC who also sits on the relevant sectoral committee. In addition, committee staff also act as 'institutional memory', as some EU legislative processes span several years (Danish parliament, EAC clerk, 21 November 2012).

Summary

Overall, the empirical analysis of the tasks of the EU staff of national parliaments confirms the criticism of existing typologies of staff roles. Firstly, the parliamentary administrations of all 28 chambers were *all* found to perform at least some functions that go beyond the merely technical. Secondly, the differences between parliamentary administrations are fairly nuanced and thus require a nuanced typology.

Interestingly, empirically *none* of the parliamentary administrations falls exclusively into the category of administrative assistant. All parliaments rely on their administrations for additional 'non-technical' support and thus allow their administrators to play some role in the scrutiny of EU affairs. In addition, only the administration of the Dutch Upper House was limited to the role of analyst, by way of giving procedural advice, for example. Five parliamentary administrations also provided content-related advice and/or drafts prior to debates and thus act as *advisors*. The vast majority of administrations, however, fall into the category of *agenda-shaper*: 21 chambers allowed their administrations to pre-select documents for parliamentary scrutiny. Finally, administrators can fulfil a coordinating function vis-à-vis other national

TABLE 3
ROLES OF PARLIAMENTARY ADMINISTRATIONS (IN 2013)*

Administrative assistant	Analyst	Advisor	Agenda-shaper
	Dutch Upper House	Austria (both)**, Finland, Portugal, UK (Lower House) (Lithuania?)***	Belgium (both), Bulgaria, Cyprus, Czech (both), Denmark, Estonia, France (both), Germany (both), Hungary, Italian Lower House, Luxembourg, Dutch Lower House, Poland (both), Romanian Lower House, Slovakia, Sweden

*The coordination function is not listed here, all parliamentary administrations play this role. Variation exists only as to the range of coordination tasks.
**The Austrian parliament has an administrative unit that conducts a pre-check for subsidiarity concerns. However, its activities are narrowly circumscribed (e.g. through politically defined key words), which makes it a borderline case between pre-selection and advice. As the drafting function of the EU staff is also limited, we count it as a strong advisor.
***The Lithuanian parliament is at least an advisor. However as information is missing on pre-selection, for example, it cannot be assessed whether it is also an agenda-shaper.

parliaments, European institutions or their own government. Table 3 reflects the relative homogeneity of tasks that officials perform across parliaments.

Overall, the preparation for and implementation of the Treaty of Lisbon has allowed administrators to play a more active role in EU affairs. Administrators have become active advisors and even 'steer' parliamentary business to some extent. Despite the fact that national parliaments are often seen to invest less energy in European issues than in domestic issues, the EU units are comparatively well staffed (e.g. in terms of EAC staff compared to sectoral committee staff) (Högenauer and Christiansen 2015). Moreover, EU staff can have more powers than domestic staff, the pre-selection role being a case in point (Spreitzer 2013). Both of these features are of course in line with delegation theory, which suggests that delegation is more likely on complex issues and on issues that are perceived to be less salient.

However, the question is also if this 'bureaucratisation' is necessarily problematic from a normative point of view, which would only be the case if officials would in fact evade the instructions of their political principals. So far, this does not appear to be the case as most interviewees agree, for instance, that the pre-selection of documents by administrators is rarely contested.

While most parliamentary administrations perform similar roles to begin with, the remaining variation between parliaments is difficult to explain conclusively on the basis of this first comparative data collection on parliamentary administrations and in the absence of prior studies. There are however some patterns that one might logically expect.

One hypothesis would be that the size and tasks of parliamentary administrations might depend on the size of the parliament. Smaller parliaments or parliaments from economically weaker member states may not have the resources for a large bureaucratic apparatus which would limit the amount of support that the administration could provide.

Alternatively, one might expect mandating systems giving rise to more political contestation as they touch upon the relationship between opposition parties, the executive and parties in government. Delegation to the administration can be expected to be more limited as political actors would be expected to want to stay in control of issues that are attributed political importance (Wlezien 2005).

Lastly, one might expect a link between proactive and engaged parliaments (O'Brennan and Raunio 2007) and strong administrations, although with a different causal direction: a strong administration might *enable* a parliament to engage actively and effectively in parliamentary scrutiny.

However, even a cursory comparison of the data in Table 3 with data on the ratio between staff numbers and MPs (Högenauer and Christiansen 2015), the level of activity of parliaments (Auel *et al.* 2015) or the existing mandating systems shows that the most wide-ranging type of role is performed both by cases that are in fact in line with the hypotheses *and* by cases that clearly contradict them (e.g. Estonia, Slovakia, Belgium and Cyprus). Similarly, the group of somewhat weaker administrations also contains very different cases (e.g. the

British House of Commons shares few characteristics with the Dutch Upper House).

The fact that many of the 'obvious' variables such as resources do not have a clear relationship with the typology of the roles of administration suggests that there may be deeper reasons for the variation: this could be less about constraints and opportunities, but rather about *choice and administrative traditions*. What *is* an appropriate role for a parliamentary administration? What *should* it do? It is possible that there is a gap between parliaments that emphasise *efficiency* (i.e. the administration carries the main burden) and parliaments that emphasise *political* control (i.e. certain tasks should fall within the scope of political masters). Our interviews reflect that the decision of the Dutch Tweede Kamer to provide only balanced arguments – rather than concrete recommendations – is rooted in the desire to stimulate political debate (Dutch Lower House, EU Affairs clerk, 9 December 2011). However, to assess these logics of appropriateness across a wider range of cases would require further in-depth studies. Ideally, in order to provide further explanation(s), the comparison should focus on the variance between parliamentary administrations that perform a comprehensive range of tasks and administrations whose tasks are limited in the context of parliaments that are otherwise very similar (when it comes to size and system of scrutiny for example).

Conclusion: Administrations on the Rise?

The Treaty of Lisbon has created new opportunities for national parliaments, but also for their administrations. In particular the work-intensive system of document-based scrutiny under the new Early Warning System has led to the delegation of certain tasks to administrators – for example the filtering and pre-selection of relevant documents. The majority of parliamentary administrations do have the opportunity to shape the agenda of their respective legislature, at least to some extent. This can be explained by the very nature of parliamentary scrutiny of EU affairs as these issues are predominantly complex and touch upon issues of low salience (Manley 1968).

In addition, EU staff play an important role in coordination between national parliaments. The permanent representatives of the respective national parliaments in the European Parliament are best placed to engage in information exchange on a regular basis and alert other parliaments to important proposals coming out of the EU's machinery.

The extent of delegation does raise the question whether bureaucratic activity is *facilitating* political control or *replacing* it. However, while parliamentary administrations play a crucial role in parliamentary scrutiny, this bureaucratisation does not necessarily present a threat to political control. The final decisions are taken by MPs in the (European Affairs or sectoral) committees and plenary, and so far the coordination between MPs and administrations is by and large devoid of conflict. As a result, parliamentary administrations can indeed be seen as a pillar of support in the context of national parliamentary control of EU policy-making. The greatest impact of administrators on the scrutiny of EU affairs stems ultimately from their attempts to promote the discussion of important European issues within their parliaments.

Nevertheless, this first comparative study of the role of parliamentary administrations in EU affairs scrutiny ends in a puzzle. There is relatively little cross-national variation, but the variation that exists does not follow any obvious patterns. One of the tasks for future research will thus be to explore further the differences between national systems of parliamentary administrative support as well as the factors explaining the variation in administrative organisation and tasks.

Acknowledgements

We are grateful to Katrin Auel, Thomas Christiansen, Desmond Dinan and Andreas Maurer for comments on earlier drafts. We would further like to thank Katjana Gattermann, Claudia Hefftler, Oliver Höing, Ariella Huff, Alexander Strelkov, Angela Tacea and Anja Thomas for their help in collecting data on parliamentary administrations. We also thank our OPAL partners at the University of Cologne, the University of Cambridge and the Institut d'études politiques, who were funded by the DFG, the ESRC and the ANR respectively.

Disclosure statement

No potential conflict of interest was reported by the authors.

Funding

The research for this article was conducted at Maastricht University as part of the NWO-funded OPAL (Observatory of Parliaments after Lisbon) project [464–10-074].

Note

1. Among the administration, interviews were primarily conducted with the EU advisors or clerks of the European Affairs Committee. In some cases, where sectoral committees play an important role in parliamentary scrutiny, interviews with sectoral committee staff were added. The interview questions covered the tasks of parliamentary administrations at different stages of the process, the interaction between parliamentary staff and politicians, party staff and MPs' assistants, the role of staff in inter-parliamentary cooperation and the key challenges for them and their parliaments in EU affairs.

References

Arnold, R. Douglas (1987). 'Political Control of Administrative Officials', *Journal of Law Economics and Organization*, 3:2, 279–86.

Auel, Katrin, and Thomas Christiansen (2015). 'After Lisbon: National Parliaments in the European Union', *West European Politics*, 38:2, 261–81.

Auel, Katrin, Olivier Rozenber, and Angela Tacea (2015). 'Fighting Back? And if Yes, How? Measuring Parliamentary Strength and Activity in EU Affairs', in Claudia Hefftler, Christine Neuhold, Olivier Rozenberg, and Julie Smith (eds.), *The Palgrave Handbook of National Parliaments*. London: Palgrave, Macmillan.

Baron, Frank (2013). 'Civil Servants: How to Support the Political Level: The French Case', in Christine Neuhold, Sophie Vanhoonacker, and Luc Verhey (eds.), *Civil Servants and Politics*. Basingstoke: Palgrave, 108–22.

Blischke, Werner (1981). 'Parliamentary Staffs in the German Bundestag', *Legislative Studies Quarterly*, 6:4, 533–58.

Campbell, Stanley, and Jean Laporte (1981). 'The Staff of the Parliamentary Assemblies in France', *Legislative Studies Quarterly*, 6:4, 521–31.

Christiansen, Thomas, Anna-Lena Högenauer, and Christine Neuhold (2014). 'The Europeanisation of National Parliaments Post-Lisbon: Bureaucratisation and Transnationalisation rather than more Democracy in the European Union?', *Comparative European Politics*, 12:2, 121–40.

Cooper, Ian (2012). 'A 'Virtual Third Chamber' for the European Union? National parliaments after the Treaty of Lisbon', *West European Politics*, 35:3, 441–65.

DeGregorio, Christine (1994). 'Professional Committee Staff as Policy Making Partners in the US Congress', *Congress & The Presidency*, 21:1, 49–65.

Dobbels, Matthias, and Christine Neuhold (2013). 'The Roles Bureaucrats Play: The Input of the European Parliament (EP) Administrators into the Ordinary Legislative Procedure: A Case Study Approach', *Journal of European Integration*, 35:4, 375–90.

Egeberg, Morten, Ase Gornitzka, Jarle Trondal, and Mathias Johannessen (2013). 'Parliament Staff: Unpacking the Behaviour of Officials in the European Parliament', *Journal of European Public Policy*, 20:4, 495–514.

Harfst, P., and Schnapp, K. (2003). 'Instrumente parlamentarischer Kontrolle der Exekutive in westlichen Demokratien', Discussion Paper SP IV 2003-201, Wissenschaftszentrum Berlin für Sozialforschung (WZB).

Hegeland, Hans (2007). 'The European Union in National Parliaments: Domestic or Foreign Policy? A Study of Nordic Parliamentary Systems', in John O'Brennan and Tapio Raunio (eds.), *National Parliaments within the Enlarged European Union: From 'Victims' of Integration to Competitive actors?* Abingdon: Routledge, 95–115.

Högenauer, Anna-Lena, and Thomas Christiansen (2015). 'The Role of Parliamentary Administrations in the EU', in Christine Neuhold, Claudia Hefftler, Olivier Rozenberg, and Julie Smith (eds.), *The Palgrave Handbook of National Parliaments*. London: Palgrave, Macmillan.

Höing, Oliver (2015). 'Testing the Limits: Parliamentary Democracy and European Integration in Germany', in Claudia Hefftler, Christine Neuhold, Olivier Rozenberg, and Julie Smith (eds.), *The Palgrave Handbook of National Parliaments*. London: Palgrave, Macmillan.

Huber, John D. (2000). 'Delegation to Civil Servants in Parliamentary Democracies', *European Journal of Political Research*, 37, 397–413.

Huber, John D., and Nolan McCarty (2004). 'Bureaucratic Capacity, Delegation, and Reform', *American Political Science Review*, 98:3, 481–94.

Kiiver, Philipp (2012). *The Early Warning System for the Principle of Subsidiarity. Constitutional Theory and Empirical Reality*. London and New York: Routledge.

Manley, John F. (1968). 'Congressional Staff and Public Policy-Making: The Joint Committee on International Revenue Taxation', *The Journal of Politics*, 30:4, 1046–67.

McCubbins, Mathew D., and Thomas Schwartz (1984). 'Congressional Oversight Overlooked: Police Patrols versus Fire Alarms', *American Journal of Political Science*, 28:1, 165–79.

Meller, Norman (1952). 'The Policy Position of Legislative Service Agencies', *The Western Political Quarterly*, 5:1, 109–23.

Neunreither, Karlheinz (2006). 'Elected Legislators and their Unelected Assistants in the European Parliament', *Journal of Legislative Studies*, 8:4, 40–60.

O'Brennan, John, and Tapio Raunio (2007). 'Introduction: Deparliamentarization and European integration', in John O'Brennan and Tapio Raunio (eds.), *National Parliaments within the Enlarged European Union: From 'Victims' of Integration to Competitive Actors?* Abingdon: Routledge, 1–27.

Olsen, Johan P. (2006). 'Maybe It is Time to Rediscover Bureaucracy', *Journal of Public Administration Research and Theory*, 16:1, 1–24.

Page, Edward C., and Bill Jenkins (2005). *Policy Bureaucracy: Government with a Cast of Thousands*. Oxford: Oxford University Press.

Patterson, Samuel C. (1970). 'The Political Staffs of Congressional Committees', *Administrative Science Quarterly*, 15:1, 22–38.

Perez, Sophie (2007). 'Parlement et administration de l'Union européenne', *Annuaire européen d'administration publique*, 29, 371–429.

Provan, James (2001). 'Legislative Assistance to Members – A Rethink,' Working Document No. 6 on Internal Reform.

Raunio, Tapio (2010). 'Destined for Irrelevance? Subsidiarity Control by National Parliaments', Europe Working Article, 2010(36), Real Instituto Elcano.

Ryle, Michael T. (1981). 'The Legislative Staff of the British House of Commons', *Legislative Studies Quarterly*, 6:4, 497–519.

Spreitzer, Astrid (2013). 'Administrating EU Affairs in the Luxembourgish Parliament', Paper presented at the ECPR General Conference, Bordeaux 4–7 September 2013.

Szalay, Karla (2005). *Scrutiny of EU Affairs in the National Parliaments of the New Member States: Comparative Analysis*. Hungarian National Assembly: Budapest.

Vehar, Primoz (2007). 'The National Assembly of the Republic of Slovenia and EU Affairs before and after Accession', in John O'Brennan and Tapio Raunio (eds.), *National Parliaments within the Enlarged European Union: From 'Victims' of Integration to Competitive Actors?* Abingdon: Routledge, 241–55.

Winzen, Thomas (2011). 'Technical or Political ? An Exploration of the Work of Officials in the Committees of the European Parliament', *Journal of Legislative Studies*, 17:1, 27–44.

Wlezien, Christopher (2005). 'On the Salience of Political Issues: The Problem with 'Most' Important Problem', *Electoral Studies*, 24, 555–79.

APPENDIX

INTERVIEWS

Austrian NPR, 22/11/2010.
Belgian House of Representatives, EAC clerk, 25/05/2012.
Belgian Senate, EAC clerk, 16/04/2012.
COSAC clerk, 09/11/2010.

Danish NPR, 09/11/2010.
Danish Parliament, EAC clerk, 21/11/2012.
Danish Parliament, EU advisor, 19/11/2012.
Danish Parliament, Environment Clerk, 20/11/2012; Danish Parliament, Food, Agriculture and Fisheries Clerk, 27/11/2012.
Dutch Lower House, EU Affairs Clerk, 9/12/2011.
Dutch Lower House, VVD MP, EAC, 23/03/2012.
Dutch NPR, 09/12/2010.
Dutch Senate, 2 EAC clerks, 11/01/2011.
Finish NPR, 16/11/2010.
Folketing, EU Advisor, 19/11/2012.
French NPR, 14/09/2010.
French Senate, advisor, 4/05/2012.
French Senate, EAC clerk (1), 25/05/2012.
French Senate, EAC clerk, 12/05/2012.
French Senate, senior EU clerk, 25/05/2012.
German Bundesrat, EAC clerk, 4/05/2012.
House of Commons, EAC clerk, 23/05/2012.
Italian Chamber of Representatives, European Affair Service, 9/11/2012.
Irish NPR, 13/01/2010).
Polish Senate, EAC advisor, 10/04/2013.
Polish Sejm, EAC clerk, 23/04/2013.
Polish Sejm, Research Bureau, 19/04/2013.
Romanian Parliament, Former EU Staff, 17/11/2011.
Romanian Senate, 2 clerks European Division, 12/04/2012.
Romanian Senate, EAC clerk, 5/04/2012.
Slovenian NPR, 16/11/2010.
Slovak Parliament, EAC clerk, 29/05/2013.
Swedish NPR, 17/11/2010.
Swedish Parliament, EAC clerk, 13/03/2012.
Swedish parliament, Social Insurance Committee clerks, 06/032,012.
Written reply, Austrian parliament, 13/11/2012.
Written reply, Belgian House of Representatives, 28/11/2012.
Written reply, Belgian Senate, 22/11/2012.
Written reply, German Bundesrat, 6/12/2012.
Written reply, Swedish parliament, 11/09/2012.

Who Controls National EU Scrutiny? Parliamentary Party Groups, Committees and Administrations

ALEXANDER STRELKOV

The article addresses the question of how parliamentary actors, namely parliamentary party groups, parliamentary administrators and committees, interact with each other in the new post-Lisbon institutional environment. On the basis of assessing scrutiny of EU proposals in the spheres of pensions and labour migration in the parliaments of Sweden, the Czech Republic and Romania, the article comes to the conclusion that despite existing opportunities for parliamentary administrators and committees to obtain greater leverage, parliamentary party groups continue to play a crucial role in defining the outcomes of the scrutiny process. Parliamentary party groups tend to focus on the division of competences between the EU and member states even when they have electoral incentives to address the content of EU proposals.

The Lisbon Treaty has expanded institutional capacities (formal rights, legal rules and existing practices) of national parliaments in EU affairs in two distinct ways. Firstly, through Lisbon Treaty provisions proper, namely by granting parliaments better information rights, allowing them to control compliance of EU proposals with the subsidiarity principle through the so-called 'Early Warning System' (EWS), etc. (Auel and Christiansen 2015). Secondly, institutional capacities of national parliaments are affected indirectly, through the adaptation of parliamentary scrutiny rules and practices to the new competences, envisaged by the Lisbon Treaty. This can be done through rulings of national constitutional courts,[1] development of new laws on executive–legislative cooperation in EU affairs,[2] revision of domestic scrutiny procedures, enhancing inter-parliamentary contacts. Such processes have taken place in the aftermath of the Single European Act or the Treaties of Maastricht and Amsterdam.[3] The Lisbon Treaty provides parliamentary actors with an opportunity to reconsider national scrutiny practices but does not prescribe any specific template: the content of the new rules and practices will depend on the bargaining between various parliamentary actors. The transformation of the scrutiny practices affects the redistribution of competences and resources, potentially putting some parliamentary actors in a privileged position.

Although previous research has made reference to political parties while studying plenary debates (Auel and Raunio 2014; de Wilde 2011; Neuhold and de Ruiter 2010) or executive–legislative relations (Holzhacker 2002, 2005) in the domain of EU affairs, their interaction with other parliamentary actors (administrators or committees) in the scrutiny process has not been addressed. This limits our understanding of factors that shape the scrutiny process.[4] Without addressing the interaction of parliamentary actors in the aftermath of the Lisbon Treaty it is impossible to provide a comprehensive assessment of scrutiny practice.[5]

The article investigates the behaviour of three key parliamentary actors: parliamentary party groups (PPGs), parliamentary committees and parliamentary administrators.[6] Political parties and committees have been traditionally identified as core organisational elements of parliaments (Shaw 1998; Strøm 1998). Parliamentary administrators are also portrayed as a distinct group of actors. Administrators cannot be considered 'neutral', as they inevitably develop a set of political preferences and do not limit themselves to purely technical tasks (Gailmard and Patty 2007; Moe 2005).

In general PPGs set the boundaries of political action by committees and administrators as well having a monopoly on the results of the scrutiny of EU affairs,[7] yet this could change in the aftermath of the Lisbon Treaty. For example, the crucial role of administrators in selecting EU documents for scrutiny and providing expertise potentially allows parliamentary staff to shape policy outcomes and develop their own political agenda (Christiansen et al. 2014; Egeberg et al. 2013). Although parliamentary committees can be dominated by governing PPGs, the challenges of acquiring expertise and coordinating amongst the MPs could lead to autonomy from partisan control (Mattson and Strøm 1995) and development of a specific *esprit du corps* amongst members of European Affairs Committees (EACs) that would cut across party lines.[8]

The article primarily aims at testing a number of theoretical propositions about the behaviour and interaction of parliamentary actors in the post-Lisbon environment.[9] The research design of the article combines elements of both inductive and deductive approaches (Bennett and Elman 2006: 467). Drawing on Dinan 2010: 97–98) and Brouard et al. (2012), the key assumption is that with the 'deepening' of European integration parliamentary actors will be more involved in EU affairs for the sake of benefit maximisation.[10]

Insights from rational choice institutionalism help establish deductive, theory-driven propositions about the behaviour and interaction of parliamentary actors. It is argued that parliamentary actors pursue their preferences according to the 'logic of calculation' and attempt to maximise their benefits in any type of institutional environment (Schmidt 2009: 126–27). In line with the rational institutionalist framework, the article focuses on the strategic interaction of political actors in the wider institutional context (Hall and Taylor 1996: 18). It considers that all types of parliamentary actors would have an interest in greater involvement in EU affairs within a new institutional environment due to either electoral or policy benefits, as in the case of PPGs, or due to incentives to increase competence and status, as in the case of parliamentary committees and administrators.

The inductive element of the study is based on the application of concepts like 'voice', 'threat of exit' and 'neglect', developed by Hirschman (1970) and Dowding *et al.* (2000). The Lisbon Treaty changes the institutional environment in which parliamentary actors attempt to pursue their preferences; they are forced to adapt their strategies of 'goal maximisation'. The concepts of 'voice', 'threat of exit' and 'neglect' help categorise these strategies of preference attainment of parliamentary actors in the post-Lisbon political environment.[11] These strategies are, however, not mutually exclusive and are considered to be used within the framework of parliamentary actors' increasing involvement in EU affairs.

The paper comes to a conclusion that in the parliaments of Sweden, Czech Republic and Romania PPGs have retained control over the scrutiny process as participation of parliamentary administrators and committees in the assessment of EU proposals has remained under partisan control. The overarching concern for both Eurosceptic and pro-European, government or opposition parties in the abovementioned parliaments has been the division of competences, while electoral benefits of using EU proposals in the sphere of pensions and labour migration to change the domestic status quo according to PPGs' own preferences have been disregarded.

The first section of the paper addresses the conceptual framework, drawing a number of propositions about the behaviour of PPGs, parliamentary administrators and committees. It also explains how the concepts of 'voice', 'threat of exit' and 'neglect' help in assessing the 'preference maximisation' strategies of parliamentary actors after the change of parliamentary institutional capacities. Later on the logic behind case selection and research methods is addressed. The following part of the article analyses the interaction between PPGs, parliamentary administrators and committees, and elaborates on the different types of reactions of parliamentary actors to the new institutional environment. The conclusion summarises the findings of the article and offers a number of insights into executive–legislative relations in EU affairs and the evolution of representative institutions in the EU.

Conceptual Framework and Research Design

The Lisbon Treaty provisions affect the institutional capacity of national parliaments to address EU affairs. Organisational theory provides a number of clues about how actors can respond to such a change in the political environment, bearing in mind that parliamentary actors are acting according to the 'logic of calculation'. Drawing on Hirschman (1970) and Dowding *et al.* (2000), these reactions could be labelled as 'voice', 'threat of exit' and 'neglect'.[12] These concepts relate to the use of new domestic scrutiny procedures in addressing EU proposals. The concepts of 'voice', 'threat of exit' and 'neglect' do not provide an explanation of the behaviour of parliamentary actors, yet they are a good heuristic tool to capture and classify the different types of reactions and 'preference maximisation' strategies of parliamentary actors in a changing institutional environment. They help us understand how parliamentary actors have tried to adapt their behaviour to the new institutional environment. 'Voice' implies the use of new institutional capacities with the aim of promoting the interests of parliamentary actors through negotiations, for example debating over the evaluation of a specific EU proposal or the design of procedural rules. 'Threat of exit' deals with a conscious strategy of parliamentary actors to involve EU-level institutions or actors in the scrutiny process if their demands are not met at the domestic level.[13] 'Threat of exit' does not simply relate to the use of the EWS by national parliaments but implies the development of contacts with MEPs, EU-level stakeholders or inter-parliamentary cooperation during the scrutiny process in order to put pressure on domestic governments. 'Neglect' describes a situation when parliamentary actors disregard one aspect of EU affairs, namely the content of EU proposals, and focus instead on the more 'straightforward' question of the division of competences. 'Neglect' does not imply less involvement in EU affairs, it refers to parliamentary actors' unwillingness/inability to maximise their gains through comprehensively addressing all aspects of the EU agenda.[14]

The propositions about the behaviour of PPGs and other parliamentary actors are drawn from rational choice institutionalism. The motivation of parliamentary actors is considered to be linked to cost–benefit calculations, as they need to find new ways to maximise their gains in a new institutional context. Most researchers (for example Auel and Raunio 2014; Ladrech 2002; Raunio 2009) agree that currently primarily marginal Eurosceptic parties address European issues in electoral competition. Centre-right and centre-left parties, whether they are pro-European or mildly Eurosceptic, are seen to keep a low profile on EU topics. However, the ability of Euroscepticism to explain variation in parliamentary activity on EU affairs was questioned (Auel et al. 2015; Winzen 2013), while other studies show that centrist parties avoided politicising EU topics even in highly salient cases (for example, Riekmann and Wydra 2013). Yet, drawing on Franklin (2010) and Green-Pedersen (2012), it can be said that the ability of parliamentary actors to address EU topics would depend on the correspondence of such issues to the traditional left–right cleavage. According to Dinan (2010: 97–98), in the aftermath of the Lisbon Treaty traditional domestic policy issues are increasingly acquiring an 'EU dimension', hence all political parties irrespective of their Eurosceptic or Europhile stance are likely to address EU issues, especially those that can be related to the domestic left–right cleavage (as is the case with pension and labour migration policies).

However, the opposition, as Holzhacker (2002, 2005) as well as Auel and Benz (2005) argue, is likely to be more engaged in the scrutiny process than the governing majority as it would try to compensate for the power asymmetry. Despite the fact that the Lisbon Treaty provisions proper (EWS, provisions on the 'passerelle clause' etc.) can be enacted only by parliamentary majority, the adaptation of domestic scrutiny rules and norms to the new competences enshrined in the Lisbon Treaty may provide the opposition with an opportunity to increase its influence on EU affairs. Such adaptation can be done through (a) change of parliamentary rules of procedure, (b) adoption of new laws on executive–legislative relations in EU affairs, and (c) enhancing contacts with MEPs, EU institutions and other parliaments. Implementation and the specific content of these measures is subject to political bargaining, hence the opposition has a chance to increase its leverage in the scrutiny process by shaping the new scrutiny norms and practices according to its interest.[15]

In relation to PPGs the article considers that:

(1) Although all political parties will start addressing EU issues, it can be expected that opposition parties will be more interested in shaping the new scrutiny rules (stemming from the transposition of the Lisbon Treaty provisions) than governing parties as this provides the opposition with opportunities to redress the power imbalance.

The incentive for parliamentary administrators to play a greater role in shaping the outcomes of the scrutiny process reflects their crucial role in preparing assessments of EU proposals for subsidiarity checks (and scrutiny in general) as MPs are dependent on the skills of parliamentary staff in complex and technical issues. For example, the key role of the EP staff in providing analysis and expertise (Dobbels and Neuhold 2013; Egeberg *et al.* 2013; Neunreither 2002) allows them to go beyond merely technical functions. Moreover, the key role of parliamentary staff in providing 'institutional memory' (Winzen 2011) as well as transposing the Lisbon Treaty provisions into domestic procedural norms allows them to shape the actions of PPGs. Yet, as Högenauer and Neuhold (2013: 20) note, any autonomous action of parliamentary administrators will be controlled by respective political parties. According to Christiansen *et al.* (2014: 135), acute inter-party conflict or rivalry between executive and legislative branches diminishes the 'steering role' of parliamentary administrators in the scrutiny process. Relations between parliamentary administrators and party groups will be dominated by attempts to define the right balance of control and autonomy. The following proposition is addressed in the article:

(2) Despite persistent control from political parties, it can be expected that parliamentary administrators will exert leverage on the outcomes of the scrutiny process as well as shape parliamentary rules and procedures as

the new institutional capacities create greater demands for information and expertise within national parliaments.

March and Olsen (1984: 738) stipulate that PPGs and committees can have divergent preferences. Academic literature provides a number of potential patterns of relations between political parties and parliamentary committees. For example, Cox and McCubbins (1993) argue that committees allow PPGs to secure compliance of parliamentary activity with the position of the majority. Other approaches argue that committees will not simply translate the position of parliamentary majority. Krehbiel (1991) suggests that parliamentary committees provide information and expertise to the whole chamber, while Shepsle and Weingast (1981) argue that committees help career advancement of MPs through specialisation in distinct policy sectors and constituency service.[16] The use of new institutional capacities acquired in the aftermath of the Lisbon Treaty not only requires expertise but also coordination of activities and sharing of information among various groups of MPs. This process can trigger closer cooperation across party lines and make individual members of parliament more independent of their respective PPGs. In fact, EACs would acquire a more autonomous political profile if their members were to interact in a cross-party mode (Arter 2003; King 1976): committee members would not follow ideological party lines but would develop a distinct *esprit de corps* on the basis of their technical expertise. Hence, the third proposition of the article is:

(3) Due to creating greater demands for information, expertise and coordination the new institutional capacities can be expected to allow EACs to limit partisan control and develop a more autonomous political profile.[17]

Case Selection and Methodology

The paper is based on the analysis of three qualitative case studies (small *N*). The selection of cases was conducted according to the 'diverse' case selection strategy (Gerring 2007), illuminating variation in terms of types of parliamentary government (majority or minority cabinets), political systems (consensual and majoritarian) as well as attitudes of parliamentary party groups towards the EU. Sweden is selected as an example of a consensual political system with a minority cabinet and mostly pro-European political parties. The Czech Republic represents a more adversarial political system with a majority coalition and a large segment of Eurosceptic political parties. Romania stands for a majoritarian political system with a majority cabinet and generally pro-European political parties. Moreover, Sweden, Czech Republic and Romania represent strong, medium-strong and weak parliaments respectively, the selection being based on the typology of Magone (2011) and the budgetary power index of Wehner (2006). The case selection is intentionally biased towards Central and

East European member states as parliamentary scrutiny of EU affairs in this region remains under-researched.

It is acknowledged that the article cannot comprehensively represent the behaviour of parliamentary actors in all strong, medium-strong and weak parliaments in the post-Lisbon environment as not all variations in national partisan and parliamentary contexts can be taken into account. Instead, the article provides insights for 'possibilistic generalisation' (Blatter and Haverland 2012: 136–37) which can help define patterns of interactions between parliamentary actors as well as their reaction to the new institutional capacities in Swedish, Czech and Romanian parliaments but cannot fully predict the actions of parliamentary actors in other institutional environments.[18]

In order to assess how parliamentary actors interact during the scrutiny process, two EU policy proposals were selected on the basis of 12 exploratory interviews with parliamentary representatives in Brussels (October–December 2010) and the information from the IPEX database. Two EU documents were selected:[19]

(1) Green paper towards adequate, sustainable and safe European pension systems (COM 2010 0365);
(2) Proposal for a directive on the conditions of entry and residence of third-country nationals for the purpose of seasonal employment (COM 2010 0379 final).

The proposals[20] were selected as 'critical cases' for two reasons: (a) electoral saliency and (b) inclusion in the 'traditional' left–right cleavage. Firstly, despite the fact that scrutiny of EU affairs is not bringing much electoral added-value (Auel and Raunio 2014), the issues of pensions and migration are very important for voters and affect PPGs' policy preferences, hence they are likely to invest resources in the scrutiny of EU proposals in these domains. Secondly, political parties will be more prepared to address EU issues that can easily be subsumed into the existing pattern of party competition, for example the left–right cleavage (Raunio 2011: 319). The fact that pension and labour migration issues can be framed within the left–right dimension makes it easier for PPGs to address the EU dimension of these policies. Ultimately, these cases are considered 'critical' because if parliamentary actors do not invest in the scrutiny of these electorally salient proposals, it is unlikely that they would do so in the case of more technical issues. It is acknowledged that the selected policy cases may not be sufficiently representative to draw comprehensive generalisations about parliamentary activity in EU affairs. However, these cases provide clues to how parliamentary actors behave and interact if EU proposals affect core national policies in the socio-economic domain.

Open-ended semi-structured interviews with parliamentary clerks, members of national parliaments and the European Parliament (EP), party staff, domestic experts and stakeholders served as the key source of information.[21] Between

October 2010 and November 2013 a total of 165 interviews[22] were conducted, the majority of them being recorded.[23]

Parliamentary Party Groups and Parliamentary Administrators

The proposition about greater ability of parliamentary administrators to shape the rules of procedure and outcomes of the scrutiny process does not find support. The data from Sweden, Czech Republic and Romania indicates that although parliamentary administrators can in principle exert some political leverage, such activities are always controlled by political parties.

Parliamentary administrators found it difficult to shape partisan positions on EU affairs during the scrutiny process. For example, in the Swedish Riksdag parliamentary staff have the task of transposing party positions on EU affairs into resolutions and explaining the content of EU documents to MPs, acting as 'interpreters' (S2a, S2b, S6a, S6c, S9). Although this allows parliamentary staff to shape party positions, PPGs always conduct control of materials provided by parliamentary staff with respect to compliance with their ideological views (S2a, S6a). Even when PPGs do not have a clear standpoint, for example on EU topics (S2b, S6b, S6c, S38), and parliamentary administrators could shape the content of the Riksdag's resolution, parliamentary staff phrase resolutions in the broadest possible way so that they would be acceptable to all political parties (S2a).

The key role of parliamentary staff in the provision of expertise and information does not automatically lead to greater political leverage. For example, during the scrutiny of the Green Paper on pensions and the Proposal for a directive on seasonal migrants neither the staff of the Riksag, nor the administrators in the Romanian parliament,[24] produced detailed impact assessments. However, this was done by the administration of the Czech parliament (C10, C27, C31). In relation to the Proposal for a directive, the Czech parliamentary staff had concerns about the document's compliance with the subsidiarity principle. They also highlighted several aspects of the Green Paper on pensions which could be used by both supporters and opponents of the current Czech pension system (C10, C27). Nevertheless, administrators were unable to force MPs to take up these issues in the ensuing parliamentary debate (C16a, C20, C31, 39).[25]

The inability of parliamentary staff to capitalise on their role in information provision can be explained by the following factors. Firstly, the low interest of MPs in EU affairs limits the demand for 'EU expertise' (R2) and does not allow parliamentary staff to have more political leverage. Administrators from both Czech (C5, C8b, C35, C36) and Romanian (R1c, R9) parliaments mentioned a continuous sense of frustration as they received few requests from MPs to conduct assessment of EU proposals. To a certain extent a similar process takes place in Sweden, as, according to a high-ranking member of the Riksdag (S9), MPs cannot get electoral bonuses for dedicating themselves to EU issues, 'decreasing' the demand for EU expertise. Secondly, interviewees from the Czech Republic and Romania argue that high levels of inter-party conflict in respective parliaments precludes the ability of parliamentary staff to shape the scrutiny process (B6c, C5, C7b, R1a, R3). Such conflicts generate little demand for expert-based assessment of EU proposals. Moreover, attempts to politicise parliamentary staff[26] have taken place in the Czech and Romanian parliaments, while no evidence of such behaviour has been found in the Riksdag. In the Czech and Romanian parliaments pressure was exerted on parliamentary staff in order to provide 'ideologically correct' analysis or nominate specific candidates in order to secure party dominance in parliamentary structures (C1a, C5, C17, R1c).

Parliamentary Party Groups and Parliamentary Committees

In contrast to the abovementioned proposition, EACs in Sweden, Czech Republic and Romania have not become more autonomous from PPGs.

Firstly, there are few signs of cross-party cooperation in the European Affairs Committees. In the Swedish Riksdag the EAC acts according to partisan logic, its role being connected to formalising inter-party agreements (S9, B39a). In fact, members of the EAC in the Swedish Riksdag largely reiterated the assessment of the Green Paper on pensions and the Proposal for a directive on seasonal migrants which was voiced earlier by their fellow party members in the Committee on Social Insurance[27] (S2, S36).

The practice in the Czech parliament also illustrates the dominance of partisan logic in the functioning of EACs. For example, resolutions of the EAC in the Czech Senate, headed by a minority party in the upper house, were continuously checked for compliance with the views of the Senate's majority (C2, C6, C7b, C8a, C16a). According to practitioners from the Chamber of Deputies and the Senate, voting in respective EACs has been continuously conducted on the basis of partisan affiliation with few signs of cross-party consensus (C6, C16a. C16b, C18, C31b).

The practice in the Romanian parliament is somewhat ambiguous. Although during the assessment of the Green Paper on pensions in the Romanian EAC some inter-party division did occur, interviewees mentioned that the positions of the Romanian European Affairs Committee are often unanimous[28] (R8a). According to practitioners from the Romanian parliament this is primarily a sign of MPs' limited interest in EU affairs (R1c, R9, R22).

Secondly, the pattern of contacts between EACs and other standing committees seems to affect the former's political autonomy. In the Riksdag close contacts between standing committees and the EAC are primarily used to resolve any potential controversies between parties (S10, S35). In contrast to the Swedish parliament (S6a; Hegeland 2011), the relationship between the EACs and standing committees in the parliaments of Czech Republic and Romania is rather ad hoc (Suchman 2010; C16a, R8a, R9). For example, the Czech EAC informed other standing committees of the Czech Chamber of Deputies about its resolution on the Proposal for a directive on seasonal migrants only after it already adopted the document (C16a), denying other parliamentary bodies an opportunity to influence the scrutiny process. In fact, as interviewees from the Czech (C25) and Romanian (R8a) parliaments claim, standing committees often resist greater contacts with respective EACs in order to avoid extra workload and safeguard the informal political balance between committees. This hinders information exchange and prevents EACs from developing their own *esprit du corps* as communication between committees is conducted along informal partisan lines.

Thirdly, the rather low status of the European Affairs Committee in the internal hierarchy of the Swedish, Czech (C1a, C8b, C16a, C10) and Romanian parliaments (R5, R9) prohibits greater political autonomy of EACs. For example, even in the strong Riksdag both administrators (S38) and members (S9) concur that concentrating on EU affairs does not increase chances of re-election and few members of the Swedish parliament have a genuine interest in EU affairs. Romanian interviewees (R5, R9, R19) are sceptical about a distinct 'committee' identity of the respective EAC, arguing that the nomination procedure allows political parties to be in full control of committee activities. This results in a situation where very few members of an EAC are policy-seekers who can develop cross-party compromises in order to reach their goals. In general, the majority of EAC members are not political 'heavyweights' and hence they depend on following the partisan line for the development of their career and increasing status within respective political parties. This results in weak political autonomy of parliamentary committees from PPGs.

Behaviour of Parliamentary Party Groups

The propositions about the behaviour of PPGs in the aftermath of the Lisbon Treaty have been partially refuted. Firstly, opposition parties have in principle been more active in shaping the new scrutiny rules, yet the context of their involvement depends on the pattern of relations between PPGs – consensual or majoritarian. Secondly, although all political parties have addressed EU issues, they have focused primarily on the division of competences between the EU and national governments despite the fact that addressing the content of EU proposals could have brought electoral benefits.

Sweden provides an interesting example of how inter-party relations in the scrutiny process are shaped by consensual practices. As Sweden has a minority government, the necessity to reach consensus between the centre-right ruling majority and centre-left opposition creates conditions for systematic involvement of the opposition in the policy-making process (S7, S35, S38). In fact, the opposition has used the debate about the content and setup of new scrutiny rules and practices in order to sustain and increase its influence in the scrutiny of EU affairs. Social Democrats, for example, have developed cooperation between the national party office and fellow members of the European Parliament in the aftermath of the Lisbon Treaty (B39a, S11a, S11b), a practice that was not repeated by the members of the governing coalition. The debate on the report of the EUMOT working group[29] provides another good illustration. The working group was tasked with developing suggestions on upgrading the Swedish scrutiny system in the aftermath of the Lisbon Treaty. Amongst other aspects, the working group proposed delegating mandating rights to standing committees as well as allowing the government to conduct the selection of 'A' points[30] for parliamentary scrutiny. The opposition parties (the Green and the Left) vetoed this proposal as they feared this would diminish their access to EU information and agenda-setting powers (S3, S6b, S6c, S38). The largest opposition party, the Social Democrats, also vetoed the idea to delegate mandating rights to sectoral committees as this could limit its capacities for influencing the parliamentary agenda (S3).

In contrast to the Riksdag, acute inter-party rivalry and majoritarian trends in the parliaments of the Czech Republic and Romania do not allow for systematic involvement of the opposition in the scrutiny of EU affairs. For example, in 2010–2013 the lower and the upper chambers of the Czech parliament were dominated, respectively, by the ruling coalition and the opposition. The opposition was constantly outvoted in the lower chamber, yet in the Senate EU-related items proposed for discussion by the governing centre-right Civic Democratic party were repeatedly taken out of the agenda by the Social Democrats who wanted to demonstrate the power of the opposition (C6, C8a, C16a). Within the given time-period there were few signs of inter-party cooperation (C5, C10, C31b). The Czech opposition also tried to use new scrutiny practices (stemming from the transposition of the Lisbon Treaty provisions) to increase its leverage: it tried to put pressure on the government through direct contacts with EU institutions, for example in the case of the allegedly limited involvement of the Czech parliament in discussing matters related to the 'European Semester' (B28, R1c).[31] In the Romanian case the negotiations over the establishment of a legal framework of executive–legislative cooperation in EU affairs could have provided the opposition with an opportunity to increase its leverage in parliamentary scrutiny.[32] However, the attitude of the opposition towards this law has been ambiguous. For example, since 2006 the Social Democratic party pushed for providing the Romanian parliament with the right to mandate the government, yet as interviewees claim each time the final voting was to take place the Social Democrats withdrew their support (R1c, B2c, R6). Allegedly, the opposition was using the law on executive–legislative cooperation in EU affairs as leverage to obtain informal concessions and benefits, having no genuine interest in EU topics as such.

The focus on the division of competences during the scrutiny process has been observed amongst both parliamentary majorities and opposition parties, regardless of their pro-European or Eurosceptic stance. This happens in parliaments with both consensual and majoritarian practices. For example, in the Riksdag both the ruling coalition and the opposition tend to focus on subsidiarity during the scrutiny process and not so much on the content of EU proposals (S6b, S22). According to parliamentary administrators, the discussion of the Proposal for a directive on seasonal migrants was stopped as soon as it became clear that no PPG had concerns about subsidiarity (S2a). The assessment of the Green Paper also focused on the undesirability of granting the European Commission more competences in the pension sector. An interviewee from the opposition Social Democratic party (S32) acknowledged that the main concern of all parties during the discussion of the abovementioned documents was to prevent further EU interference in the Swedish system. Reports from the Riksdag Committee on the Constitution also mention that in general the scrutiny process addresses primarily subsidiarity issues and not the content of the EU proposals.[33]

Despite the prevalent inter-party rivalry in the Czech and Romanian parliaments, during the discussion of the Green Paper on pensions as well as the Proposal for a directive on seasonal migrants both majority and opposition parties focused on the division of competences between the EU and member states. As parliamentary administrators argue (B6b, C10, C20, C27, C31, C39), the discussion of the two documents in the Czech parliament paid little attention to policy solutions and focused on subsidiarity. During the scrutiny of the abovementioned documents in the Romanian parliament, important issues, like potential access of seasonal migrants to national social security systems, have been overlooked (R1a, R8a, R9, R13).

Such behaviour is striking as these proposals directly impact on the PPGs' policy preferences and could be exploited for electoral gains. For example, the pro-European Swedish Social Democrats have not used the 'seasonal migrants directive' to push for the reintroduction of labour market tests, which could have found support amongst trade union members, their traditional electorate. Nor have the Eurosceptic Czech Civic Democrats, members of the governing coalition, mobilised their voters against the Green paper on pensions, which could be considered to infringe on the sovereign rights of the member states. Romanian political parties have also not connected the debate on the Green Paper on pensions to the ongoing discussions over the Romanian social security system reform.

Reactions of Parliamentary Actors to the New Institutional Capacity

It has been shown that neither parliamentary administrators nor EACs have been able to use the new institutional capacities to play a more autonomous role in the scrutiny process. PPGs continue to determine how parliaments react to the new post-Lisbon environment: the concepts of 'voice', 'threat of exit' and 'neglect' refer to the behaviour and 'preference maximising' strategies of PPGs.

'Voice' is widely used by PPGs. However, the use of 'voice' depends on the mode of PPG interaction as it would determine how partisan interests are promoted. One could compare the consensual negotiations of Swedish PPGs over the report of the EUMOT working group (S3, S6b) with the adversarial relations between the Romanian ruling and opposition parties over the new law on executive–legislative relations in EU affairs (R1c, B2c). The pattern of cooperation between EACs and standing committees could also affect the use of 'voice'. While PPGs in the Riksdag benefit from such cooperation (S9, S12, S36), the lack of regular contacts between EACs and standing committees in the Czech Republic and Romania denies PPGs an opportunity of filtering and discussing their views.

'Threat of exit' seems to be predominantly used by opposition PPGs. Sweden and Czech Republic provide examples of how MP–MEP relations and contacts with EU institutions could be used to put pressure on the government (S11, B28, R1c). However, occasions when 'threat of exit' is used remain limited and its ability to change respective government's policies is questionable. It is noteworthy that during the scrutiny of the Green Paper on pensions and the Proposal for a directive on seasonal labour neither rapporteurs/shadow rapporteurs in the European Parliament (B15, B19–25) nor representatives of the Brussels-based stakeholders (B14, B26), nor the relevant DGs of the European Commission (B9–11, B13) were consulted by any of actors from the parliaments of Sweden, Czech Republic or Romania.

PPGs in both strong (Sweden) and relatively weak (Czech Republic, Romania) parliaments have 'neglected' the opportunity to maximise their benefits through the new institutional capacities in one particular way. It has been shown above that during the scrutiny of the Green Paper on pensions and the Proposal for a directive on seasonal labour migrants PPGs focused on the division of competences and disregarded the content of EU proposals, although addressing it could maximise their electoral benefits (S2a, C31, R8a). This does not imply that in each and every case Swedish, Czech and Romanian PPGs disregard the content of EU proposal; it demonstrates that even when electoral benefits can be drawn from in-depth assessment of the content of EU documents, PPGs may wish not to use this opportunity and limit the debate to the issues of subsidiarity.

Conclusion

Transposition of the Lisbon Treaty provisions into the rules of procedure of national parliaments provided for a new institutional environment where parliamentary party groups, committees and administrators reconsidered their relationship to each other. Evidence from the parliaments of Sweden, Czech Republic and Romania shows that PPGs have remained in control of the scrutiny process, although both parliamentary administrators and committees could have been expected to play a greater role in shaping the course of parliamentary deliberations in EU affairs.

Despite the fact that parliamentary staff is crucial for analysing EU proposals, administrators in Sweden, Czech Republic and Romania have not developed their own political preferences as well as the ability to consistently shape the outcomes of the scrutiny process. This seems to relate to the fact that specialisation in EU affairs does not increase MPs' chances of re-election. As a result, there is little demand for expertise in EU affairs and administrators have few means to increase their political leverage. Moreover, as parliamentary practice in Romania and Czech Republic demonstrates, acute inter-party rivalry also diminishes the ability of parliamentary administrators to shape the scrutiny process as in such situations MPs are more focused on ideological divisions than on technical expertise.

Neither in strong (Sweden), nor in relatively weak parliaments (Czech Republic, Romania) have the EACs been able to obtain more autonomy from political parties. Through controlling the nomination procedure to the EACs and being in charge of contacts between committees PPGs diminish the opportunities for EACs to have autonomous input into the scrutiny process.

Although there is evidence that opposition parties have attempted to use the new institutional capacities in order to increase their leverage in the scrutiny process, it seems that the pattern of interaction between ruling and opposition PPGs largely depends on the presence of consensual or majoritarian traits in the national political system. Consensus-seeking practices as well as minority governments allow opposition in the Riksdag more influence than permanent inter-party rivalry in the parliaments of Romania and the Czech Republic as only in the former case are the views of opposition parties systematically taken into account. At the same time, analysis of debates around the Green Paper on pensions and the Proposal for a directive on seasonal labour migrants highlights the fact regardless of their governing or opposition status as well as pro-European or Eurosceptic attitudes, parties have focused on subsidiarity issues despite the fact that addressing the content of EU proposals could have brought electoral benefits.

Given the fact that PPGs in Sweden, Czech Republic and Romania have not allowed other types of parliamentary actors to increase their influence in the scrutiny process, the concepts of 'voice', 'threat of exit' and 'neglect' can be applied primarily to the benefit maximisation strategies of PPGs within the framework of the post-Lisbon environment. PPGs do promote their interests in EU affairs on the domestic level through inter-party negotiations ('voice'). Developing contacts with EU-level institutions and stakeholders in order to pressure national governments ('threat of exit') does not seem to be used very often and its ability to change decisions of the governing majority remains questionable. Nevertheless, actors in both strong and weak parliaments often focus on the division of competences and 'neglect' the content of EU proposals, even if doing otherwise could bring electoral benefits.

It remains to be seen to what extent this trend is present in all 28 national parliaments, although data from Sweden, Czech Republic and Romania suggests that both strong and weak national parliaments can exhibit 'shallow involvement' in EU affairs. Despite the fact that parliamentary institutions have acquired new capacities, parliamentary actors are often unwilling or unable to make full use of them in the scrutiny process. National parliaments may run the risk of considering EU issues as a simple 'yes–no' dichotomy if they do not address the content of EU proposals. This could shift the discussion of EU affairs out of the parliamentary arena, relegating it to social movements, advocacy groups or other political actors. This raises doubts about the ability of national representative institutions to secure accountability of the EU political system. For example, Bellamy (2010: 15–16) claims that 'non-majoritarian mechanisms of the EU can be legitimised so long as their scope and operation is controlled by the majoritarian systems of the member-states'. Yet it is exactly the members of these majoritarian institutions (national parliaments) that often have little motivation to engage in profound assessment of the content of EU proposals and tend to limit their interest in EU affairs to 'constitutional change' and the division of competences, hindering the debate on the policy solutions proposed by the EU.

Acknowledgements

I would like to express my gratitude to the guest editors, anonymous reviewers and members of the OPAL project, especially Professor Neuhold and Dr Högenauer, for their constructive criticism and comments. The usual disclaimer applies.

Disclosure Statement

No potential conflict of interest was reported by the author.

Notes

1. For example, the German Constitutional Court's ruling on the Lisbon Treaty created a de facto obligation for the German parliament to be actively involved in EU affairs, while the Czech Constitutional Court stipulated that the procedure for parliamentary scrutiny of EU affairs has to be decided on the political level and it has no competences to address the issue.
2. In the aftermath of the Lisbon Treaty such laws have been modified, for example, in Germany and Romania.
3. For specific details see Raunio (1999).
4. For an overview of factors responsible for cross-national differences see Bergman (1997), Saalfeld (2005), Raunio (2005), Karlas (2012) and Winzen (2013).
5. The article draws primarily on qualitative studies of national parliaments and EU integration. Although there is a large number of quantitative contributions to the sub-field (de Ruiter 2013; Finke and Danwolf 2012; Karlas 2012; Saalfeld 2005), the article's primary objective is to analyse the practices and 'micro-level' of parliamentary scrutiny (Kropp *et al.* 2011: 228–30), about which there is limited information. According to George and Bennett (2005: 45), qualitative approaches are precisely the tool to address such issues.
6. They are all considered collective actors.
7. PPGs can be considered as principals of parliamentary administrators and committees, who act as agents. However, the article does not explicitly draw on the principal–agent theory. See Saalfeld (2005) and Strøm *et al.* (2003) on issues of delegation, agency and legislative politics.
8. Parliamentary committees are seen as distinct actors and not as arenas controlled by political parties. It could be expected that greater demands for analysis of EU affairs could push the interaction of political parties within EACs towards a cross-party mode (King 1976) and weaken partisan control. As a result respective committees would be more 'technocratic' rather than 'ideological' and develop towards an 'ideal type' of US Congress committees (Campbell and Davidson 1998). See Shaw (1998) and Arter (2003) for the development of argument about committee's independent input into parliamentary affairs.

9. It should be stressed that the article does not aim to provide a direct comparison between the pre- and post-Lisbon environment, as the timeframe of comprehensive introduction of the Lisbon Treaty provisions into parliamentary rules of procedure varies between Sweden, Czech Republic and Romania. Rather, the article develops the assumption that the new competences increase information processing costs for national parliaments (de Ruiter 2013), which could potentially lead to a change of relationship between parliamentary actors.

10. This means that increasing interconnectedness between EU and national issues will increase parliamentary involvement in EU affairs, not that parliamentary actors will become more or less supportive of EU integration.

11. While the deductively formulated propositions relate to the interaction of parliamentary actors in the post-Lisbon environment, the inductive categories of 'voice', 'threat of exit' and 'neglect' address the strategies these actors use to maximise their benefits.

12. Hirschaman's concept of 'loyalty' has not been included in the theoretical framework as it remained difficult to justify what would be the common reference point for 'loyalty' amongst different types of parliamentary actors.

13. 'Threat of exit' does not imply a lack of interest in EU affairs; it means that MPs address EU-level bodies in order to promote their views about an EU proposal.

14. For example, while the Swedish Riksdag and the Czech Senate may disregard the content of EU proposals, these chambers are clearly not uninterested in EU affairs as such, judging by the large numbers of their contributions to the Early Warning System and the Political Dialogue. See COM (2014) 507 as well as the European Parliament annual report 2013/2014 on relations with national parliaments.

15. The article does not aim to provide a comprehensive overview of all the procedural changes in the parliaments of Sweden, Czech Republic and Romania. The goal is to trace how opposition parties were involved in key procedural reforms that were triggered by the transposition of the Lisbon Treaty provisions.

16. The three perspectives on parliamentary committees are classified as 'partisan', 'information' and 'distributive' respectively (see Martin 2014; Martino 2006).

17. Parliamentary committees can achieve a certain measure of political autonomy only if a regular dialogue between the EACs and standing committees is established. Otherwise knowledge about the EU would remain highly centralised and committees would not be aware of the added value of scrutiny for policy-shaping. The article does not aim to measure the level of EAC 'political autonomy'. Instead, on the basis of interview data, it looks for evidence that could support the interaction of PPGs in a cross-party mode.

18. It is acknowledged that the article only constitutes a probe into the behaviour of parliamentary actors in Sweden, Czech Republic and Romania in the post-Lisbon environment. Addressing plenary debates, scrutiny of other EU proposals and widening the timeframe of analysis to account for electoral change would provide more opportunities to test propositions about the behaviour of parliamentary actors.

19. Both legislative and non-legislative proposals were selected in order to provide a more representative sample. However, it is acknowledged that the article cannot provide a comprehensive comparison between parliamentary scrutiny of legislative and non-legislative proposals.

20. The Green Paper was discussed by EU institutions between July 2010 and February 2011, while the Proposal for a directive on seasonal labour migrants was discussed between October 2010 and February 2014. The author has found no evidence of national parliaments' involvement in the negotiations at EU level, apart from a single meeting in November 2010 between MPs and MEPs on the issue of seasonal labour migrants. For background information on these policy documents and the assessment of their discussion in EU institutions see author's unpublished PhD thesis and Cooper (2013).

21. Due to complications in getting access, only 10 MPs were interviewed in Sweden, five in the Czech Republic, two in Romania. This may limit the robustness of claims made in the article. However, contacts with other groups of interviewees not only provided additional information

about the interaction of PPGs with other types of parliamentary actors but allowed the validity of interview data from the few questioned MPs to be cross-checked.
22. The full list of interviews can be accessed in the web appendix to the article.
23. It should be acknowledged that the paper cannot fully account for changes in parliamentary scrutiny after general elections. The bulk of data collection was conducted between early 2011 and late 2013, with only Romania and Czech Republic holding general elections within this period.
24. Information sheet of the Romanian Chamber of Deputies No. 77. October 2010; Information note of the Romanian Chamber of Deputies No. 40 / 661, 15 December 2010.
25. Senate of the Czech Republic, 312th resolution of the Committee on EU affairs, 6 October 2010; Senate of the Czech Republic, 307th Resolution of the Committee on EU affairs, 21 September 2010.
26. It can be argued that politicisation of parliamentary administrators implies that their activities are not conducted on the basis of serving the general interests of a parliament but are focused on supporting the position of one specific parliamentary party group.
27. Stenographic records of the EAC meeting 2010/11: 2; Statement 2010/11: SfU5; 2011/12: SfU15; Stenographic records of the EAC meeting 2009/10: 54.
28. Inter-party rivalry in Romania is not related to partisan differences in EU issues (Soare 2012) but is primarily linked to power-sharing struggles within various governing coalitions and opposition parties.
29. 2010/11: URF2.
30. 'A' points are items on the COREPER agenda that are scheduled to be taken into account without debate. In the Riksdag parliamentary staff have to look at them and select which points have to be put on the agenda of the EAC.
31. This was done outside the framework of the EWS or Political Dialogue.
32. The law was adopted in December 2013.
33. 2010/11: KU18, 2011/12: KU4, 2013/14: KU5.

References

Arter, David (2003). 'Committee Cohesion and the 'Corporate Dimension' of Parliamentary Committees: A Comparative Analysis', *Journal of Legislative Studies*, 9:4, 73–87.
Auel, Katrin, and Arthur Benz, eds. (2005). *The Europeanization of Parliamentary Democracy*. London: Routledge.
Auel, Katrin, and Thomas Christiansen (2015). 'After Lisbon: National Parliaments in the European Union', *West European Politics*, 38:2, 261–81.
Auel, Katrin, and Tapio Raunio (2014). 'Debating the state of the Union? Comparing Parliamentary Debates on EU Issues in Finland, France, Germany and the United Kingdom', *Journal of Legislative Studies*, 20:1, 13–28.
Auel, Katrin, Olivier Rozenberg, and Angela Tacea (2015). 'To Scrutinize or Not to Scrutinize? Explaining Variation in EU-Related Activities in National Parliaments', *West European Politics*, 38:2, 282–304.

Bellamy, Richard (2010). 'Democracy without Democracy? Can the EU's Democratic "Outputs" Be Separated from the Democratic "Inputs" Provided by Competitive Parties and Majority Rule', *Journal of European Public Policy*, 17:1, 2–19.

Bennett, Andrew, and Colin Elman (2006). 'Qualitative Research: Recent Developments in Case Study Methods', *Annual Review of Political Science*, 9, 455–67.

Bergman, Torbjørn (1997). 'National Parliaments and EU Affairs Committees: Notes on Empirical Variation and Competing Explanations', *Journal of European Public Policy*, 4:3, 373–87.

Blatter, Joachim, and Markus Haverland (2012). *Designing Case Studies. Explanatory Approaches in Small-N Research*. New York, NY: Palgrave.

Brouard, Sylvain, Costa Olivier, and Thomas König (2012). *The Europeanization of Domestic Legislatures. The Empirical Implications of the Delors' Myth in Nine Countries*. New York: Springer.

Campbell, Colton, and Roger Davidson (1998). 'US Congressional Committees: Changing Legislative Workshops', in Lawrence Longley and Roger Davidson (eds.), *The New Roles of Parliamentary Committees*. London: Frank Cass, 124–42.

Christiansen, Thomas, Högenauer Anna-Lena, and Christine Neuhold (2014). 'National Parliaments in the Post-Lisbon European Union: Bureaucratization rather than Democratization', *Comparative European Politics*, 12:2, 121–40.

Cooper, Ian (2013). 'Deliberation in the Multilevel Parliamentary Field: The Seasonal Workers Directive as a Test Case', in Ben Crum and John Fossum (eds.), *Practices of Inter-Parliamentary Coordination in International Politics. The European Union and beyond*. Colchester: ECPR Press, 51–70.

Cox, Gary, and Mathew McCubbins (1993). *Legislative Leviathan: Party Government in the House*. Berkeley and Los Angeles: University of California Press.

Dinan, Desmond (2010). 'Institutions and Governance: A New Treaty, a Newly Elected Parliament and a New Commission', *Journal of Common Market Studies*, 48:s1, 95–118.

Dobbels, Mathias, and Christine Neuhold (2013). '"The Roles Bureaucrats Play": The Input of European Parliament (EP) Administrators into the Ordinary Legislative Procedure: A Case Study Approach', *Journal of European Integration*, 35:4, 375–90.

Dowding, Keith, John Peter, Mergoupis Thanos, and Mark van Vugt (2000). 'Exit, Voice and Loyalty: Analytic and Empirical Developments', *European Journal of Political Research*, 37:4, 469–95.

Egeberg, Morten, Åse Gornitzka, Jarle Trondal, and Mathias Johannessen (2013). 'Parliamentary Staff: Unpacking the Behaviour of Officials in the European Parliament', *Journal of European Public Policy*, 20:4, 495–514.

Finke, Daniel, and Tanja Danwolf (2012). 'Whistle Blowing and Opposition Control. Parliamentary Scrutiny in the European Union', *European Journal of Political Research*, 50:6, 715–46.

Franklin, Mark (2010). 'Cleavage Research: A Critical Appraisal', *West European Politics*, 33:3, 648–58.

Gailmard, Sean, and John Patty (2007). 'Slackers and Zealots: Civil Service, Policy Discretion, and Bureaucratic Expertise', *American Journal of Political Science*, 51:4, 873–89.

George, Alexander, and Andrew Bennett (2005). *Case Studies and Theory Development in Social Sciences*. Cambridge, MA: Harvard University Press.

Gerring, John (2007). *Case Study Research. Principles and Practices*. Cambridge: Cambridge University Press.

Green-Pedersen, Christoffer (2012). 'A Giant Fast Asleep? Party Incentives and the Politicization of European Integration', *Political Studies*, 60:1, 115–30.

Hall, Peter, and Rosemary Taylor (1996). 'Political Science and the Three New Institutionalisms', MPIFG Discussion Paper 96/6.

Hegeland, Hans (2011). 'The European Union as a Foreign Policy or Domestic Policy? EU Affairs in the Swedish Riksdag', in Persson Thomas and Wiberg Matti (eds.), *Parliamentary Government in the Nordic Countries at a Crossroads. Coping with Challenges from Europeanisation and Presidentialisation*. Stockholm: Santerus Academic Press, 139–60.

Hirschman, Albert (1970). *Exit, Voice, and Loyalty: Responses to Decline in Firms, Organizations, and States*. Cambridge, MA: Harvard University Press.

Högenauer, Anna-Lena, and Christine Neuhold (2013). 'National Parliaments after Lisbon: Administrators on the Rise? OPAL Online Paper Series. № 12.

Holzhacker, Ronald (2002). 'National Parliamentary Scrutiny over EU issues. Comparing the Goals and Methods of Government and opposition Parties', *European Union Politics*, 3:4, 459–79.

Holzhacker, Ronald (2005). 'The Power of Opposition Parliamentary Groups in European Scrutiny', *Journal of Legislative Studies*, 11:3–4, 428–45.

Karlas, Jan (2012). 'National Parliamentary Control of EU Affairs: Institutional Design after Enlargement', *West European Politics*, 35:5, 1095–113.

King, Anthony (1976). 'Modes of Executive-Legislative Relations: Great Britain', *France and West Germany, Legislative Studies Quarterly*, 1:1, 11–36.

Krehbiel, Keith (1991). *Information and Legislative Organisation*. Ann Arbor: University of Michigan Press.

Kropp, Sabine, Jonas Buche, and Aron Buzogány (2011). 'Parlamentarisch-exekutive Steuerung in europäischen Fachpolitiken ein Blick auf die Mikroebene', in Gabriele Abels and Annegret Eppler (eds.), *Auf dem Weg zum Mehrebenenparlamentarismus? Funktionen von Parlamenten im politischen System der EU*. Baden-Baden: Nomos Verlag, 227–39.

Ladrech, Robert (2002). 'Europeanization and Political Parties: Towards a Framework for Analysis', *Party Politics*, 8:4, 389–403.

Magone, José (2011). *Contemporary European Politics. A Comparative Introduction*. Oxon: Routledge.

March, David, and Johan Olsen (1984). 'The New Institutionalism: Organizational Factors in Political Life', *The American Polical Science Review*, 78:3, 734–49.

Martin, Shane (2014). 'Committees', in Shane Martin, Thomas Saalfeld and Kaare Strøm (eds.), *The Oxford Handbook of Legislative Studies*. Oxford: Oxford University Press, 352–68.

Martino, Nancy (2006). 'Balancing Power: Committee System Autonomy and Legislative Organization', *Legislative Studies Quarterly*, 31:2, 205–34.

Mattson, Ingvar, and Kaare Strøm (1995). 'Parliamentary Commitees', in Herbert Döring (ed.), *Parliaments and Majority Rule in Western Europe*. Mannheim: Mannheim center for European Social Research, 249–307.

Moe, Terry (2005). Power and Political Institutions, *Perspectives on Politics*, 3:2, 215–33

Neuhold, Christine, and de Ruiter, Rik. (2010). 'Out of REACH? Parliamentary Control of EU Affairs in the Netherlands and the UK', *Journal of Legislative Studies*, 16:1, 57–72

Neunreither, Karlheinz (2002). 'Elected Legislators and Their Unelected Assistants in the European Parliament', *Journal of Legislative Studies*, 8:4, 40–60.

Raunio, Tapio (1999). 'Always One Step Behind? National Parliaments and European Integration', *Government and Opposition*, 34:2, 180–202.

Raunio, Tapio (2005). 'Holding Governments Accountable in European Affairs: Explaining Cross-National Variation', *Journal of Legislative Studies*, 11:3–4, 319–42.

Raunio, Tapio (2011). 'The gatekeepers of European integration? The functions of national parliaments in the EU political system', *Journal of European integration*, 33:3, 303–21.

Raunuio, Tapio (2009). 'National Parliaments and European Integration: What We Know and Agenda for Future Research', *Journal of Legislative Studies*, 15:4, 317–34.

Riekmann, Sonja, and Doris Wydra (2013). 'Representation in the European State of Emergency: Parliament against Governments?', *Journal of European Integration*, 35:5, 565–82.

de Ruiter, Rik (2013). 'Under the Radar? National Parliaments and the Ordinary Legislative Procedure in the European Union', *Journal of European Public Policy*, 20:8, 1196–212.

Saalfeld, Thomas (2005). 'Deliberate Delegation or Abdication? Government Backbenchers, Ministers and European Union Legislators', *Journal of Legislative Studies*, 11:3–4, 343–71.

Schmidt, Vivien (2009). 'Comparative Institutional Analysis', in Todd Landman and Neil Robinson (eds.), *The SAGE Handbook of Comparative Politics*. London: Sage, 125–43.

Shaw, Malcolm (1998). 'Parliamentary Committees: A Global Perspective', *Journal of Legislative Studies*, 4:1, 225–51.

Shepsle, Kenneth, and Barry Weingast (1981). 'Structure-Induced Equilibrium and Legislative Choice', *Public Choice*, 37:3, 503–19.

Soare, Sorina (2012). 'The Romanian Party System's Europeanization: An Open Bet', in Erol Kulahci (ed.), *Europeanisation and Party Politics. How the EU Affects Domestic Actors, Patterns and Systems*. Colchester: ECPR Press, 145–56.

Strøm, Kaare (1998). 'Parliamentary Committees in European Democracies', *The Journal of Legislative Studies*, 4:1, 21–59

Strøm, Kaare, Wolfgang Muller, and Torbjorn Bergman, eds. (2003). *Delegation and Accountability in Parliamentary Democracies*. Oxford: Oxford University Press.

Suchman, Jaroslav (2010). 'Czech Republic', in Iglesias Gil and Blanco Luiz Blanco (eds.), *The Role of National Parliaments in the European Union*. Madrid: FIDE XXIV Congress, 145–65.

Wehner, Joachim (2006). 'Assessing the Power of the Purse: An Index of Legislative Budget Institutions', *Political Studies*, 54:4, 767–85.

de Wilde, Peter (2011). 'Ex Ante Vs. Ex Post: The Trade-off between Partisan Conflict Visibility in Debating EU Policy-Formulation in National Parliaments', *Journal of European Public Policy*, 18:5, 672–89.

Winzen, Thomas (2011). 'Technical or political? An exploration of the work of officials in the committees of the European Parliament', *Journal of Legislative Studies*, 17:1, 27–44.

Winzen, Thomas (2013). 'European Integration and National Parliamentary Oversight Institutions', *European Union Politics*, 14:2, 297–323.

National Parliaments and the Eurozone Crisis: Taking Ownership in Difficult Times?

KATRIN AUEL and OLIVER HÖING

The eurozone crisis suggests a significant reinforcement of executive dominance in EU policy-making. Opaque emergency decisions taken at European summits as well as treaties established outside of the EU legal framework facilitate the side-lining of democratically elected chambers. This development entails the risk of a new wave of de-parliamentarisation in EU policy-making. An effective scrutiny of crisis management by national parliaments is, however, indispensable for taking national ownership of the reforms in the Economic and Monetary Union (EMU). This paper investigates national parliaments' involvement in the development of instruments to combat the crisis. Based on a quantitative dataset of crisis-related parliamentary activities in 2010–2012, the article observes a very uneven engagement in the scrutiny of crisis management. Institutional prerogatives in EU affairs as well as macro-economic factors can partly explain the observed variation. Surprisingly, however, crisis-related parliamentary activity is not a reaction to Eurosceptic attitudes either in parliament or among the public.

National parliaments (NPs) were for a long time perceived as the 'institutional Cinderellas of European integration' (Dinan 2012: 85): they invested little time in the scrutiny of their governments in EU affairs or in the scrutiny of European actors. Given the continuous transfer of legislative competences to the European level, this led many observers to lament the erosion of parliamentary involvement in EU affairs (among many, Laursen and Pappas 1995; Norton 1996). Only more recently was this 'de-parliamentarisation thesis' called into question (see for example Auel and Benz 2005a; O'Brennan and Raunio 2007; Winzen 2012, 2013): national parliaments acquired new formal participation rights, and many are now in a position to exert a stronger influence in EU affairs.

These recent improvements, however, seem to have been thwarted by the eurozone crisis. Decisions to tackle the crisis were not only taken under conditions of increased executive dominance and time pressure, making it difficult for parliaments to get involved and to take ownership of the crisis management; core instruments of the new EU economic governance also directly affect the budgetary sovereignty of national parliaments – conventionally seen as the 'crown jewels' (Puntscher Riekmann and Wydra 2013: 565) of democratically elected chambers. In addition, enhanced economic coordination at the European level increasingly reduces the political leeway at the national level in economic policy. Does this development indicate a renewed trend of de-parliamentarisation of EU affairs, and are all parliaments affected to the same degree?

Against this background, the aim of the paper is to analyse the crisis-related activities of the 27 national parliaments between 2010 and 2012. The paper proceeds as follows: we briefly discuss the changes to European economic governance and their impact on national parliaments by highlighting the executive dominance during the crisis management as well as the increasing number of initiatives outside the EU legal framework. We then outline the theoretical framework to explain variation in the level of parliamentary scrutiny activity, drawing on agency theory and the broad literature on national parliaments in the EU. This literature has identified domestic institutional strength and Euroscepticism as the most important factors for the development of tight scrutiny procedures. We expand these more conventional explanations by including macro-economic factors, given that we focus on a very specific area of EU politics. We then introduce the data, a quantitative dataset on crisis-related parliamentary activities established within the OPAL (Observatory of Parliaments after Lisbon) project (see Auel *et al.* 2015a). As our analysis reveals, institutional strength and macro-economic conditions are the strongest predictors for legislative scrutiny, while Euroscepticism plays – surprisingly – no role. The final section discusses the results and concludes.

Economic Governance Reform and its Impact on National Parliaments

Drudi *et al.* (2012: 881) propose dividing the financial crisis into three main phases: 'the financial turmoil (September 2008), the global financial crisis (September 2008–May 2010) and the eurozone sovereign debt crisis (May 2010–the present)'. During the first two phases, the crisis did not (yet) have a specifically European dimension. It fully reached the EU when Greece requested financial assistance in early 2010. Since then, the crisis has spread to other member states, most notably Ireland, Portugal, Spain and Cyprus.[1] EU member states have since then agreed on a number of economic governance reforms to manage and overcome what is now often labelled the 'eurozone crisis' (for an overview see Table 1 and Kunstein and Wessels 2012).

The crisis has impacted national parliaments in a number of ways. First and foremost, parliaments of financially threatened member states not only lose part of their freedom of action due to their dire financial situation, but must also comply with strict obligations to consolidate their budgets as a condition for receiving financial assistance from international funds, such as the European Stability Facility (EFSF) or the European Stability Mechanism (ESM). The so-called Memoranda of Understanding place massive burdens in terms of salary and

TABLE 1
CRISIS MANAGEMENT AND ECONOMIC GOVERNANCE REFORM 2010–2012
(MAIN INSTRUMENTS)

Instrument	Within EU legislative framework	Role of NPs
European Financial Supervision: European Systemic Risk Board (ESRB) and European System of Financial Supervisors (ESFS)	Based on EU secondary legislation. Participants: *EU Member States*	
European Financial Stabilisation Mechanism (EFSM)	Commission involved in defining general EU-wide policy goals regarding National Reform as well as Stability and Convergence Programmes	Domestic scrutiny procedures and subsidiarity check by NPs apply.
European Economic Policy Coordination:		
European semester; Six-Pack; Two-Pack		

Instrument	Outside EU legislative framework	Role of NPs
European Financial Stability Facility (EFSF)	Private company owned by the *eurozone* members. European Commission involved in implementation (conditionality)	
European Stability Mechanism (ESM)	Intergovernmental organisation owned by the *eurozone* members. Its establishment required a limited change of the EU treaties by all MS. European Commission involved in implementation (conditionality).	NPs had to ratify all new treaties outside the EU legal framework, but involvement in the decision-making depends on specific procedures; general scrutiny procedures do not necessarily apply.
Euro-Plus-Pact	Intergovernmental agreement. Adopted by the *eurozone* members as well as *Bulgaria, Denmark, Latvia, Lithuania, Poland and Romania.* European Commission involved in monitoring.	
Treaty on Stability, Coordination and Governance (TSCG)	Intergovernmental treaty signed by *all EU MS except the Czech Republic and the UK.* European Commission involved in monitoring. Obligation to introduce national debt brake subject to jurisdiction of the ECJ.	

Source: Kunstein and Wessels (2012), with modifications.

117

pension cuts or the retrenchment of social welfare programmes (see for instance Pisani-Ferry *et al.* 2013). But even donor countries must follow demands to consolidate national budgets within the revised Stability and Growth Pact or the Treaty on Stability, Coordination and Governance in the Economic and Monetary Union (TSCG), also known as the Fiscal Compact (for the Italian case see Hopkin 2012). Additionally, they must shoulder large financial guarantees that may severely limit their future financial room for manoeuvre.

A second development is a further strengthening of European executives. With the EU in full crisis mode, the European Council has become the most important forum for decision-making in EMU affairs. Crisis management 'by summit' has become the norm (Schulz 2012), shifting the decision-making mode even further towards European executives who can more easily bypass parliaments at the national and European level (Eriksen and Fossum 2011: 158). Executives in the Eurozone have also set up the Euro Summit, a new decision-making body consisting of the Heads of State and Government of the eurozone which meets prior to European Council sessions. The European Council, the Euro Summit as well as the Eurogroup have therefore turned into something similar to a European economic government (Wessels and Rozenberg 2013).

And, third, some of the measures have been implemented within the EU legal framework and others outside. Instruments such as the EFSF/ESM, the Euro Plus Pact (EUPP) or the Fiscal Compact are based on treaties outside of the EU legal framework and apply to participating countries only. This differentiation implies that national parliaments in and outside the Eurozone increasingly face different legal and political set-ups, as well as very different economic conditions. Additionally, national governments treated (or tried to treat) intergovernmental agreements as foreign rather than EU policy, thus limiting their parliaments' involvement.

How did parliaments respond to these developments? First empirical evidence reveals a growing asymmetry of parliamentary power during the course of the crisis (Benz 2013): some parliaments gained strong (formal) participation rights in new rescue mechanisms (e.g. Austria, Estonia, Finland, Germany or the Netherlands with regard to the EFSF and ESM) while others, especially parliaments in debtor countries, were in the firm grip of austerity measures imposed by international financiers (see for instance Katsikas 2012; Ladi 2013; Scharpf 2012). While this growing asymmetry refers primarily to formal parliamentary prerogatives, we know only little about whether and how parliaments made use of them. Their *actual* involvement is, however, imperative to take 'national ownership' of the crisis management. If the crisis management is perceived as a dictate from non-elected 'bureaucrats in Brussels', this cuts off the vital legitimacy chain that national parliaments ought to provide.

Delegation and Ownership in Times of Crisis

Our concept of ownership is closely related to agency theory and the principal–agent model, which have become prominent approaches to the study of political representation in general and the role of national parliaments in EU affairs in particular. Kiewiet and McCubbins (1991: 239–40) define an agency relationship as 'established when an agent has delegated ... the authority to take action on behalf of ... the principal'. Applied to national parliaments, the underlying assumption is that they (or more specifically the governing parties) delegate authority in EU affairs to their agent – the government – and can then employ various means of control to prevent agency loss (see also Winzen 2012). The concept of ownership, however, goes beyond the prevention of agency loss and takes into account that parliaments are also agents of their citizens. To fulfil this role, parliaments must not only accompany decision-making processes by scrutinising and controlling their governments, but also by communicating EU crisis politics to their citizens.

Whether or not MPs will invest their scarce resources in activities aimed at taking ownership of EU politics rather than simply abdicating them to their agents depends on both institutional opportunities – i.e. the *capacity* – and on incentives – i.e. the *motivation* to engage in scrutiny of EU affairs (see Auel and Christiansen 2015). So far, most of the literature on national parliaments in the EU[2] has focused on the institutional adaptation to EU affairs, i.e. the development of the institutional capacities. Two factors were identified as being most important: domestic institutional strength and Euroscepticism. Institutional strength has been measured with a variety of variables such as the overall institutional strength of parliaments prior to and independent of integration, the power balance in legislative–executive relations or the type of government (especially minority governments) (Bergman 1997, 2000; Dimitrakopoulos 2001; Holzhacker 2005; Karlas 2012; Martin 2000; Maurer and Wessels 2001; Raunio 2005; Saalfeld 2005). 'Indeed, research on explaining cross-national variation in the level of scrutiny in EU matters indicates that the overall strength of the legislature "spills over" to European affairs, with stronger control of the government in domestic matters producing also tighter cabinet scrutiny in European affairs' (Raunio 2009: 330, fn. 11). The second factor draws on motivation-based explanations and can be summarised under the heading of public and/or elite opinion, including the degree of public support for the EU in the member state and/or the existence of Eurosceptic parties (Raunio and Wiberg 2000; Raunio 2005; Winzen 2013). In Raunio's comparative study (2005), based on a fuzzy-set QCA analysis, the power of parliament independent of integration emerged as the only necessary condition, whereas the combination of having a powerful parliament and a Eurosceptic electorate were sufficient conditions for producing tighter procedures for the control of the government in EU matters.

In the following, we draw on these findings to develop hypotheses on the impact of both institutional capacity and political motivation on the level of activity in crisis affairs. Although the literature presented above is mainly concerned with institutional aspects, it can also be applied to parliamentary behaviour: MPs not only need institutional opportunities, but also incentives to invest limited resources in the scrutiny of European Affairs. In addition, given that we are analysing behaviour in a very specific area of EU politics – i.e. the management of the eurozone crisis – we add a hypothesis on macro-economic factors.

Parliamentary Capacities – Institutional Strength

Although formal prerogatives in EU affairs do not necessarily equate actual activities (see for instance Auel 2007; Pollak and Slominski 2003), they must be regarded as an important precondition for activity. They define instruments and establish procedures, which can also impact more indirectly on executive–legislative relations (Winzen 2012: 662): The Danish government, for example, cooperates closely with the Folketing in EU affairs to avoid receiving narrow mandates or even no mandate at all (see also Auel and Benz 2005b).

H1a: Institutional strength I: *The greater the institutional strength of national parliaments in EU affairs, the greater their level of crisis-related activity.*

Second, in line with the literature outlined above, we expect the overall balance of power between government and parliament to affect the level of parliamentary activities. According to Lijphart's (1999) conceptualisation, majoritarian systems are – inter alia – characterised by a greater dominance of the executive within the political system. In consensus systems, in turn, executive–legislative relationships are more balanced, and coalition governments provide opportunities and incentives for MPs to 'police the bargain' (Martin and Vanberg 2004, see also Saalfeld 2005), i.e. to control whether ministers from other coalition partners respect parliamentary positions. Minority governments, finally, cannot rely on their own parliamentary majority, providing (at least part of) the opposition with direct policy influence.

H1b: Institutional strength II: *The less the dominance of the executive within the political system, the greater the level of parliamentary crisis-related activity.*

Political Motivation

Incentives for Scrutiny I: Euroscepticism. The literature presented above suggests that institutional capacities are not the only factors explaining parliamentary involvement, but that political motivation also matters. MPs in member states where public opinion is generally more critical of EU integration are considered to have a greater electoral incentive to become active in EU affairs due to the potential electoral impact of EU politics. This is even more relevant since European issues have gained more salience and public attention with the outbreak of the crisis (Serrichio *et al.* 2013: 57). The greater the level of public Euroscepticism, the more MPs and their parties have an incentive to scrutinise crisis affairs to assure their voters that they will defend their interests at the European level.

H2a: Euroscepticism in public opinion: *The stronger the Euroscepticism in public opinion, the greater the parliamentary level of crisis-related activity.*

In addition, the literature has suggested that the presence of Eurosceptic parliamentary party groups or party factions within parliament has a positive impact on the development of tighter scrutiny procedures (e.g. Raunio and Wiberg 2000). Accordingly, we assume that they also have an incentive to make use of these institutional capacities, both for electoral reasons and to gain policy influence. We expect this electoral incentive to be greatest for Eurosceptic parties, many of which have achieved electoral successes since the beginning of the eurozone crisis. Where these parties are represented in parliament, they can publicly pressure the government on EU issues to sharpen their profile by politicising the crisis (De Vries and Edwards 2009).

H2b: Share of Eurosceptic parties: *The greater the share of Eurosceptic parties in parliament, the higher the level of parliamentary crisis-related activity.*

However, Eurosceptic parties are often found on the fringes of the political spectrum and are too small to exert significant influence within parliament. Mainstream parties, in contrast, usually publicly support European integration – but they are rarely perfectly united on this issue. Indeed, many mainstream parties experience medium to high levels of party dissent over European integration issues (Bakker *et al.* 2012; Edwards 2009). Intra-party dissent can be expected to have a negative impact on parliamentary activities, as party leaders will try to avoid issues on which the party is divided (De Vries 2010; see also Auel and Raunio 2014). We therefore expect that parliaments with an overall greater share of dissenting Eurosceptic MPs will scrutinise EU (crisis) affairs less actively (H2c).

H2c: Level of parliamentary Euroscepticism: *The greater the share of dissenting Eurosceptic MPs in parliament, the lower the level of parliamentary crisis-related activity.*

Incentives for Scrutiny II: Macro-economic Conditions

In addition, we need to take into account that the motivations to engage in scrutiny of EU affairs may also be affected by the distinct macro-economic conditions that parliaments faced in the 2010–2012 period (see among others Buti and Carnot 2012; De Grauwe and Ji 2012). While Northern European countries could, for instance, easily refinance their government expenditures at record low prices, many Southern European countries experienced significant increases in the interest rates of their long-term government bonds which put the sustainability of their debt levels at risk (see for instance Drudi *et al.* 2012: 888). Some of them were forced to implement austerity programmes in exchange for financial assistance, while 'countries such as Germany, Netherlands and Finland fear[ed] that a bailout would create a lasting relationship of dependency of the debtor nations on their more creditworthy neighbours' (Hopkin 2012: 36).

Without question, member states drawing on financial EU–IMF assistance have been severely constrained by the commitment to implement economic and adjustment programmes that were 'designed in discussions between the *national authorities* and the so-called Troika, consisting of the European Commission, the European Central Bank and the International Monetary Fund' (European Commission 2014: 7). Parliaments, as well as other national authorities of programme countries, have hardly exercised any influence during these negotiations. As Scharpf puts it: 'In the euro crisis, debtor states have completely lost fiscal autonomy, and the exercise of wide ranges of their economic, social and labor-market competences has been subjected to direct European control' (Scharpf 2012: 27). However, not only debtor countries were affected. As of 2012, 23 EU member states were under the excessive deficit procedure for exceeding – to varying degrees – the limit to either the annual government deficit (3% of annual GDP) or the government debt (exceeding 60% as the ratio of gross government debt to GDP).[3] Financial predicament therefore increases the odds that a country must follow recommendations by European actors to correct economic imbalances. We assume that these economic and financial constraints altered the motivation of parliaments to engage in the scrutiny of the crisis management.

H3: 'Relevance' of crisis: *Parliaments of economically weak member states show lower levels of crisis-related parliamentary activity.*

Finally, we added the level of participation in different treaties of the Economic and Monetary Union (EMU) as a control variable. This takes into account that participation in different EMU treaties (TSCG, EUPP) varies within non-eurozone countries, while eurozone countries can be distinguished according to donor and debtor status.

Data

Dependent Variable

The empirical analysis is based on a dataset generated by a broader study within the OPAL project (see also Auel *et al.* 2015a). It provides, for the first time, detailed comparative empirical data on parliamentary activities in EU affairs between 2010 and 2012 across all 40 parliamentary chambers of the EU.[4] The data covers (some of) the most important means of national parliaments to get involved in and take ownership of EU politics: resolutions/mandates providing parliaments with the opportunity to give their opinion on EU documents and the government's negotiation position (policy-influencing function), plenary debates serving public deliberation and control (communication function), and reasoned opinions within the EWS as well as opinions within the Political Dialogue[5] (policy influence directly at the EU level). For the purpose of this paper, we selected all crisis-related activities from the larger dataset[6] and focus on lower chambers only. In financial and economic affairs, the competences of lower chambers are usually more pronounced; furthermore, data for some of the independent variables was available for lower chambers only. The final dataset on crisis-related activities consists of 993 parliamentary activities and therefore represents roughly 19 per cent of the overall EU activities of the lower chambers (5,124 activities).

Our dependent variable is a score for the level of activity based on the three types of activities (mandates/resolutions, debates, opinions) calculated for each parliament and year. The indicators for the crisis-related activity score are presented in Table 2. The values for the indicators were first normalised on a scale from 0 to 1,[7] added up to an overall score and divided by three.

Two caveats need to be mentioned. First, the data does omit other activities, especially committee activities as well as more informal means of influence and control. This omission is due to unavailable data. While much of the EU activity takes place in European Affairs Committees[8] as well as – depending on the scrutiny system – within standing committees, it is impossible to obtain data on the share of committee time spent on scrutinising and debating crisis issues compared to other (EU) issues. The omission of more informal means of influence and control is, unfortunately, part of the trade-off between large and small N studies. Investigating informal strategies not only relies on qualitative data sources, but is also difficult to quantify.

Second, simply measuring the level of activity reveals little about the *impact* of parliamentary involvement, i.e. whether more active parliaments succeed in controlling and influencing their governments effectively. Since the actual impact of parliamentary activity in terms of influence is extremely difficult to measure, we can only capture what parliaments do, but not whether they are actually successful.

Independent Variables

To test the hypotheses on institutional strength (H1), we draw on the OPAL score (Auel *et al.* 2015a), which measures parliamentary strength in EU affairs along three dimensions: access to information, the parliamentary infrastructure and oversight powers. To take the special character of the crisis measures into

TABLE 2
INDICATORS AND MEASUREMENT OF THE ACTIVITY SCORE

Indicator	Measurement
Mandates/ resolutions	Number of crisis-related mandates/resolutions by year
Debates	Two indicators combined: number of crisis-related debates and percentage of plenary time spent on crisis issues by year
Opinions	Absolute number of reasoned opinions (EWS) x 2, plus absolute number of Political Dialogue opinions on crisis-related documents by year

Note: Reasoned opinions were given double weight because they are not only more important in terms of potential impact, but also require parliaments to focus on a highly specific argumentation.

account, we expanded the original OPAL score by adding a fourth indicator (with double weight to account for its importance) capturing the specific parliamentary prerogatives within the EFSF:[9] whether parliaments are only informed about payouts through the EFSF, whether they have the right to vote on them or whether they are not involved at all. The data was provided by a frequently cited study by the Deutsche Bank (Deutsche Bank 2011) and cross-checked with the relevant parliamentary committees. For the measurement of the dominance of the executive we use two alternative variables. First, we draw on an updated indicator of Lijphart's (1999) dimension 'Executives–parties' developed by Armingeon *et al.* (2013), which focuses on the key elements that characterise executive–legislative relations and the power balance between government and parliament. As this is a highly aggregated indicator, we use the percentage of minority governments in 2010–2012, based on the ParlGov database (Döring and Manow 2014) as an alternative variable.

For the Euroscepticism hypotheses, we draw on three different indicators measuring public and party Euroscepticism. *Public Euroscepticism* (H2a) measures the percentage of citizens per year that stated they had 'a negative image of the EU' (annual average of the Eurobarometer Surveys 73–78).[10] The indicator reflects a more nuanced form of Euroscepticism in contrast to, for instance, whether EU membership is generally perceived as 'a bad thing'. Parliamentary Euroscepticism was measured with two variables: the strength of *Eurosceptic parties* within parliaments based on the seat share of all Eurosceptic parties for each parliament using the Chapel Hill 2010 dataset (Bakker *et al.* 2012)[11] (H2b); and *dissenting Eurosceptic MPs* by the share of no-votes and abstentions regarding the parliamentary ratification of the ESM Treaty (H2c).[12]

For the macro-economic hypothesis (H3), we use two variables. First, we calculated the average sovereign credit rating per year by the three largest rating agencies (Moody's, Standard and Poor's and Fitch Ratings) between 2010 and 2012 with data provided by Rogers *et al.* (2013). Based on the 16 highest classifications used by all three rating agencies, we assigned numbers from 16 ('prime rating', 'triple A') to 0 ('substantial risk' or 'default') and calculated averages for each country by year. Credit ratings combine a number of economic indicators

TABLE 3
OVERVIEW OF THE DEPENDENT AND INDEPENDENT VARIABLES

Variable	Mean	Std. Dev.	Min	Max
Score parl. activity	18.62	13.77	0	62
OPAL score inst. strength	48.35	17.80	20	88
Lijphart index	−0.00077	0.93	−2.28	1.9
Minority governments	33.83	39.90	0	100
Public Euroscepticism	24.24	8.64	9	46.5
Strength of Eurosceptic parties	13.93	14.09	0	48.58
Elite Euroscepticism	20.46	13.93	09	47.74
Credit rating by year	11.84	4.10	0	16
Gov't deficit (% of GDP)	−4.59	4.35	−30.6	4.3
EMU involvement	2.92	1.34	0	4

and contain future expectations of a country's economic development. Second, we used data on the yearly government deficit in percentage of GDP 2010–2012 (European Central Bank 2014: 45) to capture the economic condition a country faced specifically in the period under investigation.

EMU involvement, finally, is captured by a variable that assigns the value 1 for participation in the Fiscal Compact, the Euro Plus Pact, the eurozone as well as for EFSF/ESM donor status. Values thus range from 0 to 4.

Table 3 provides an overview of our dependent and independent variables.

Dealing with the Crisis from the Backbenches

As Table 4 shows, the crisis did indeed play a significant role for national parliaments. Between 2010 and 2012 national parliaments spent nearly 1,000 hours debating crisis issues in 454 debates in the plenary and issued close to 440 mandates or resolutions on crisis-related issues. In contrast, the Political Dialogue with the European Commission, and especially the Early Warning System, were less important with regard to crisis legislation.

To some extent, the crisis has been business as usual for national parliaments (see also Auel and Höing 2014). When it comes to mandates/resolutions or the two types of opinions (Political Dialogue and EWS) – and thus to activities where parliaments mainly react to documents sent by the European Commission (both legislative proposals and other preparatory documents) – the share of crisis-related activities out of all EU activities is fairly similar (around 14 and 11.1 per cent). This roughly reflects the ratio of crisis-related documents out of all documents published by the Commission in 2010–2012 (Auel

TABLE 4

COMPARISON OF PARLIAMENTARY ACTIVITIES CONCERNING THE CRISIS AND OTHER EU ISSUES

	Type of activities				
	Number of plenary debates	Hours of plenary debates	Mandates/ resolutions	Reasoned opinions on subsidiarity	Political dialogue opinions
Crisis activities Abs. (av.)	454 (17)	998 (37)	438 (16)	12 (0.4)	89 (3.3)
Other EU activ. Abs. (av.)	625 (23)	1106 (41)	2697 (100)	96 (3.6)	713 (26)
All EU activities Abs. (av.)	1079 (40)	2104 (78)	3153 (117)	108 (4)	802 (30)
% Crisis out of all EU activities	42.1%	47.4%	14%	11.1%	11.1%

Note: For all activities, the table provides the absolute number of all observations for 2010 to 2012, and the averages in parentheses.
Source: Author's data.

and Höing 2014: 1188). The crisis did, however, have a greater impact on the debating activity of national parliaments. Over 40 per cent of the EU debates, and almost half of the plenary time spent on EU issues were focused on the crisis.

The aggregate numbers do, however, obscure vast differences in the level of activity by individual parliaments. Figure 1 therefore provides an overview over the activity scores per year.

To test the hypotheses developed above, we ran a multiple linear regression analysis using STATA 13.1. Since we have data for three years for each parliament, we used a regression with clustered standard errors ($N = 78$, groups = 26) (Table 5). We omitted the Portuguese Assembleia from the analysis of the overall activity level because the extremely large number of inconsequential opinions sent within the Political Dialogue led to an inflated activity score not comparable to the other parliaments.[13] Given the relatively small number of cases, we interpret the regression coefficients as broad rather than highly precise indicators for the influence of different variables.

The first three models test the association between parliamentary activity and the three sets of indicators plus the control variable according to our sets of hypotheses (model 1: *institutional capacity*; model 2: Incentives for Scrutiny I – *Euroscepticism*; model 3: Incentives for Scrutiny II – *macro-economic conditions*). In model 1 we also varied the measure of executive dominance between the Lijphart index (Model 1a), and minority governments (Model 1b). Model 4 then includes the full set of variables, again using the Lijphart index (model 4a) once and the minority government variable (model 4b) once.

As all variants of the model show, institutional strength in EU affairs is the most important predictor for parliamentary activity. The findings support assumptions in the literature that formal prerogatives are a vital precondition for activity. The formal prerogatives include, among others, access to

FIGURE 1
CRISIS-RELATED ACTIVITY SCORES 2010–2012

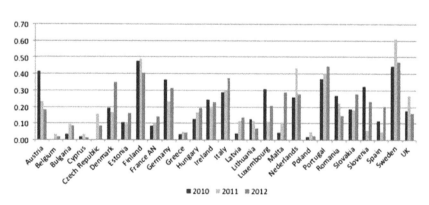

Source: Authors' data.

TABLE 5
REGRESSION MODELS

Variables	Model 1	Model 1a	Model 2	Model 3	Model 4a	Model 4b
OPAL score inst. strength	0.480***	0.503***			0.479***	0.512***
	(0.110)	(0.122)			(0.126)	(0.117)
Lijphart index	0.243				1.528	
	(1.437)				(1.615)	
Minority governments		0.051				0.057
		(0.049)				(0.035)
Public Euroscepticism			0.134		0.160	0.248
			(0.290)		(0.190)	(0.143)
Strength of Eurosceptic parties			0.088		0.044	0.064
			(0.250)		(0.148)	(0.151)
Elite Euroscepticism			−0.023		−0.310	−0.294
			(0.268)		(0.193)	(0.195)
Credit rating by year				1.452**	0.269*	0.852*
				(0.465)	(0.380)	(0.368)
Gov't deficit (% of GDP)				0.248	−0.216	0.221
				(0.483)	(0.367)	(0.395)
EMU Involvement	−1.668	−1.733	1.194	−0.495	−2.009	−1.876
	(1.879)	(1.736)	(2.126)	(1.847)	(2.013)	(1.810)
Constant	0.284	−2.358	11.121	4.008	−10.957	−14.563
	(6.145)	(6.074)	(10.094)	(6.117)	(7.2382)	(6.816)
Adjusted R^2	0.345	0.364	0.019	0.203	0.462	0.478
N/groups	78/26	78/26	78/26	78/26	78/26	78/26

Notes: Dependent variable: score of parliamentary activity in crisis-related EU affairs. Entries are coefficients with standard errors in parentheses.
*$p < 0.05$; **$p < 0.01$; ***$p < 0.001$. All models exclude Portugal.

information as well as a well-functioning parliamentary infrastructure. Both help overcome information deficits as a precondition for tighter control of the 'agents'. This is particularly important in times of crisis, when decisions are taken quickly and national executives can more easily circumvent democratically elected chambers. It is therefore not surprising that the 'Northern European' parliaments with a well-functioning parliamentary infrastructure – such as Denmark, Finland, Germany, Netherlands or Sweden – are in the group of countries with the highest crisis-related activity levels. Exceptions, however, are the Czech Republic, Estonia, Lithuania and Slovenia, all rather powerful parliaments with little activity.

The assumption that executive dominance impacts on activity levels is, in contrast, not confirmed. The specific advantages of consensus systems – i.e. the greater balance of power between the executive and the legislature as well as the incentives to control the coalition partner – did not influence the use of formal parliamentary instruments of control. One reason could be that under conditions of crisis governing parties were under greater pressure to support their governments, reducing the possibilities of 'policing the bargain' and making them more similar to majoritarian systems. In addition, we are measuring formal activities and cannot capture more informal negotiations and agreements between governing parties and the executive. Similarly, the simple fact of having a minority government does not increase parliamentary activity. Indeed, among the parliaments with minority governments we find both parliaments that are powerful and active in EU affairs (Sweden, Denmark, The Netherlands) and weaker and much less active ones (Belgium, Bulgaria, or Spain).

Surprisingly, and contrary to findings in the literature, public Euroscepticism did not spur parliaments into greater activity regarding the crisis. One explanation is that MPs felt compelled to scrutinise, and especially to communicate, crisis-related matters to their citizens irrespective of their citizens' attitude towards the EU – and possibly precisely to avoid (further) increases in public Euroscepticism. This is underlined by the fact that the crisis accounts for more than 40 per cent of all debates on EU issues in the period under investigation. Thus, parliaments seem to have been generally more willing to poke the famous 'sleeping giant' (van der Eijk and Franklin 2004) when it comes to the crisis, but this was not a reaction to public demands.

Our hypothesis on elite Euroscepticism was also not confirmed. Although a greater share of dissenting Eurosceptic MPs decreased the level of parliamentary activity, the result is not significant at the 95 per cent level. Similarly, the hypothesis on the share of Eurosceptic parties is also clearly disconfirmed: Eurosceptic parties have either been unable or unwilling to exploit the crisis via activities in parliament. Thus while parliamentary Euroscepticism is a factor explaining the institutional adaptation of national parliaments, the same is not true for the actual *use* of scrutiny provision. The reason could well be that parliamentary instruments, such as resolutions and opinions, require support by a majority and thus cannot be used by – often small – Eurosceptic parties on their own. In addition, resolutions or opinions usually gain little public attention. They are therefore simply not attractive instruments for Eurosceptic parties aiming at politicising the EU via the crisis. Plenary debates, in contrast, do indeed serve such a purpose, but here the impact of Eurosceptic parties is possibly cancelled out by the fact that (a) smaller parties are also often constrained in their ability to put issues on the plenary agenda *on their own* and (b) mainstream parties also seem to have felt compelled to communicate crisis-related matters to their citizens. Within this result for the EU 26 we do find exceptions, however. For Finland, for example, Raunio (2014) shows that the True Finns – after their electoral success in 2011 – were able to use the eurozone crisis to trigger a major domestic politicisation of Europe in the Eduskunta, which led, inter alia, to a marked increase in plenary debates.

Macro-economic factors, finally, explain about 20 per cent of the variation, and credit rating is an important predictor in all models, while the government deficit has no impact. The latter suggests that the current fiscal condition of a member state made little difference with regard to the parliamentary scrutiny of crisis issues. A high credit rating, in contrast – which also takes expectations about the future economic outlook into account – does impact positively on parliamentary activity levels. Rating agencies can downgrade countries if they believe the government is not pursuing a certain economic policy rigorously enough. Credit ratings can thus influence the political credibility of a country to implement prudent economic policies; they also have a highly symbolic value for policy-makers. The fear of being downgraded, hence losing creditworthiness and possibly future foreign investors, does seem to provide incentives for greater activity regarding crisis issues.

That the level of EMU integration, finally, does not have an impact at all seems to be a somewhat contradictory result. A rather straightforward expectation would have been that deeper EMU integration has a positive impact on activity levels. Our data shows, however, that this assumption is too simplistic: Member states outside the eurozone were clearly affected by the crisis as well. Indeed, we find parliaments with high levels of activity both within the eurozone (such as Austria, Finland, Germany, Italy or the Netherlands) as well as outside: Sweden (TSGC participation), Denmark (both TSCG and EUPP) or the UK (no participation). Among the parliaments with less than average activity levels within the eurozone are those of Belgium, Estonia, France, Slovakia (donor status) or Greece (debtor status); outside of the eurozone we find those of the Czech Republic (no participation), Bulgaria, Latvia or Poland (all TSGC and EUPP). One reason why the predictor is negative (albeit not significant at the 95 per cent level) could be that most of the less active parliaments in the eurozone are also among the least powerful in terms of formal institutional strength. Especially economically weak parliaments depending on current financial aid through the EFSF/ESM – or under threat to depend on such assistance possibly in the future (Cyprus and Spain) – were under great pressure to agree to crisis decisions without much delay through parliamentary scrutiny.

Conclusion

Unsurprisingly, our data reveals that there is no simple answer to the question of how parliaments responded to the European crisis management. As in EU politics in general, we can find both rather active parliaments and scrutiny 'laggards' – and a large field in between. Thus, at least regarding the scrutiny of the management of the crisis, to speak of a general 'de-parliamentarisation' is too simplistic. So far, there is no indication that the crisis generally shocked parliaments into inertia.

As expected, formal institutional capacities do provide parliaments with the necessary prerequisites for parliamentary engagement in scrutiny, as demonstrated by the strong Northern European parliaments. Institutional opportunities are, however, not always neatly translated into actual activity. Some of the more powerful parliaments, such as those of Estonia, Lithuania or Slovenia, have been far less active than would have been expected, while the opposite is true for some of the weaker parliaments, most notably the Irish Dail. This supports the expectation that MPs need additional incentives to become involved. Surprisingly, and this is a second important finding, neither public nor parliamentary Euroscepticism provided such incentives with regard to the crisis. Potential future threats related to the crisis, however, and especially the threat to lose a symbolically important credit rating, does seem to be an incentive for MPs to become active. Thus, the more member states potentially have to lose in case of a failure of crisis management, the more active they are. Where this outlook is bleaker to start with, in contrast, MPs seem to lose incentives to scrutinise the crisis measures closely. Quite worryingly, it is therefore harder for weak parliaments of financially troubled member states to take national ownership of crisis management.

Acknowledgements

The research for this article has been conducted as part of the OPAL (Observatory of Parliaments after Lisbon) research consortium and was funded by the *Agence Nationale de Recherche* and the *Deutsche Forschungsgemeinschaft*. We also thank our OPAL partners at Science Po Paris and the Universities of Cambridge, Cologne and Maastricht, the coders who supported us with the data collection, the anonymous reviewers as well as Christian Deubner, Peter Grand, Mark Hallerberg and Jan Rovny for their helpful advice. All errors are our own.

Disclosure Statement

No potential conflict of interests was reported by the authors.

Notes

1. During our period of investigation (2010–2012), only Greece, Ireland, Portugal and Spain (late 2012) received financial assistance. Cyprus followed in early 2013.

2. Due to space limitations, this article cannot present a comprehensive overview of the literature, but Goetz and Meyer-Sahling (2008), Raunio (2009), Winzen (2010) and Rozenberg and Hefftler (2015) provide excellent reviews.
3. http://europa.eu/rapid/press-release_MEMO-12-7_en.htm.
4. Data was collected from parliamentary websites and the European Commission website for the Political Dialogue (http://ec.europa.eu/dgs/secretariat_general/relations/relations_other/npo/index_en.htm) and cross-checked through the Interparliamentary EU Information Exchange (IPEX) database. Coders also requested and confirmed data from parliamentary information offices. In addition, a questionnaire sent to national parliaments provided data on the average length of EU plenary debates as well as the overall debate time in the plenary. After a third reminder, the return rate was 100 per cent, although some specific data was missing in a few cases which was added through the authors' own calculations.
5. For details on the Early Warning System – the parliamentary subsidiarity check introduced with the Lisbon Treaty – see Auel and Christiansen (2015) as well as Gattermann and Hefftler (2015) in this volume. On the political Dialogue with the European Commission, introduced with the Barroso initiative in (2006), see Jančić (2012).
6. This included all activities on (1) crisis-related EU legislative proposals and pre-legislative documents, (2) all intergovernmental measures initiated outside the legal EU framework, and (3) all activities where the content showed sufficient relation to the crisis. The latter is based on a qualitative assessment and included, for instance, general debates on the crisis or parliamentary resolutions dealing with the crisis independent of specific EU proposals.
7. Unity-based normalisation: $X_{i, 0 \text{ to } 1} = (X_i - X_{Min})/(X_{Max} - X_{Min})$, where X_i = each data point I, X_{Min} = the minima among all the data points, X_{Max} = the maxima among all the data points, $X_{i, 0 \text{ to } 1}$ = the data point i normalised between 0 and 1.
8. For an analysis of the factors explaining, inter alia, time spent in EAC meetings in EU affairs in general see Auel et al. (2015b). We have also tested whether the ability of the committees to take decisions on behalf of the plenary has an impact on the number of debates. We assigned 0 = committees can decide on behalf of the plenary, 1 = committees can in some cases decide, and 2 = plenary has to decide. There is no statistically significant correlation with the number of plenary debates on crisis issues during our period of analysis (Pearson's $r = 0.171$, $p = 0.391$).
9. Given that the ESM entered into force only in October 2012, EFSF participation rights are more pertinent for our period under investigation. We included the non-eurozone countries, assigning them the lowest score (0 = not involved). The fact that they do not provide financial guarantees in the framework of the EFSF could be a reason to exclude them from this indicator. However, the functioning of the EFSF (and later the ESM) is vitally important for the whole EU and not just for the eurozone. We therefore regarded the fact that non-eurozone countries have no say over decisions regarding some of the main measures to combat the crisis as an institutional constraint.
10. The data was retrieved through the Eurobarometer Interactive Search System, online at: http://ec.europa.eu/public_opinion/cf/index.cfm?lang=en.
11. The Chapel Hill data is based on expert surveys; respondents were asked to assess 'the general position on European integration that the party leadership took over the course of 2010' on a scale from 1 = strongly opposed to 7 = strongly in favour. Parties with a score of 3.5 or lower were considered Eurosceptic. Where the Chapel Hill data does not provide data (for Cyprus, Luxembourg and Malta or data for new parties that entered parliaments after 2010), national experts provided additional data upon request.
12. The ESM treaty is one of the most far-reaching changes to the EU institutional architecture in recent years. All parliaments had to ratify the modification of article 136 TFEU; parliaments in the Eurozone additionally ratified the ESM treaty. The share of votes not supporting the treaty allows the capture of potential divisions within political parties and not only between them. In most cases, the share of non-supporters also differs substantially from the share of Eurosceptic parties.

13. The Portuguese *Assembleia* adopts opinions within the Political Dialogue on virtually all documents sent by the European Commission. However, most of these opinions do not include any comments on the document other than a statement that the Assembleia has not found a breach of the subsidiarity principle. The Commission no longer replies to these supportive opinions (http://ec.europa.eu/dgs/secretariat_general/relations/relations_other/npo/index_en.htm).

References

Armingeon, Klaus, Romana Careja, David Weisstanner, Sarah Engler, Panajotis Potolidis, and Marléne Gerber (2013). *Comparative Political Data Set III 1990–2011*. Berne: University of Berne, Institute of Political Science.

Auel, Katrin (2007). 'Democratic Accountability and National Parliaments – Re-Defining the Impact of Parliamentary Scrutiny in EU Affairs', *European Law Journal*, 13:4, 87–504.

Auel, Katrin, and Arthur Benz (2005a). 'Europeanisation of Parliamentary Democracy', *Journal of Legislative Studies*, 11:3–4, 303–18.

Auel, Katrin, and Arthur Benz (2005b). 'The Politics of Adaptation: Europeanisation of National Parliamentary Systems', *Journal of Legislative Studies*, 11:3–4, 372–93.

Auel, Katrin, and Oliver Höing (2014). 'Parliaments in the Euro Crisis: Can the Losers of Integration Still Fight Back?', *Journal of Common Market Studies*, 52:6, 1184–93.

Auel, Katrin, and Tapio Raunio (2014). 'Debating the State of the Union?: Comparing Parliamentary Debates on EU Issues in Finland, France, Germany and the United Kingdom', *Journal of Legislative Studies*, 20:1, 12–28.

Auel, Katrin, and Thomas Christiansen (2015). 'After Lisbon: National Parliaments in the European Union', *West European Politics*, 38:2, 261–81.

Auel, Katrin, Olivier Rozenberg, and Angela Tacea (2015a). 'Fighting Back? And If Yes, How? Measuring Parliamentary Strength and Activity in EU Affairs', in Claudia Hefftler, Christine Neuhold, Olivier Rozenberg, and Julie Smith (eds.), *Palgrave Handbook of National Parliaments and the European Union*. Houndsmills/Basingstoke: Palgrave Macmillan, 60–93.

Auel, Katrin, Olivier Rozenberg, and Angela Tacea (2015b). 'To Scrutinise or Not to Scrutinise? Explaining Variation in EU-Related Activities in National Parliaments', *West European Politics*, 38:2, 282–304.

Bakker, Ryan, Catherine de Vries, Erica Edwards, Liesbet Hooghe, Seth Jolly, Gary Marks, Jon Polk, Jan Rovny, Marco Steenbergen, and Milada Vachudova (2012). 'Measuring Party Positions in Europe: The Chapel Hill Expert Survey Trend File, 1999–2010', *Party Politics*, 1–16 (published before print).

Benz, Arthur (2013). 'An Asymmetric Two-Level Game. Parliaments in the Euro Crisis', in Ben Crum and John Erik Fossum (eds.), *Practices of Interparliamentary Coordination in International Politics*. Colchester: ECPR Press, 125–40.

Bergman, Torbjörn (1997). 'National Parliaments and EU Affairs Committees: Notes in Empirical Variation and Competing Explanations', *Journal of European Public Policy*, 4:3, 373–87.

Bergman, Torbjörn (2000). 'The European Union as the Next Step of Delegation and Accountability', *European Journal of Political Research*, 37:3, 415–29.

Buti, Marco, and Nicolas Carnot (2012). 'The EMU Debt Crisis: Early Lessons and Reforms', *Journal of Common Market Studies*, 50:6, 899–911.

De Grauwe, Paul, and Yuemei Ji (2012). 'Mispricing of Sovereign Risk and Macroeconomic Stability in the Eurozone', *Journal of Common Market Studies*, 50:6, 866–80.

De Vries, Catherine E. (2010). 'EU Issue Voting: Asset or Liability? How European Integration Affects Parties' Electoral Fortunes', *European Union Politics*, 11:1, 89–117.

De Vries, Catherine E., and Erica E. Edwards (2009). 'Taking Europe to Its Extremes: Extremist Parties and Public Euroscepticism', *Party Politics*, 15:1, 5–28.

Deutsche Bank (2011). 'EFSF – Where Do National Parliaments Have a Say in the EMU?', *Frankfurt Am Main: Deutsche Bank Research*, available at http://www.dbresearch.com/PROD/ DBR_INTERNET_EN-PROD/PROD0000000000280052.pdf (accessed 28 March 2014).

Dimitrakopoulos, Dionyssis (2001). 'Incrementalism and Path Dependence: European Integration and Institutional Change in National Parliaments', *Journal of Common Market Studies*, 39:3, 405–22.

Dinan, Desmond (2012). 'Governance and Institutions: Impact of the Escalating Crisis', *Journal of Common Market Studies*, 50: annual review, 85–98.

Döring, Holger, and Philip Manow (2014). *Parliament and Government Composition Database (ParlGov): An Infrastructure for Empirical Information on Parties, Elections and Governments in Modern Democracies*. Active version, available at www.ev.parlgov.org.

Drudi, Francesco, Alain Durré, and Francesco Paolo Mongelli (2012). 'The Interplay of Economic Reforms and Monetary Policy: The Case of the Eurozone', *Journal of Common Market Studies*, 50:6, 881–98.

Edwards, Catherine E. (2009). 'Products of Their Past? Cleavages and Intra-Party Dissent over European Integration', *IHS Political Science Series*, 118, 1–36.

Eriksen, Erik Oddvar, and John Erik Fossum (2011). 'Bringing European Democracy Back in-or How to Read the German Constitutional Court's Lisbon Treaty Ruling', *European Law Journal*, 17:2, 153–71.

European Central Bank (2014). 'Statistics Pocket Book (Full Report)', available at http://sdw.ecb. europa.eu/reports.do?node=1000002994_ALLPDF (accessed 28 March 2014).

European Commission (2014). *The Troika and Financial Assistance in the Euro Area: Successes and Failures*. Brussel: Study on the request of the Economic and Monetary Affairs Committee.

Gattermann, Katjana, and Claudia Hefftler (2015). 'Beyond Institutional Capacity: Political Motivation and Parliamentary Behaviour in the Early Warning System', *West European Politics*, 38:2, 305–34.

Goetz, Klaus H. and Jan-Hinrik Meyer-Sahling (2008). 'The Europeanisation of National Political Systems: Parliaments and Executives', *Living Review in European Governance* 3: 2, available at http://www.livingreviews.org/lreg-2008-2.

Holzhacker, Ronald (2005). 'National Parliamentary Scrutiny of EU Decision-Making: The Role of Opposition Parties' *Journal of Legislative Studies*, 11:3–4, 428–45.

Hopkin, Jonathan (2012). 'A Slow Fuse: Italy and the EU Debt Crisis', *The International Spectator*, 47:4, 35–48.

Jančić, Davor (2012). 'The Barroso Initiative: Window Dressing or Democratic Boost?', *Utrecht Law Review*, 8:1, 78–91.

Karlas, Jan (2012). 'National Parliamentary Control of EU Affairs: Institutional Design after Enlargement', *West European Politics*, 35:5, 1095–113.

Katsikas, Dimitrios (2012). 'The Greek Crisis and the Search for Political Leadership', *The International Spectator*, 47:4, 49–56.

Kiewiet, Roderick D., and Mathew D. McCubbins (1991). *The Logic of Delegation*. Chicago, IL: University of Chicago Press.

Kunstein, Tobias, and Wolfgang Wessels (2012). 'What We Hope, What We Fear, What We Expect: Possible Scenarios for the Future of the Eurozone', *European View*, 11:1, 5–14.

Ladi, Stella (2013). 'Austerity Politics and Administrative Reform: The Eurozone Crisis and Its Impact upon Greek Public Administration', *Comparative European Politics*, 12:2, 184–208.

Laursen, Finn, and Spyros A. Pappas, eds. (1995). *The Changing Role of Parliaments in the European Union*. Maastricht: EIPA.

Lijphart, Arend (1999). *Patterns of Democracy: Government Forms and Performance in Thirty-Six Countries*. New Haven, CT: Yale University Press.

Martin, Lisa L. (2000). *Democratic Commitments. Legislatures and International Cooperation*. Princeton: Princeton University Press.

Martin, Lanny W., and Georg Vanberg (2004). 'Policing the Bargain: Coalition Government and Parliamentary Scrutiny', *American Journal of Political Science*, 48:1, 13–27.

Maurer, Andreas, and Wolfgang Wessels, eds. (2001). *National Parliaments on Their Ways to Europe: Losers or Latecomers?* Baden-Baden: Nomos.

Norton, Philip, ed. (1996). *National Parliaments and the European Union*. London: Frank Cass.

O'Brennan, John, and Tapio Raunio (2007). *National Parliaments within the Enlarged European Union*. London and New York: Routledge.

Pisani-Ferry, Jean, André Sapir, and Guntram Wolff (2013). *EU-IMF Assistance to Euro-Area Countries: An Early Assessment*. Brussels: Bruegel Blue Print Series.

Pollak, Johannes, and Peter Slominski (2003). 'Influencing EU Politics? The Case of the Austrian Parliament', *Journal of Common Market Studies*, 41:4, 707–29.

Puntscher Riekmann, Sonja, and Doris Wydra (2013). 'Representation in the European State of Emergency: Parliaments against Governments?', *Journal of European Integration*, 35:5, 565–82.

Raunio, Tapio (2005). 'Holding Governments Accountable in European Affairs: Explaining Cross-National Variation', *Journal of Legislative Studies*, 11:3–4, 319–42.

Raunio, Tapio (2009). 'National Parliaments and European Integration: What We Know and Agenda for Future Research', *Journal of Legislative Studies*, 15:4, 317–34.

Raunio, Tapio (2014). 'When Party Politics and Institutional Culture Collide: The Politicization of EU Affairs in the Finnish Eduskunta', paper prepared for Workshop on National Parliaments in the EU, Delmenhorst, 6/7 March 2014.

Raunio Tapio and Matti Wiberg (2000). 'Does Support Lead to Ignorance? National Parliaments and the Legitimacy of EU Governance', *Acta Politica*, 35:2, 146–68.

Rogers, Simon, Ami Sedghi, and John Burn-Murdoch (2013). 'Credit Ratings: How Fitch, Moody's and S&P Rate Each Country', *The Guardian Datastore*, available at http://www.theguardian. com/news/datablog/2010/apr/30/credit-ratings-country-fitch-moodys-standard#data.

Rozenberg, Olivier, and Claudia Hefftler (2015). 'Introduction', in Claudia Hefftler, Christine Neuhold, Olivier Rozenberg, and Julie Smith (eds.), *Palgrave Handbook of National Parliaments and the European Union*. Houndsmills/Basingstoke: Palgrave Macmillan, 1–39.

Saalfeld, Thomas (2005). 'Delegation or Abdication? Government Backbenchers, Ministers and European Integration', *Journal of Legislative Studies*, 11:3–4, 343–71.

Scharpf, Fritz (2012). 'Legitimacy Intermediation in the Multilevel European Polity and Its Collapse in the Euro Crisis', *Cologne: Working Paper Max Planck Institute*, 1–39.

Schulz, Martin (2012). *'Democratic Europe – 10-Point Plan to Put the EU on a New Democratic Footing'*, Berlin: Speech at the Humboldt University, available at http://www.europarl.europa.eu/ the-president/de-en/press/press_release_speeches/speeches/sp-2012/sp-2012-may/speeches-2012-may-4.html.

Serrichio, Fabio, Myrto Tsakatika, and Lucia Quaglia (2013). 'Euroscepticism and the Global Financial Crisis', *Journal of Common Market Studies*, 51:1, 51–64.

Van der Eijk, Cees, and Mark Franklin (2004). 'Potential for Contestation on European Matters at National Elections in Europe', in Gary Marks and Marco R. Steenbergen (eds.), *European Integration and Political Conflict*. Cambridge: Cambridge University Press, 32–50.

Wessels, Wolfgang, and Olivier Rozenberg (2013). *Democratic Control in the Member States of the European Council and the Euro Zone Summits*. Brussels: European Parliament Study, available at http://www.europarl.europa.eu/committees/fr/studiesdownload.html?languageDocument=EN&file=90910.

Winzen, Thomas (2010). 'Political Integration and National Parliaments in Europe', *Living Reviews in Democracy* 2, available at http://www.livingreviews.org/lrd-2010-5.

Winzen, Thomas (2012). 'National Parliamentary Control of European Union Affairs: A Cross-National and Longitudinal Comparison', *West European Politics*, 35:3, 657–72.

Winzen, Thomas (2013). 'European Integration and National Parliamentary Oversight Institutions', *European Union Politics*, 14:2, 297–323.

Executive Privilege Reaffirmed? Parliamentary Scrutiny of the CFSP and CSDP

ARIELLA HUFF

The EU's Common Foreign and Security Policy (CFSP) and Common Security and Defence Policy (CSDP) occupy a unique space in EU governance. Both policies have supranational elements, yet their formally intergovernmental status shields them from the increased scrutiny powers granted to national parliaments after Lisbon. National parliamentary scrutiny of these policy areas has thus received relatively little attention. Using an analytical framework of 'authority, ability and attitude', this paper argues that attitude, meaning MPs' willingness to scrutinise CFSP, is the most important factor in explaining the empirical variation in the quantity and quality of national parliamentary scrutiny of CFSP. Drawing on qualitative research and interviews conducted as part of the OPAL project, the paper demonstrates that formal powers do not, in practice, equate to 'strong' scrutiny, arguing that the strongest parliaments are those that make CFSP scrutiny a systematic, normalised and culturally accepted part of parliamentarians' everyday work.

The EU's Common Foreign and Security Policy (CFSP) and Common Security and Defence Policy (CSDP) are situated at the nexus of two fields that have generally proven problematic for parliamentary scrutiny: foreign and security policy, and EU integration. Many European legislatures have long treated foreign policy as a matter for executive competence, having limited involvement in policy-making and weak scrutiny mechanisms relative to other fields. This problem is often exacerbated in CFSP/CSDP, where policy-making takes place at a level even further removed from national parliaments. The cases of CFSP and CSDP thus provide special insight into how national parliaments oversee non-legislative aspects of EU policy, in which scrutiny activity may be more ad hoc, less automatic, and less institutionalised than it is for EU legislation. Essentially, these policy areas pose the question: if national parliaments are not required automatically to scrutinise an aspect of EU policy, will they do so anyway, and under what circumstances?

Despite removing the Maastricht pillar structure to reflect the various dimensions of the EU's external relations, the Lisbon Treaty perpetuated this insofar as it reiterated the 'intergovernmental' decision-making processes, explicitly forbidding the use of legislative acts in CFSP and preserving the unanimity requirement for CSDP (Art. 31 Treaty on European Union [TEU]). Moreover, the European Parliament's powers remain severely limited in this field, relative to its role as a co-legislator. Thus, with the exception of the provision on establishing an interparliamentary forum for debate on CFSP/CSDP issues (Art. 10, Protocol 1 Treaty of Lisbon), the Treaty implicitly maintained the intergovernmental model of oversight, whereby the democratic scrutiny of CFSP/CSDP is provided primarily by national parliaments monitoring the actions of their governments.

However, despite its decision-making structures, many scholars have noted that CFSP/CSDP is not purely intergovernmental, but rather carried out at multiple levels comprising both intergovernmental and supranational elements (e.g. Lord 2011; Stavridis 2006; Wagner 2005, 2006a) – even before taking into account the wider field of 'external relations', which includes many areas of EU competence including trade and development policy. Helene Sjursen, for example, has argued that CFSP policy-making structures, particularly after the establishment of the European External Action Service (EEAS), have become so intricate that it has created a 'fuzziness' about where responsibilities lie (Sjursen 2011: 1084). This has allowed the European Parliament to expand its role by, for example, exercising control over the financing of the EEAS, but has done little to help national parliaments gain any leverage over their governments in areas that remain dominated by intergovernmental decision-making processes.

This problem is further compounded by the particular nature of foreign and security policy scrutiny, which, as Hänggi (2004: 15) notes, tends to be relatively weak in most political systems. This field is often characterised by considerable information asymmetry, with parliaments lacking the expertise or access to sensitive information necessary for effective scrutiny of government (Kesgin and Kaarbo 2010: 21). Events may move quickly, leaving parliaments able only to question their governments after actions have already been taken. Concerned with domestic matters that are perceived as more important to voters, parliaments may also lack the will to pursue governments aggressively in this field, and may be wary of undermining their governments' standing abroad (Greene 2004: 30; Kesgin and Kaarbo 2010: 21). These problems are magnified in the case of CFSP/CSDP, where the urgency, opacity and secrecy of the 'complex bargaining games' involved in decision-making hinder the capacity of parliaments to control and oversee their governments' decisions at European level (Bono 2006: 441–43).

In the case of CSDP, scholars have used detailed process-tracing to show how parliaments have scrutinised particular case study missions (Bono 2005; Peters *et al.* 2008, 2010, 2011; Wagner 2006b). However, with respect to issues decided under the CFSP framework more broadly – including military and civilian crisis management, declarative diplomacy, the issuing of sanctions against third countries and the EU's participation in international negotiation and mediation – there remains almost no empirical, comparative evidence of how, in practice, national parliaments approach and attempt to mitigate the challenges outlined above, both formally and informally. What types of powers can parliaments exercise over issues decided under the framework of CFSP and how can strength or weakness be evaluated? Do parliaments have access to sufficient time and resources to make effective use of those powers? Do MPs even display any interest in scrutinising CFSP in the first place and if not, why not?

This paper attempts to answer these questions and, in turn, to develop an initial explanatory model for variation between parliaments in terms of scrutiny outcomes. The paper is organised around a comparative framework developed by Born and Hänggi in their work on parliamentary control over the use of military force under international auspices, evaluating parliaments on the basis of three criteria: *authority*, *ability* and *attitude* (Born and Hänggi 2004, 2005). In essence, this formulation splits the concept of 'capacity', outlined in the Introduction to this volume, into two interlinked parts (formal powers and resource access), with the role of 'attitude' addressing the question of 'motivation' (cf. Auel and Christiansen 2015). Although Born and Hänggi apply this framework specifically to parliamentary scrutiny of the use of military force, it is equally useful for studying how parliamentary scrutiny of all CFSP-related issues is carried out in practice, as it allows for in-depth comparisons between individual parliaments whilst accounting for their very different practices and cultures. None of the three elements is sufficient to explain parliamentary activity in this field, but each is necessary. Born and Hänggi describe these three concepts as interlinked, attaching no priority to any one in terms of which is most important in determining scrutiny outcomes. Similarly, Peters *et al.* (2011: 18) argue that there is 'no clear hierarchy' in the relative importance of formal powers and attitudes. However, in practice the bulk of the existing scholarship on the question of parliamentary scrutiny of CFSP/CSDP has focused primarily on authority, specifically with respect to parliamentary 'war powers' (e.g. Anghel *et al.* 2008; Dieterich *et al.* 2008, 2010; Peters *et al.* 2008, 2010; Wagner 2006a). Although this literature is detailed and valuable, it tells us little about the formal powers that parliaments have to oversee the decisions their governments make on the vast majority of CFSP issues that do not involve military force.[1]

The questions of ability and attitude have received even less systematic attention, despite Bono's finding that a parliaments' level of formal powers cannot fully account for the practice of parliamentary scrutiny (Bono 2005: 220). To a large extent, this may simply reflect practical considerations. Born and Hänggi identify large defence committees, administrative and expert support, as well as access to timely and accurate information, as the constituent elements of ability (Born and Hänggi 2005: 5–9; Peters *et al.* 2011: 2). However, these factors are difficult to evaluate, as their most easily measured components – the size of a committee, for example, or the number of support staff – do not account for more qualitative, subjective considerations like the level of staff or parliamentarian expertise. In the case of attitude, Born and Hänggi suggest that assessing a given chamber's attitude toward CFSP scrutiny requires extensive qualitative analysis of the political conditions and dynamics in each country, which makes data difficult to acquire and compare (Born and Hänggi 2005: 11). Like Bono, Peters *et al.* use the concept in evaluating the roles played by national parliaments in scrutinising specific CSDP operations, but although this provides great detail on how parliaments tackled individual missions, this approach cannot be used to make systematic comparisons (Peters *et al.* 2011: 2).

First, this paper will use the tripartite formula to map the authority, ability and attitude of the case study parliaments, paying as much attention to the latter two categories as to formal powers. Second, the paper takes this framework a step further by using the interaction between the three elements to propose a model for explaining variation between different parliaments in terms of their scrutiny activity in CFSP/CSDP. Are the most active and effective scrutinisers simply those with the strongest formal powers to hold their governments accountable *ex ante* and *post hoc*? Is there a direct correlation between strong formal powers, good access to resources and parliamentarians' willingness to hold governments accountable? If not, what appears to be the most important of the three factors in explaining how active and effective a parliament is in scrutinising CFSP?

A further advantage of this tripartite framework is that it facilitates holistic definitions of parliamentary strength and scrutiny across a number of dimensional axes. First, it can present a more realistic empirical picture of parliamentary 'strength' or 'weakness', based both on the capacity of parliaments *and* on their willingness to use that capacity to control or question their governments (cf. Auel and Christiansen 2015). Assessments of 'strength' as employed here are also reflective, deriving in part from how parliamentarians actually perceive the quality and effectiveness of their own scrutiny efforts. Second, the choice to de-emphasise the importance of formal powers facilitates a definition of scrutiny that can incorporate what Auel and de Wilde have noted are the dual functions of a parliament: private accountability of government to parliament (i.e. traditional concepts of 'influence') *and* providing an arena for public debate (Auel 2007: 504; de Wilde 2011: 686). This approach allows for a comparative analysis that still takes into account the individual role and political context of each parliament, evaluating them both in relation to each other and with reference to the particular roles they play in their country's political system. For example, based on a more simplistic and absolute conception of 'strength' as formal power and 'scrutiny' as control, the Folketing clearly emerges as much stronger in CFSP scrutiny than the relatively powerless House of Lords. Yet although this concept of strength cannot be ignored altogether, within the context of the Lords' role in the British political system as an arena for debate and provider of expert advice to government, the House should arguably be seen as 'stronger' than its lack of formal authority would suggest.

Taking a sociological institutionalist approach, as outlined in the Introduction to this volume, this paper argues that the *attitude* of MPs toward CFSP scrutiny constitutes the most important factor in explaining scrutiny outcomes – and, thus, variation across parliaments – because the policy's non-legislative status means that scrutiny is rarely automatic and thus depends on MPs' willingness to engage with the topic (cf. Auel and Christiansen 2015). Although formal powers and resources can constrain or empower MPs, having a profound intervening effect on the ultimate quality and scope of scrutiny, whether parliaments choose to make full use of their capacity is largely contingent on the broader normative context in which they operate, which in turn is influenced by parliamentary culture, political salience and party-political fault lines.

The paper focuses on seven case study countries – Britain, Poland, Germany, the Netherlands, Denmark, France and Italy. This group offers wide variation with respect to formal powers of control in CFSP, and includes both 'working parliaments' with largely committee-focused scrutiny and 'debating chambers' that tend to conduct more scrutiny through the plenary.[2] Some of the comparative tables refer only to lower chambers for the sake of simplicity and coherence, but the qualitative discussions that follow draw on examples from both upper and lower chambers where possible.

The paper draws on in-depth qualitative research carried out as part of the Observatory of Parliaments After Lisbon (OPAL) project. In order to understand the empirical reality of the practice of scrutiny, and how formal rules and capabilities actually interact with MPs' individual interests and attitudes, the paper presents evidence from semi-structured interviews carried out with parliamentarians and parliamentary staff across the case study countries. The next three sections evaluate these seven parliaments in terms of authority, ability and attitude, in turn. The conclusion then examines how the inclusion of ability and, more importantly, attitude challenges and changes a typology of 'strong' and 'weak' based purely on formal powers, and suggests a research agenda for the future study of this under-explored field. Finally, it should be acknowledged here that the paper focuses specifically on CFSP rather than 'external relations' as a whole, despite the evident links between all aspects of EU foreign policy, as the goal of the study is to contribute to a broader understanding of how parliaments scrutinise non-legislative aspects of EU policy. By the same token, it must also be acknowledged that many of the examples cited are drawn from CSDP, reflecting the existing literature's heavy emphasis on parliamentary scrutiny of the defence aspect of EU foreign policy. However, data and illustrations from the wider field of CFSP are employed wherever possible.

Authority: Formal Powers

The concept of *authority* refers to the formal powers available to parliaments to legislate on foreign and security policy and to scrutinise and oversee their governments. This can be further sub-divided into *ex ante* powers (mandates and troop deployment vetoes), *post hoc* powers (ability to ask questions, conduct inquiries and hold votes of confidence), and budgetary control. Table 1 shows the range of authority available to each of the seven case studies. On the basis of the powers outlined in Table 1, the authority level of each case study parliament would suggest the rough typology of parliamentary strength presented in Table 2.

The ability to issue mandates to ministers before Council meetings remains arguably the most potent instrument available to parliaments to exert influence over, and to scrutinise, government decision-making in CFSP. Germany boasts a formal mandating system, while the Dutch parliament employs a system of informal mandates that are considered to have de facto binding status, including for CFSP. These mandates tend to be formulated in a flexible manner to give governments some negotiating leeway, but governments comply with them in practice, meaning that MPs are relatively satisfied with their level of formal power (although this is particularly true of MPs from majority parties) (Bundestag MP, 24 May 2012; Bundestag clerk, 20 June 2012; TK clerk, 27 March 2012; EK MP, 23 October 2012).[3] Perhaps counter-intuitively this suggests that, for mandating parliaments, foreign and security policy conducted under EU auspices may be easier to scrutinise than national foreign and security policy, because their control over the decisions of ministers in the Council is often greater than their control of ministers in bilateral negotiations or other intergovernmental fora, where mandating is not used.

The British, Polish, French and Italian parliaments, by contrast, have no ability to dictate or control the government's negotiating position in CFSP matters *ex ante*.[4] These parliaments are empowered to ask questions, conduct inquiries and publish reports, but scrutiny of CFSP effectively takes place on a *post hoc* basis. *Post hoc* scrutiny of this kind, although generally considered to be less effective than *ex ante* mandating or veto power, can still provide a way for legislatures to hold their governments publicly accountable for their actions and thus to exert political pressure on future decisions (Dieterich *et al.* 2008: 8–9). However, the use of these procedures is not systematic, but rather heavily dependent on whether MPs are willing to expend time, energy and resources on interrogating their governments after CFSP decisions have already

TABLE 1
FORMAL POWERS OVER CFSP AND CSDP: LOWER CHAMBERS ONLY

Power (lower chambers only)	UK	PL	DE	NL	DK*	FR	IT
Binding mandating (*ex ante*)	–	–	√	√†	√	–	–
Troop dispatch veto (*ex ante*)	–	–	√	–	N/A	–	√
Post hoc questioning/inquiry	√	√	√	√	√	√	√
Budget veto over individual missions	–	–	√**	–	N/A	–	√
Ability to amend or veto overall FP budget	–	√	√	√	√	√	√

*Denmark does not participate in the CSDP.
**The Bundestag does not have an explicit budgetary veto, but budgets are included in the mission proposal.
†The Dutch mandating system is not legally formal, but is considered politically binding.
Sources: Born and Hänggi (2005); Dieterich *et al.* (2010); Smith *et al.* (2012); OPAL research.

TABLE 2
'STRENGTH' IN CFSP SCRUTINY: AUTHORITY ONLY

Very strong	Strong	Weak	Very weak
Germany	Netherlands	Poland	France
Denmark	Italy		UK

been made. Moreover, mandating systems have the additional advantage of, by definition, requiring ministers to appear before parliament at a relatively early stage in CFSP negotiations, before decisions have been made. In the British, Polish and French systems, by contrast, ministers are not formally required to appear before parliament to discuss the agenda for upcoming Council meetings. As a result, it remains up to individual committee chairs and members whether they choose actively to pursue a particular CFSP-related topic (HoC clerk A, 23 May 2012; Sejm MP, 18 April 2013).

With respect to vetoes over the dispatch of troops and 'power of the purse', meanwhile, interviews suggested that these aspects of authority are considerably less important than mandating in determining the quality of scrutiny. In large part this reflects the fact that both apply to military CSDP missions, which comprise only a small fraction of CFSP-related decisions. Moreover, rejection of proposed missions, mission budgets or mandate extensions takes place at a very late stage in the policy-making process, long after the decision to launch a mission has been taken at the European level, and after negotiations about the potential mission's size, scope, budget and mandate. At this point, proposed missions have a certain momentum; in the Italian case, votes have even been taken after missions had begun (CdD clerk, 7 November 2012; CdD clerk, 15 November 2012; Senato clerk, 14 November 2012). Similarly, the role of 'power of the purse' over foreign and defence policy expenditure is in practice quite limited (Dieterich *et al.* 2008: 15). As Table 1 shows, most of the case study legislatures have the power to amend or at least to approve foreign and defence policy budgets, with the exception of the UK parliament, which has no power to amend proposed expenditures and in practice votes through all government appropriations en bloc (Smith *et al.* 2012: 91). However, with the exception of some of the costs of military CSDP missions, CFSP as a whole is funded from the Community budget and is thus not open to indepth, line-item scrutiny from national parliaments, except insofar as they can control and/or debate their governments' contributions to the overall EU budget, which is considerably removed from the actual point of CFSP expenditure.

Ability: The Structure of Scrutiny

The question of ability relates to the resources and support available to parliaments to enable them to make use of their formal authority. On the whole, the evidence suggests that parliaments in which CFSP scrutiny is fully mainstreamed (i.e. systematically involves the Foreign Affairs and Defence Committees) are better equipped to oversee the policy than those in which the EU Affairs Committee alone is responsible for it, as CFSP can be integrated into oversight of national foreign policy more generally, and the scrutiny process benefits from the policy expertise of Foreign Affairs Committee (FAC) members (Gatterman *et al.* 2013: 7–8). Table 3 offers an overview of the relative levels of involvement of FACs and Defence Committees (DCs) in CFSP scrutiny across the case study parliaments, using lower chambers only in this case for effective comparison (many upper chambers have different arrangements – e.g. the French Sénat's combined Foreign Affairs and Defence Committee).

Those committees described as having a 'high' level of involvement in CFSP scrutiny have full responsibility for the policy area or share responsibility equally with the EU Affairs Committee (EAC); those with a 'medium' level have some input in an advisory capacity, or scrutinise CFSP on an ad hoc basis alongside the EAC; finally, the committees with 'low' involvement in scrutiny are neither formally nor informally considered responsible for scrutinising CFSP (note: this does not take into account whether the committee in question *actually conducts* CFSP scrutiny, but rather simply whether such scrutiny is technically considered to be its responsibility). In general, across all cases FACs take a stronger role in both CFSP and CSDP scrutiny than DCs, which tend to be more occupied with questions of national defence and procurement than small CSDP missions.

The Tweede Kamer provides a good example of how a fully mainstreamed system can benefit CFSP scrutiny. Its Foreign Affairs and Defence Committees have full responsibility for oversight of the policy; they choose their own priority areas for scrutiny and ministers must report directly to them both before and after Council meetings. Moreover, these committees are well supported by cross-cutting EU staff who provide information on Council agenda items and other issues at MPs' request (TK clerk, 27 March 2012; TK MP, 20 June 2012). The Bundestag is structured in a similar way, with the FAC taking overall responsibility for both CFSP and CSDP with the European Affairs and Defence Committees playing advisory roles (Bundestag MP, 23 May 2012; Bundestag clerk, 20 June 2012). Several upper chambers are also well configured for CFSP scrutiny. In the French Sénat, the incorporation of Foreign Affairs and Defence into a single committee is particularly effective for scrutinising CFSP; the Committee has issued several reports on a range of CFSP topics (Sénat clerk, 14 June 2013). Similarly, the House of Lords European Union Select Committee has six sub-committees focusing on particular policy areas, with Sub-Committee C (External Affairs) responsible for a wide range of CFSP-related issues, as well as for development and trade policy.

Chambers in which FACs and/or DCs are not specifically and systematically tasked with CFSP scrutiny, by contrast, on the whole engage in far less discussion of CFSP issues. In the House of Commons, EU affairs are concentrated in the European Scrutiny Committee (ESC), with other committees involved only on an ad hoc basis. The Foreign Affairs and Defence Committees can choose to investigate CFSP issues if they wish, but are not required to

ROLE OF FOREIGN AFFAIRS AND DEFENCE COMMITTEES IN CFSP/CSDP SCRUTINY: LOWER CHAMBERS ONLY

	UK	PL	DE	NL	DK	FR	IT
Level of FAC involvement in **CFSP** scrutiny	Medium	Low	High	High		Medium	High
Level of DC involvement in **CSDP** scrutiny	Low	Low	Medium	High	N/A	Medium	High

High ■ Medium ▨ Low □

Source: OPAL research (see list of interviews).

do so, and scrutiny is not automatic or routine. For example, renewals or extensions of CSDP mission mandates are not typically scrutinised (HoC clerk A, 23 May 2012). The policy must compete alongside other pressing concerns for space on the agenda and can thus be overlooked, particularly if the members have little interest in pursuing it (HoC clerk A, 23 May 2012). Similarly, no one committee has full responsibility for CFSP scrutiny in either chamber of the Polish parliament. The Sejm FAC typically allocates only one meeting per annum to discussion of CFSP/CSDP, and does not consider scrutiny of this area to be a major responsibility – even though several of its members sit on both the FAC and EAC (Sejm clerk, 25 April 2013; Sejm MP, 18 April 2013). As a result, CFSP tends to fall between two stools in both chambers, with neither the FAC nor the EAC taking systematic responsibility for scrutinising it (Sejm clerk, 25 April 2013; Sénat clerk, 23 April 2013).

Despite the clear differences between mainstream and non-mainstream parliaments, there remains one problem relating to ability cited across the board: access to timely information, particularly for members of opposition parties.[5] This confirms the contention of much of the literature that information asymmetry remains a particular problem in this field (Born and Hänggi 2005: 5–9; Kesgin and Kaarbo 2010: 21). Members of the Bundestag EAC, for example, complained that the legislature did not obtain information about the impending launch of Operation Atalanta until almost immediately before the deployment, despite the formal requirement for parliament to approve German participation in the operation (Bundestag MP, 23 May 2012; Bundestag clerk, 20 June 2012). Similarly, an Italian parliamentary clerk claimed that the government gave so little information to the Senato before the operation that most of what senators knew when voting to approve the mission could have been found 'on the Internet'; another Italian suggested that the Camera Dei Deputati received 'almost nothing' on CFSP (Senato clerk, 14 November 2012; CdD clerk, 15 November 2012). It has long been a bugbear of the House of Commons ESC that the majority of overrides to the scrutiny reserve – the practice whereby the government is expected to refrain from making decisions at EU level until parliament has had sufficient time to consider the issue – are made by the Foreign Office in relation to CFSP/CSDP decisions, usually when parliament is in recess (House of Commons 2013: 42). This problem is especially pronounced in the British case given the document-oriented nature of the scrutiny system; since CFSP documents such as action plans are classed as 'non-legislative', they are often not sent to parliament for scrutiny (House of Commons 2013: 41). Even members of the Folketing sometimes use informal networks to acquire information, as neither government nor EU sources always deliver documents in time to conduct proper scrutiny (Danish former MEP, 27 November 2012). This problem therefore also highlights the critical role of political will in ensuring adequate CFSP scrutiny, as MPs must often pro-actively seek or agitate for access to relevant documents.

Attitude: Domestic Parliamentary Culture, Political Salience and Party Politicisation

Yet how can the political will to hold government accountable – i.e. 'attitude' – be evaluated, and how can it be compared across parliaments in a systematic way? This problem is also reflected in the attempts to explain how attitudes are formed. The literature has largely defined attitude as influenced by 'pressures from government, media and public opinion' as well as the merits of each proposed operation or decision (Born and Hänggi 2005: 11; Peters *et al.* 2011: 2). Although there is clear empirical validity to this argument, its reliance on the specific context of each individual decision or operation in each individual parliament renders effective comparisons quite difficult.

Yet it remains possible to develop a conception of attitude and its constituent elements that can be used to compare, albeit in somewhat broad brush-strokes, across parliaments. In its discussion of sociological institutionalist explanations for the 'motivation' of MPs to participate in EU affairs scrutiny more generally, the Introduction to this volume highlights the importance of parliamentary culture and expectations and norms regarding the appropriate roles for parliamentarians vis-à-vis government (Auel and Christiansen 2015). Applying these concepts to parliamentary scrutiny of CFSP, we can expect MPs to be interested in actively pursuing CFSP scrutiny in parliaments where scrutiny of both EU affairs and foreign policy are perceived as important elements of MPs' work, at least within the relevant committees. Taking into account the party-political dimensions suggested by Born and Hänggi, we might also expect MPs to be more willing to scrutinise CFSP in cases where it is of high political salience, and moreover where there is a high level of polarisation between parties (Born and Hänggi 2005: 11). This is likely to be especially true where political contestation over CFSP can be mapped easily onto existing government/opposition or party-political dynamics.

A Culture of Executive Privilege?

With respect to the role of parliamentary culture as it relates to foreign policy and EU affairs scrutiny, empirical evidence indeed suggests that a parliament that tends to perceive foreign and security policy as matters for executive control is unlikely to put significant energy into CFSP and CSDP oversight (and, conversely, that parliaments where MPs consider it important to scrutinise CFSP will generally attempt to do so). Crucially, this does not appear in all cases to reflect, or stem from, the level of formal power that a legislature has over CFSP. In some cases, notably the Dutch, German and Danish, there is a relatively straightforward 'fit' between high levels of formal power over CFSP and willingness to use those powers, with MPs citing foreign policy oversight – in these three cases, largely in the context of committee work – as an important aspect of their jobs (Folketing MP, 22 November 2012; TK MP, 20 June 2012; Bundestag MP, 24 May 2012; Bundestag clerk, 20 June 2012). A staff member in the Bundestag even commented that the chamber kept tighter control over the executive on foreign policy issues than other national parliaments such as the French (Bundestag clerk, 20 June 2012). This coheres with existing studies that find formal power to be a strong indicator of parliamentary activity (e.g. Raunio 2005). However, the other case studies present a much more nuanced and mixed picture that challenges the division of certain parliaments into 'strong' and 'weak' based on formal powers alone, and suggest that attitude can trump both authority and ability in terms of determining the real quantity and quality of CFSP scrutiny.

The Italian parliament appears, on paper, to be among the stronger of the case study chambers, with extensive powers of formal control (cf. Tables 1 and 2). Moreover, the Foreign Affairs Committee in both chambers takes full responsibility for CFSP scrutiny; in the Camera dei Deputati, the FAC even has a sub-committee for EU foreign policy, which approximates to the previous section's understanding of an ideal-type structure for maximising ability. Yet there remains a long-standing, entrenched normative convention that foreign and defence policy should be a matter for executive control, and an 'unwritten rule' that the legislature's main responsibility is to support government action (CdD clerk, 7 November 2012; CdD clerk, 14 November 2012; Senato clerk, 14 November 2012). This appears to be particularly true in cases of relatively low political salience or public interest, as is usually the case for CFSP (see below) (CdD clerk, 14 November 2012). As such, despite the strong 'author-ity' of the Italian parliament in terms of CFSP scrutiny, in practice such scrutiny is extremely limited and, where it does take place, has been described as 'mockery' and 'theatre' (CdD clerk, 14 November 2012, Italian senator, 14 November 2012; Senato clerk, 14 November 2012).

On the other side of the spectrum stands the House of Lords, which is among the weakest chambers in this study in terms of authority (although its level of ability is comparatively high, given both the structure of its scrutiny system and the unusually high degree of expertise of its members). Yet this chamber is extraordinarily active in CFSP scrutiny, issuing an average of two large-scale reports per year on CFSP- and CSDP-related topics (see http://www.parliament.uk). This reflects the chamber's self-perception as taking a 'longer view' on policy than the lower house, its own internal culture emphasising con-sensus and technical expertise rather than party-political antagonism, and its role as a 'constructive' advisor to government (HoL Peer, 5 June 2013).

The other chambers in this study fall on a spectrum in between these two extremes, with wide variation in terms of perceived responsibility for CFSP/CSDP scrutiny. In no cases was a culture of executive dominance in foreign policy discussed as explicitly as in the Italian, but the importance of individual members' interests was regularly cited as critical in determining the quantity and quality of scrutiny (HoC clerk A, 23 May 2012; Sejm clerk, 25 April 2013; Polish senator, 15 May 2013; Sénat clerk, 14 June 2013). One clerk in the House of Commons commented that if MPs in sectoral committees like the FAC do not care about EU issues, they cannot be forced to undertake scrutiny of those issues (HoC clerk B, 23 May 2012). The Polish, French and UK parliaments, although the weakest of the seven cases in terms of formal war powers, all display regular and sustained interest in general foreign and defence policy scrutiny, particularly in cases of high political salience in those countries (e.g. the Syrian conflict for Britain and France, which both parliaments debated at length; or the Ukraine protests which have generated much discussion in the Polish parliament). However, their interest in CFSP is considerably more sporadic. We must therefore turn to the question of political salience to explain when MPs are willing to invest time and resources in CFSP scrutiny, and when they are not.

Political Salience – or Lack Thereof

The level of CFSP's political salience is difficult to compare systematically, since it varies over time and depending on the specific issue or mission under discussion. CFSP *in general* is of relatively low salience across the board, particularly since the advent of the financial and eurozone crises which have captured so much public and political attention since 2008. According to the autumn 2013 Standard Eurobarometer data, 'The EU's influence in the world' is cited as a major concern by less than 10 per cent of respondents in all cases except the Netherlands, where 11 per cent of respondents cited it as important.[6] This coheres with interview evidence from several countries, which suggested that the EU's foreign policy was relatively low on the priority list of many MPs, and had a relatively low profile compared to issues perceived as 'national' foreign and security policy (Bundestag MP, 24 May 2012; Sénat clerk, 14 June 2013; CdD clerk, 14 November 2012). In the UK, for example, an informal tradition has begun to emerge whereby the government consults parliament before large, controversial troop deployments, as it did in 2003 for Iraq and in 2013 regarding a proposed operation in Syria; however, no votes have ever taken place in advance of CSDP operations, nor are debates held routinely in committee sessions (HoC clerk A, 23 May 2012).

Moreover, there appears to be little correlation between anti-CFSP sentiment in public opinion and MPs' willingness to scrutinise the policy. Although Raunio (2005) has demonstrated that the presence of a Eurosceptic public is correlated with more parliamentary scrutiny of EU affairs, this does not appear to be the case for CFSP specifically. Table 4 shows support and opposition to CFSP according to 2013 Eurobarometer data across the seven case studies.

Although we might expect the presence of significant popular opposition to CFSP to result in greater levels of scrutiny activity, this is not the case for the UK – where activity has declined relative to the early 2000s, although the level of popular support for CFSP has remained roughly constant at 35–45 per cent – and neither Danish nor Dutch interviews suggested that members of parliament felt compelled to scrutinise CFSP due to popular opposition. On the opposite side of the spectrum, the two states with by far the highest levels of support for

	For	Against	Don't know
UK	42	45	13
DK	44	53	3
NL	53	41	6
FR	61	30	9
IT	66	22	12
PL	73	18	9
DE	75	19	6

Source: Standard Eurobarometer 79, Spring 2013: http://ec.europa.eu/public_opinion/archives/eb/eb79/eb79_anx_en.pdf.

CFSP – Germany and Poland – are worlds apart in terms of MPs' willingness to scrutinise the policy, with German MPs taking significant interest in CSDP while Polish MPs give it very little attention (Bundestag MP, 24 May 2012; Bundestag clerk, 20 June 2012; Sejm MP, 25 April 2013; Sejm MP, 18 April 2013; Polish senator, 15 May 2013; Sejm policy analyst, 19 April 2013).

Party-Political Polarisation

One major difficulty in translating public opinion to the parliamentary level is that it rarely maps perfectly onto the split of opinion within parliaments and political parties. Writing on EU integration issues more generally, Raunio (2011: 321) suggests that parties might push for more debate in cases where the specific policy issue can be 'incorporated into the cleavages structuring domestic policy contestation (mainly the left–right dimension)', particularly with respect to public mechanisms such as plenary debates, interpellations and PQs. One might therefore expect that the extent of party-political polarisation over CFSP may affect MPs' attitudes toward scrutiny; in cases where there is great dissension, we might see greater interest among MPs in holding governments accountable for their actions.

The Chapel Hill Expert Survey includes a measure on parties' support for a common EU foreign policy. By taking the standard deviation of the average score for all parliamentary parties' positions on CFSP, one can infer, albeit somewhat crudely, the extent of party-political polarisation on this issue within each of the seven case studies.[7] If such polarisation does increase MP's eagerness to scrutinise CFSP, we should expect some degree of correlation between those parliaments with high levels of polarisation and those where MPs display a strong interest in CFSP scrutiny.

However, as Table 5 shows, no such pattern is evident. The two parliaments in which MPs have the greatest willingness to scrutinise CFSP, according to the interview data – the Dutch and German – are in the bottom half of the polarisation scale. In both of these cases, the Chapel Hill survey and the

TABLE 5
STANDARD DEVIATION OF PARTY-POLITICAL SUPPORT LEVELS FOR CFSP, IN
ASCENDING ORDER

IT	NL	DE	DK	UK	PL	FR
1.13	1.48	1.49	1.66	1.81	1.81	1.89

Source: Bakker *et al.* (2012).

interview data suggest broad cross-party support for CFSP among the major parties, with only Eurosceptic and far-left parties dissenting (Bakker *et al.* 2012; Bundestag MP, 23 May 2012; Bundestag MP, 24 May 2013; TK clerk, 27 March 2012; TK MP, 20 June 2012; EK MP, 23 October 2012). By contrast, Poland scores highly for polarisation, but its MPs remain largely uninterested in CFSP, compared to other aspects of foreign and defence policy (Sejm MP, 25 April 2013; Sejm MP, 18 April 2013; Polish senator, 15 May 2013; Sejm policy analyst, 19 April 2013). As such, polarisation on its own appears to offer little potential explanatory value for analysing the empirical variation in attitudes between parliaments, unless treated in concert with parliamentary culture and the related question of intra-party coherence.

Intra-Party Coherence

In line with Raunio's (2011: 321) argument that parties are likely to publicise aspects of EU affairs that fit well into established party-political cleavages, we may expect CFSP to receive relatively little attention if it divides opinion within parties. This is particularly relevant for parliaments classed as 'debating arenas', where much activity takes place in the plenary (see Auel *et al.* 2014). In arguably the best example of a 'debating arena', the House of Commons, public debates and discussion about CSDP reached a peak during the early 2000s, as the Conservative Party adopted the issue as a pillar of its broader Eurosceptic narrative against the Labour government.[8] Since that time the volume of public, politicised debate on the issue has dropped sharply, especially after the 2010 elections that brought the Conservatives to power in coalition with the more pro-European Liberal Democrats. The coalition partners are now reluctant to initiate major debates on the policy since it exposes cleavages both between and within them; meanwhile Labour, in opposition, has little reason to draw attention to a policy for which its support is lukewarm and ambivalent at best. Despite occasional flurries of activity relating to specific operations or, in December 2013, to the European Council summit on defence issues, these debates typically feature a small but consistent handful of MPs who have objected to the concept of a common EU foreign and defence policy for many years.[9] However, more extensive qualitative research at the level of individual parties will be required to determine the relative explanatory power of intra-party coherence in determining MPs' attitudes toward CFSP scrutiny.

Conclusion: Can't Scrutinise, Won't Scrutinise?

Taking into account the evaluations of ability and attitude presented here, one can suggest re-arranging the typology of parliaments presented in Table 2 as shown in Table 6. Thus the Netherlands moves from 'Strong' to 'Very strong' on the basis of its members' enthusiasm for actively pursuing CFSP/CSDP scrutiny, while the Folketing's relative lack of interest in the topic, compounded by the lack of integration between EU and Foreign Affairs committees, takes it from 'Very strong' to 'Strong'. Meanwhile, both Italy and Poland drop to 'Weak' and 'Very weak' respectively, on the basis of their members' self-reported unwillingness to hold their governments privately and/or publicly accountable for CFSP decision-making. The UK system is split: the House of Commons remains weak due to the ad hoc nature of its scrutiny, but moves up one category in acknowledgement of its willingness to debate publicly a range of CFSP issues. Finally, the House of Lords is described as 'strong', which may initially seem counterintuitive given its relative lack of formal powers. Yet within the constraints of its limited authority it boasts a well-developed and active system of CFSP scrutiny, with members who take their scrutiny role very seriously.

This is not to argue that formal authority or ability are irrelevant to scrutiny outcomes. Both serve to constrain or empower MPs in their scrutiny efforts, and have a strong effect on the quality and quantity of scrutiny. For all its activity and the high quality and visibility of its scrutiny work, the House of Lords cannot reasonably be deemed 'stronger' than the Tweede Kamer or Bundestag, both of which can influence government decision-making *ex ante,* enjoy relatively high levels of access to expertise and support (through mainstreamed scrutiny systems), and are keenly interested in making use of their capacity. However, when evaluating the relative 'strength' or 'weakness' of parliamentary scrutiny, this paper argues that it is critical to judge parliaments not only in relation to one another, but in relation to their own, individual approach to parliamentary oversight. After all, the UK parliament does not formally control its government's decision-making *ex ante* in any policy field, but rather acts as an arena for public debate on key political issues; to ignore that nuance is to render comparisons between parliaments too artificial to be meaningful.

The empirical findings of this paper challenge the widespread association between formal power and 'strength' in national parliamentary scrutiny of EU affairs, commonly asserted by the literature on legislative scrutiny. Unlike scrutiny of EU legislation, oversight of the EU's foreign policy generally remains ad hoc, non-automatic and non-systematic, even in archetypically 'strong' parliaments like the Folketing. In this context, parliamentarians must first choose

TABLE 6
'STRENGTH' IN CFSP SCRUTINY, RECONSIDERED

Very strong	Strong	Weak	Very weak
Germany	Denmark	Italy	France
Netherlands	UK House of Lords	UK House of Commons	Poland

to make use of their authority and ability; if they remain uninterested in doing so, then scrutiny either does not happen at all (as is typical in the Polish case) or is largely a matter of going through the motions and rubber-stamping government actions (as in Italy). Thus, the elements of both authority and ability that best indicate strength are those that serve to make scrutiny a systematic, normatively accepted part of everyday parliamentary work.

The paper has also begun tentatively to explore the potential constituent elements of attitude, arguing that parliamentary culture, political salience, polarisation and intra-party coherence may all have some effect, albeit through complex interaction with one another. However, despite their critical role in determining scrutiny outcomes, the attitudes of MPs toward CFSP scrutiny remain under-researched and poorly understood. Future researchers should aim to test both qualitatively and quantitatively the explanatory value of each of these factors on attitudes, and might also explore some potential external influences including, for example, national strategic culture and the attitude of government ministries toward CFSP.

Although this represents only an initial foray into developing a comprehensive conceptual and empirical understanding of national parliamentary scrutiny of CFSP, it has profound implications for the debate on the policy's democratic legitimacy. In an intergovernmental policy area, the role of national parliaments remains critical in holding member state governments both publicly and privately accountable for decisions on topics as significant as the EU's response to the Arab Spring and the issuing of sanctions against third countries. Yet it seems that although some parliaments strive to ensure adequate scrutiny of this field, others remain incapable, uninterested or both. Granting additional formal oversight powers can address only one part of this problem. Issues such as information access may be mitigated by increased interparliamentary cooperation, but many parliaments are strongly resistant to any cooperation that might lead to a greater role for the supranational level in CFSP (see Herranz-Surrallés 2014). In a policy area from which many parliaments have been excluded since long before the advent of CFSP, encouraging more and better scrutiny will require significant shifts in parliamentary practices, cultures and norms.

Acknowledgements

I would like to thank the Editors of this Special Issue and the two anonymous reviewers for their helpful feedback, and the entire OPAL team for their constructive criticisms of this paper. I particularly wish to thank my Cambridge colleagues Julie Smith and Geoffrey Edwards for their help, advice and comments at all stages of the paper's development. I am also very grateful to all those who agreed to be interviewed as part of this research. The usual disclaimer applies.

Disclosure Statement

No potential conflict of interests was reported by the author.

Notes

1. This includes most CSDP missions, of which two-thirds are civilian in nature and therefore not subject to the same parliamentary approval procedures.
2. These seven case studies were selected by the OPAL project for in-depth research. The case of Slovakia was also examined closely by the OPAL project, but there was not enough data on CFSP scrutiny to include it in this study.
3. The Folketing also has a formal mandating system, but it does not apply for defence issues, or for EU defence due to the Danish opt-out. As a result the Folketing remains somewhat marginalised in terms of CSDP.
4. The Polish parliament has a 'soft' mandating system for EU legislation that obliges the government to adopt the same position as the European Union Committee, or else to explain its decision. This does not apply to CFSP.
5. In their study of parliamentary scrutiny of Operation Atalanta, Peters *et al.* (2011: 7) found that members of opposition parties often had less access to information than their counterparts in governing parties. This was echoed in interviews for OPAL.
6. See Standard Eurobarometer 80, First Results: http://ec.europa.eu/public_opinion/archives/eb/eb80/eb80_first_en.pdf, p. 16 (accessed 22 December 2013).
7. To obtain a result reflective of the dynamic within each parliament, only parties with national parliamentary representation on 31 December 2013 were included in these calculations (thus, for example, the United Kingdom Independence Party was excluded).
8. See, for example, the PMQ session and plenary debates held on 22 November 2000 (House of Commons, Hansard vol. 357) and the Opposition Day debate of 27 October 2003 (House of Commons, Hansard vol. 412).
9. For example, a debate on EUTM Mali and EUTM Somalia took place in the European Committee – an ad hoc body to which a number of MPs are appointed to debate specific issues on the recommendation of the ESC – on 16 January 2013. The transcript is available at http://www.publications.parliament.uk/pa/cm201213/cmgeneral/euro/130,116/130116s01.htm.

References

Anghel, Suzana, Hans Born, Alex Dowling, and Teodora Fuior (2008). 'National Parliamentary Oversight of ESDP Missions.' in Peters Dirk, Wagner Wolfgang, and Deitelhoff Nicole (eds.), *The Parliamentary Control of European Security Policy*. ARENA Report No. 7/08, RECON Report No. 6. Oslo: ARENA, 51–76.

Auel, Katrin (2007). 'Democratic Accountability and National Parliaments: Redefining the Impact of Parliamentary Scrutiny in EU Affairs', *European Law Journal*, 13:4, 487–504.

Auel, Katrin, and Thomas Christiansen (2015). 'After Lisbon: National Parliaments in the European Union', *West European Politics*, 38:2, 261–81.

Auel, Katrin, Olivier Rozenberg, and Angela Tacea (2014). 'Fighting Back? And If Yes, How? Measuring Parliamentary Strength and Activity in EU Affairs', in Heftler Claudia, Neuhold Christine, and Rozenberg Olivier; Smith Julie, and Wessels Wolfgang, *The Palgrave Handbook of National Parliaments and the European Union*. Palgrave.

Bakker, Ryan, Catherine de Vries, Erica Edwards, Lisbet Hooghe, Seth Jolly, Gary Marks, Polk Jonathan, Jan Rovny, Marco Steenbergen, and Milada Vachudova (2012). 'Measuring Party Positions in Europe: The Chapel Hill Expert Survey Trend File, 1999–2010', *Party Politics*, 21:1, 143–52. doi:10.1177/1354068812462931.

Bono, Giovanna (2005). 'National Parliaments and EU External Military Operations: Is There Any Parliamentary Control?' *European Security* 14:2, 203–29.

Bono, Giovanna (2006). 'Challenges of Democratic Oversight of EU Security Policies', *European Security*, 15:4, 431–49.

Born, Hans, and Heiner Hänggi (2005). 'The Use of Force under International Auspices: Strengthening Parliamentary Accountability,' DCAF Policy Paper no. 7. Geneva: Centre for the Democratic Control of Armed Forces.

Dieterich, Sandra, Hartwig Hummel, and Stefan Marschall (2008). 'Strengthening Parliamentary "War Powers" in Europe: Lessons from 25 National Parliaments,' DCAF Policy Paper no. 27. Geneva: Centre for the Democratic Control of Armed Forces.

Dieterich, Sandra, Hartwig Hummel, and Marschall Stefan (2010). 'Parliamentary War Powers: A Survey of 25 European Parliaments,' DCAF Occasional Paper No. 21. Geneva: Centre for the Democratic Control of Armed Forces.

Gatterman, Katjana, Anna-Lena Högenauer, and Ariella Huff (2013). 'National Parliaments after Lisbon: Towards Mainstreaming of EU Affairs?' OPAL Online Paper Series 13/2013, available at http://www.opal-europe.org/tmp/Opal%20Online%20Paper/13.pdf (accessed 30 May 14).

Greene, Owen (2004). 'Democratic Governance and the Internationalisation of Security Policy: The Relevance of Parliaments', in Hans Born and Heiner Hänggi (ed.), *The Double Democratic Deficit: Parliamentary Accountability and the Use of Force under International Auspices*. Aldershot: Ashgate, 19–32.

Hänggi, Heiner (2004). 'The Use of Force under International Auspices: Parliamentary Accountability and "Democratic Deficits', in Hans Born and Heiner Hänggi (ed.), *The Double Democratic Deficit: Parliamentary Accountability and the Use of Force under International Auspices*. Aldershot: Ashgate, 3–18.

Herranz-Surrallés, Anna (2014). 'The EU's Multilevel Parliamentary (Battle)Field: Explaining Inter-Parliamentary Cooperation and Conflict in the Area of Foreign and Security Policy.' *West European Politics*, 37:5, 957–75.

House of Commons European Scrutiny Committee (28 November 2013). 'Reform of the European Scrutiny System in the House of Commons.' 24th Report of Session 2013–2014. London: The Stationary Office Limited.

Kesgin, Baris, and Juliet Kaarbo (2010). 'When and How Parliaments Influence Foreign Policy: The Case of Turkey's Iraq Decision', *International Studies Perspectives*, 11:1, 19–36.

Lord, Christopher (2011). 'The Political Theory and Practice of Parliamentary Participation in the Common Security and Defence Policy', *Journal of European Public Policy*, 18:8, 1133–50.

Peters, Dirk, Wolfgang Wagner, and Nicole Deitelhoff (2008). 'Parliaments and European Security Policy: Mapping the Parliamentary Field.' in Dirk Peters, Wolfgang Wagner, and Nicole Deitelhoff (eds.), *The Parliamentary Control of European Security Policy*. ARENA Report No. 7/08, RECON Report No. 6. Oslo: ARENA.

Peters, Dirk, Wolfgang Wagner, and Nicole Deitelhoff (2010). 'Parliaments and European Security Policy: Mapping the Parliamentary Field.' in Sophie Vanhoonacker, Hylke Dijkstra, and Heidi Maurer (eds.), *Understanding the Role of Bureaucracy in the European Security and Defence Policy*. European Integration online Papers, 14(1), available at http://eiop.or.at/eiop/index.php/eiop/article/view/2010_012a (accessed 28 February 2013).

Peters, Dirk, Wolfgang Wagner, and Cosima Glahn (2011). 'Parliamentary Control of Military Missions: The Case of the EU NAVFOR Atalanta,' RECON Online Working paper 2011/24, available at http://www.reconproject.eu/main.php/RECON_wp_1124.pdf?fileitem=5456368 (accessed 28 February 2013).

Raunio, Tapio (2005). 'Holding Governments Accountable in European Affairs: Explaining Cross-National Variation', *Journal of Legislative Studies*, 11:3–4, 319–42.

Raunio, Tapio (2011). 'The Gatekeepers of European Integration? The Functions of National Parliaments in the EU Political System', *Journal of European Integration*, 33:3, 303–21.

Sjursen, Helene (2011). 'Not so Intergovernmental After All? On Democracy and Integration in European Foreign and Security Policy', *Journal of European Public Policy*, 18:8, 1078–95.

Smith, Julie, Ariella Huff, and Geoffrey Edwards (2012). 'Towards a More Comprehensive, Strategic and Cost-Effective EU Foreign Policy: The Role of National Parliaments and the European Parliament'. Report prepared for the European Parliament Budgetary Affairs Committee. Brussels: European Parliament.

Stavridis, Stelios (2006). 'Why the EU's Constitutionalization and Parliamentarization Are Worsening the Existing Democratic Deficit in European Foreign and Defence Policies,' JMWP Working Paper no. 59, available at http://aei.pitt.edu/6113/1/jmwp59.pdf (accessed 20 February 2013).

Wagner, Wolfgang (2005). 'The Democratic Legitimacy of European Security and Defence Policy.' Occasional Paper no. 57. Paris: European Union Institute for Security Studies.

Wagner, Wolfgang (2006a). 'The Democratic Control of Military Power Europe', *Journal of European Public Policy*, 13:2, 200–16.

Wagner, Wolfgang (2006b). *Parliamentary Control of Military Missions: Accounting for Pluralism*, Occasional Paper no. 12. Geneva: Centre for the Democratic Control of Armed Forces.

de Wilde, Pieter (2011). '*Ex ante vs Ex* Post: the Trade-Off Between Partisan Conflict and Visibility in Debating EU Policy-Formulation in National Parliaments', *Journal of European Public Policy*, 18:5, 672–89.

Interviews (anonymous)

Bundestag MP & advisor, Left Party, 23/05/12
Bundestag MP, CDU, 24/05/12
Bundestag clerk, 20/06/12
House of Commons clerk A, 23/05/12
House of Commons clerk B, 23/05/12
House of Lords Peer & clerk, EU Select Committee, 05/06/13
Danish former MEP, 27/11/12
Folketing MP, Social Democratic Party, 22/11/12
Sejm clerk, 25/04/13
Sejm MP, Law and Justice, 18/04/13
Sejm MP, Law and Justice, 25/04/13
Sejm MP, Civic Platform, 26/04/13
Sejm policy analyst, 19/04/13
Senat, Senator, Law and Justice, 15/05/13
Senat clerk, 23/04/13
Sénat clerk, 14/06/13
Camera dei Deputati clerk, 07/11/12
Camera dei Deputati clerk, 15/11/12
Camera dei Deputati clerk, 14/11/12
Senato della Republica clerk: 14/11/12
Senato della Republica Senator, Defence Committee, 14/11/12
Tweede Kamer clerk, 27/03/12
Tweede Kamer MP, D66, 20/06/12
Eerste Kamer MP, VVD, 23/10/12

Index

INDEX

Weingast, Barry 100
Weßels, Bernhard 12
Winzen, Thomas 8, 79
Woldendorp, Jaap 37

yellow cards 7, 46, 49, 56, 62–3
Yläoutinen, Sami 33

Zeng, Langche 52

www.ingramcontent.com/pod-product-compliance
Ingram Content Group UK Ltd.
Pitfield, Milton Keynes, MK11 3LW, UK
UKHW020350010325

455677UK00021B/385